D0422938

THE SLOW LEARNER IN THE CLASSROOM

NEWELL C. KEPHART
Purdue University

THE SLOW LEARNER
IN THE CLASSROOM

CHARLES E. MERRILL BOOKS, INC.

Columbus, Ohio

First printing . . . . July 1960
Second printing. . . . . June 1961
Third printing . . . . November 1962
Fourth printing . . . . May 1964
Fifth printing . . . . July 1965
Sixth printing . . . . October 1965
Seventh printing . . . . December 1965
Eighth printing. . . . . September 1966
Ninth printing. . . . . January 1967

Library of Congress Catalog Card Number: 60-14419

Printed in the United States of America

iv

to MAK

Preface

This book is written for the classroom teacher who has a few pupils who never seem quite able to learn what others are learning readily and eagerly. Teachers of special groups will also find the book valuable, since many problems of the special student are similar to those of the slow learner.

The difficulties shown by this small group of children begin early in the first grade, perhaps in beginning reading and even in the "readiness" work which precedes reading. As the school year progresses, these children fall further and further behind until they are no longer able to participate with the rest of the group in academic work. The longer they remain in the school system, the more confused they become and the more constantly they are faced, both formally and informally, with their failure to achieve.

The book is divided into three parts. Part I contains a description of some of the major learning areas in the development of the pre-school child. Over a number of years, research studies have indicated that slow-learning children lack basic readiness skills which, it is often assumed, the average child brings with him when he enrolls in kindergarten or the first grade. Since these skills enter into a major portion of the activities prescribed by the school, the child who has not developed them will find a large number of school tasks impossible.

The teacher will require some method of identifying the child who is lacking in these early skills. Part II presents a series of performances the observation of which should yield insight into the child's status in basic learning skills.

Clinical experimentation has disclosed certain methods by which basic pre-readiness skills can be taught. In Part III, these clinical methods have been adapted for use in the classroom. Many children can be helped through these methods to develop the readiness skills which will make academic achievement possible.

The training task is easier at early ages and the problems are less complicated by compensations and alterations in learning which the child has been forced to adopt in attempting to perform the tasks assigned him. For this reason, the discussion is aimed at the kindergarten and first three grades. Teachers of older children will find the described procedures useful, however, if they alter them slightly to provide adequate motivation for older pupils.

The teacher already spends a great deal of time with the slow-learning child. Much of this time could be more profitably spent by concentrating on pre-academic skills rather than by continued drilling on the academic activities from which the child has already demonstrated that he is not ready to profit. If readiness can be achieved by giving such special attention early, many slow learners can fall in with the rest of their fellows and continue learning through the customary activities of the group. The purpose of this book is to aid the classroom teacher in making such an achievement possible.

For their valuable assistance in reviewing the manuscript of this book, grateful acknowledgment is made to Professor John Goodlad of the University of Chicago, Professor Dale Harris of Pennsylvania State University, and Professor John Horrocks of Ohio State University.

NEWELL C. KEPHART

Contents

ix

part 1

Development and Achievement

chapter 1

Introduction

THE PRINCIPLE OF ADJUSTMENT

The human organism is required to make more complex, more rapid, and more complicated adjustments than any other organism. Demands made on any type of organism occur in terms of the response which that organism is required to make to the environment which surrounds it. Such demands determine the type of behavior which the organism is required to make. If the demands are simple, the behavior can also be simple. If, however, the demands are complex, the behavior must be correspondingly complex.

The primary problem for the organism is that of developing the types of behavior required by its environment. Behavior, if it is to meet the ever-changing demands of a constantly changing environment, must be flexible. It would be a simple task for nature to produce a mechanical organism which would provide an adequate constant response to a constant environment. Our ability to produce automatic machines which will make a highly complicated series of movements is evidence of the direction in which nature could have moved if a constant environment for living organisms were possible or desirable.

Automatic machines, however, produce a specified series of movements and do not alter their activities when conditions around them change unexpectedly. Even the most miraculous-seeming electronic machines—the so-called machines that think—can alter response only to predictable changes which can be anticipated in detail and reduced to coded information which can be fed into the machine ahead of time.

Such inflexible activities are in general not adequate for the living organism. Changes in the environment surrounding the organism are seldom so predictable as those surrounding a machine. Furthermore, the changes occur more extensively. For this reason, the living organism must be adaptable. It must have available a series of activities which may be selected in terms of the momentary demands of the environment. The greater the demands, the more extensive the series must be and the more flexible the selection device.

THE NEED FOR LEARNING

Such a series of alternate behaviors and the possibility of rapid and extensive selectivity can be assured through the operation of development and learning. Adaptive behavior of this type cannot be built into an organism as we build prescribed behaviors into a machine. The necessary variability and flexibility can only be produced by learning. Through its own interchanges with the environment, the organism must develop within itself the adaptability of behavior which will permit it to survive and adjust.

Obviously, the more constant the environment and the fewer its demands for altered behavior, the less the organism depends upon development and learning and the more it can depend on built-in behavior mechanisms. Certain primitive organisms living in the depths of the sea find such a constant environment or something very close to it. Pressure and temperature remain constant, darkness is unbroken, and movement or turbulence in the surrounding water is virtually unknown. Such organisms have a very limited behavior mechanism. When a particle touches the surface of such a creature, the organism, which is fluid like a jellyfish, flows itself around the particle and begins to absorb it as food. After a period of time sufficient to digest the substance, the organism unfolds from around the particle. The same behavior occurs in any event, even if the particle is inedible.

This simple behavior is virtually the only response of which such organisms are capable. Further, it is virtually the only behavior which is required for survival and for satisfactory adjustment to this simple environment. Such simple behavior, with its lack of flexibility, has almost no necessity for learning. Therefore, we find that for the most part such organisms come into the world with their responses immediately ready to function. The initial response remains unchanged during the life of the organism; it improves very little or not at all in either quantity or quality.

With more complex environments, more complex behavior responses are required. For example, organisms which live nearer the surface of the sea have to react both to water and to air. They must be able to move to respond to currents and turbulences. They must select and pursue their food. Such a more complex environment requires correspondingly more complex behaviors. Even in these simple organisms we already see the operation of adaptability in behavior and the need for learning and development. Such organisms improve their behavior during their lifetime as a result of learning or development.

THE CHILD'S NEED FOR LEARNING

Of all environments of living organisms, that of the human organism is by far the most complex. The human being must live in all geographical environs at some time or another: on land, sea, or in the air. His geographic mobility subjects him to extremes of temperature, humidity, and climatic conditions. Above all, his development of a social environment has necessitated highly complex systems of communication, so complex that they are impossible for any lower species. Working together in groups, he has gained control over his physical environment for his own advancement. In so doing, however, he has greatly complicated the demands for adaptable behavior. He must not only respond to environmental changes as they occur but must also anticipate such changes and prepare his behavior ahead of time. Such greatly increased environmental demands require activities within the organism which are so complex that only the human species is capable of performing them. All of these advanced behaviors, because of the extreme demand for flexibility, must depend upon learning and development for their acquisition. Thus, the complex environment of the human organism leads to extreme demands for learning. Achievement is demanded of the child as it is demanded of no other organism.

It is well to stop occasionally and consider the demands which are made of the child for behavior adaptations. Not only is behavior at a high level of achievement demanded but such behavior is demanded of an organism which has not yet completed the development necessary for such adaptation. Such demands are double-barrelled: behavior is demanded on the one hand, while indirectly (and too often unknowingly) a complex learning activity is demanded as well. This underlying learning activity is most complex—so complex that no other species can even accomplish it, let alone develop efficiency.

Such learning is difficult at best. It strains the capacity of the normal child. For a child whose organism is deficient and in whom some of the physiological and neurological processes necessary for such learning do not operate normally, it becomes impossible without very special help. We must know much more about the demands we are making on the organism and much more about the skills and abilities of the organism both in performance and in learning before any child can be given the amount and kind of help he needs.

STIMULUS FLEXIBILITY

As his environment increases in complexity, man's behavior must increase in complexity accordingly and certain types of response not required of lower organisms are required of the human organism. In the first place, the behavior of lower organisms is characterized by a high degree of specificity. It is stereotyped and rigid. It lacks variability or flexibility. This specificity is shown in three facets of behavior: the stimulus, the response, and the process.

The animal responds to very specific stimuli. His ability to generalize stimulus situations is very limited. Behavior is aroused by a specific stimulus element and any modification of this element will result in failure to elicit the behavior. Thus Cinat-Thompson (1926) showed that female parakeets with the cere painted blue were attacked by male parakeets as strangers but were recognized again when the voice was heard. Schjelderup-Ebbe (1923) found that a hen was no longer recognized by her associates when her comb was fastened on the wrong side of her head.

The human being, on the other hand, is required to respond to many elements of a stimulus at once and to the relationships between these elements. He must respond in terms of a total stimulus field rather than an isolated element in that field. His response must remain unaltered even though insignificant changes in this field occur.

In young children and in pathological states, inflexibility in the stimulus can be observed. Thus, Valentine (1942) cites the example of a young child who saw his father shaving and did not recognize him because of the lather on his face. Such responses, normal in animals, are considered bizarre in children, and we immediately turn our attention to teaching a broader and more generalized mode of response.

The human organism is required to identify a stimulus as a whole in an organized stimulus field and to adapt his behavior to the totality of the relationships involved. He must be ready to respond now in terms of one element or group of elements and now in terms of another element or group, recognizing in the process changes in the meaning of elements as surrounding conditions change.

BEHAVIOR FLEXIBILITY

Just as the child is required to react to a wider configuration of stimuli than any other organism, so also he is required to respond with a wider configuration of behaviors. Lower organisms can adapt through specific responses to specific stimuli, and these responses can be used over and over again without modification. Requirements for altered behavior to meet changed conditions of the environment are rare in lower organisms when compared to their frequency in the human organism.

A white rat, for example, can be taught to go out from his cage and seek food in a feeding pan. When he has learned the new method of obtaining food, he will take the most direct route from the cage to the food. If this route is blocked, as by a gate or fence, he will continue in his attempts to go directly to the food. He will attack the barrier and try to squeeze through it or he will try to tear it down. His original response of proceeding directly to the food is not immediately modified. The process of going around the barrier requires a major modification of his original response: he must go away from the food in order to get to it. Only with great difficulty does he make this modification of behavior. After many such experiments, research workers are still not in agreement as to whether he actually learns to modify a general behavior or merely learns a new behavior. Some workers (Higgenson, 1926; Hsiao, 1929; Tolman and Honzik, 1930; and Helson, 1927) have felt that they saw evidence of a sudden insightful solution in such detour problems, while others (Valentine, 1928; Gilhousen, 1931; and Keller and Hill, 1936) obtained negative results.

Whatever the outcome of this scientific question, it seems apparent that even if the animal does show adaptive behavior of a generalized nature, he does so in a very restricted sense and such adaptive behavior is a minor part of his total responses. Increasing the length and complexity of the detour makes the problem much more difficult for the animal. If the goal is out of sight, even for a short time, the animal has great difficulty (Thorpe, 1956). With animals, such modification of behavior is the exception, not the rule, and we must construct carefully designed experiments to elicit it. Complicated detour problems such as following a winding route to school, in which the child frequently changes direction following streets and sidewalks and prescribed routes rather than direct routes, would be entirely impossible for the animal. However, we demand such complicated behavior from our children at an early age.

Even for the child such behavior is difficult. Kurt Lewin demonstrated in a motion picture how difficult it can be for a three-year-old child to seat himself on a stone. The child must first turn his back to the stone in order to establish a physical contact. Similarly, a mentally retarded child standing inside a gate may be able to use a stick to reach for an object outside. If the stick and the object are both in the same direction, he has little trouble. However, if the stick lies on one side of his body and the object on the other, so that he must obtain the stick and then turn around to approach the object, the problem becomes difficult for him (Werner, 1948, p. 192).

The child is expected to "outgrow" rapidly such rigid responses. We often forget that "outgrowing" means *learning* and that the learning requirements which have been set for the child are enormous—greater than those which could be expected from lower organisms. Not only is the child expected to complete such complicated learnings, but he is expected to do so rapidly and at an early age. We demand that he master such problems at least by the time he is ready to go to school at five or six years of age.

BEHAVIOR PROCESSES

We are often too prone to look at the results of behavior and pay little attention to the process by which the organism arrived at this result. Processes can be rigid just as single responses can be rigid. The child is required to be flexible in the processes of his behavior. He is expected to know that "dog" applies to his own dog, to the neighbor's dog, and to a class of animals, depending upon the situation in which the word is used. His behavior is expected to reflect a process either of differentiation or generalization depending upon the immediate demands. The child who, coming home from his first grade reading class, said, "I can't read that story—the dog's name is Spot and my dog's name is Rover," is, we feel, not behaving at as high a level as we would expect.

The problem of shifting the processes of behavior, of substituting one behavior for another, of learning that "there is more than one way to skin a cat," is high-level learning. Again, most animals either never learn it or learn only in a few isolated instances. Such behavior is expected of our children at an early age. We expect to be able to "take their mind off" an undesirable activity by offering a substitute activity. Many of them learn this lesson so well that they use their learning to get around us and manipulate us for their own purposes. We often forget that such abilities are not entirely undesirable. They are evidences of a high-level learning. Many parents make a practice of driving their children to school. If, on a cold winter morning, the car refuses to start, even the kindergarten child is expected to know that he can get to school by walking, by riding a bicycle, or even by "hitching" a ride with the neighbors. The goal of getting to school can be achieved through a number of different specific activities or behavior processes. This illustration is simple to the point of absurdity. However, the same kinds of alteration in behavior processes, raised to the symbolic or conceptual level, become important in education as imagination and are among the significant variables in creativity (Osborn, 1953; Guilford *et al.*, 1954).

Behavior in the lower animals often occurs as a rigid sequence of movements. When the stimulus occurs which elicits the behavior, a series of movements takes place. This series is highly ordered and must continue from one stage to another without alteration. Should unusual events or circumstances intervene, the order is not interrupted but continues on according to its original sequence.

The spider offers an example of such behavior. The cross spider captures and devours its food according to the following series of movements: it enshrouds the prey, glues it down, moves around the web away from the prey, returns to it, and then sucks the trapped insect dry. If a fly is impaled on a pin and offered to the spider outside the web, the spider moves away from the fly and back to it exactly as it would in the web before eating it. She will run on the support away from the prey, spinning a thread behind her. Before returning, she fastens this thread to the support, and only then does she return to the prey and attack it. This side excursion, which under normal circumstances would take place in the nest at the center of the web and result in a reversal of the head, after dragging in the food, in order to achieve the proper sucking position, has no significance in the present situation. However, it is a part of the rigid series of actions prescribed for the response to food and so cannot be omitted even though it now serves no purpose (Baltzer, 1923).

One part of the hen's activity in seeking food is a preliminary scratching of the ground. The hen will always scratch for its food even though the action may be purposeless. If the bird is placed on a plate strewn with corn, it will persist in scratching, even to its own detriment (Hempelmann, 1926).

Not only are such series of actions rigidly prescribed and unalterable in the sense that, once started, they must proceed by prescribed order to the end, but parts of the total series cannot be lifted out and used when needed. The thermometer bird lays its eggs on mounds of tufted, dried grass and sand. The young bird breaks through the shell and, by beating its wings, raises itself up through the loose sand. However, if the young bird is buried again in the sand from which it has just emerged successfully, it will be unable to repeat the action of beating its wings to escape and will perish. The required action cannot be lifted out of the series and used in isolation. Since the stimulus for the beginning action in the series is not present, no useful behavior can occur.

Such rigid behavior processes are not adequate for the child. We expect him, at a very early age, to show much more adaptability in his behavior. Plasticity of response is characteristic of organisms with more complex nervous systems. Having the most flexible nervous system of all animals, man has the possibility of greatest plasticity. As Sherman and Sherman (1929) have pointed out, intelligent behavior depends upon the ability to modify reactions. Rigid behavioral processes do not allow such modification. The greater the freedom for modification, however, the greater the demands upon development and learning.

Natural curiosity drives children to see how things work. This curiosity needs to be stimulated and opportunities need to be provided for its exercise. (Courtesy of Donald A. Boose from Alpha Photo Associates, Inc.).

A MODERN DILEMMA

THE NEED FOR PRACTICE

As Bühler (1929, p. 92) has pointed out to us, organisms with plastic and adaptable systems have to perfect themselves by practice. The early, simple games of the child are intended to develop his sense organs and his motor system. The child experiments with things, looks at them, feels them from all angles, smells them, and taps them to produce sound. Such games can be called games of experience. By the manipulation of things and of his own body in relation to things, he is perfecting the sensory-motor process and is learning to match sensory data to motor data. He is building up a plastic, adaptive perceptual-motor process which will allow him to fit his behavior to the varied demands of the situations in which he will later find himself.

An enormous amount of such random experimentation is necessary. The child needs first to try out all the possible muscular responses of which his body is capable in order to find out what his body and its parts can do and what neurological patterns he has to develop in order to cause them to do so. He must observe how he can obtain sensory data concerning things and learn how these sensory data vary with his own position relative to the thing. He must learn to make a sensory impression the basis for an appropriate motor response which will change his relation toward a thing in the direction in which he wishes it to change. Finally, he must observe the relationships between things and how things operate together. He needs to take things apart and discover how they work and, later, perhaps even put them together again. At each stage of these developments, massive amounts of experimentation are necessary. Such experimentation needs to be, from our adult point of view, random. It must be child-centered, not adult-centered. It must be designed by him to help him acquire the mass of experiential data necessary for the organized skills he is building up. As such, it follows his own needs, not some externally determined logical order of procedure.

MODERN CIVILIZATION AND THE CHILD

Our modern world demands these learnings of the child as no previous civilization has demanded them. Our society has become so complicated and the types of response necessary to adjustment have become so varied, that plasticity and variability of behavior are more important than ever before. Whereas, only a few years ago, a limited number of highly skilled behaviors would suffice, modern man needs countless different behaviors dictated by the things and processes which surround him. Each advance in our technical development surrounds us with machines and devices which make increased demands on our ability to alter behavior. Each new device carries with it a behavior pattern necessitated by its use and hence a variation of behavior depending on whether it is present in the situation or not. As a result, countless new types of behavior are demanded of us and countless modifications of response are dictated by the devices surrounding us at any moment.

As we have seen, increased plasticity means increased learning and increased demands upon elementary skills which underlie all types of behavior. We cannot compensate by specific learned responses for deficiencies in basic skills as we could a few years ago. Consider for a moment the things with which a modern child comes in contact and which he is expected to behave toward at a very early age. Television sets, automobiles, electrical appliances, plumbing, and many other gadgets must influence his behavior. We expect him at a very young age to modify his behavior in terms of these devices. He is expected in any one day to behave adaptively toward large numbers of things. In Colonial days, the things toward which he was expected to behave were much more concrete and hence the different types of behavior demanded in any given period were less extensive and more direct.

Not only our technology but also our social organization has greatly increased in complexity. We are highly organized socially and we expect our children to reflect that organization early in life. A child must belong to, and participate in, many varied social groups and situations. The skills of social adjustment, however, depend upon the more basic skills which allow the child to adjust to concrete objects and things. He must see the same thing and it must elicit the same type of response before there is a basis for social contact with another individual.

THE DILEMMA

Our modern civilization demands more of the child than ever before and its demands are increasing daily. However, the very civilization which is increasing its demands is *decreasing* the opportunity which it offers the child for the very necessary experimentation with basic skills which we have discussed above. We have said that the child needs to experiment randomly with things around him and with his own body in relation to these things. Such basic experimentation is more and more difficult in our present-day life for two reasons.

First, the things with which the child is surrounded are so complicated that, if he experiments with them, they will break and a highly expensive expert will be required to put them together again. Forty years ago, children often took the percolator apart and saw how it was put together. From this experience, they learned many very useful things—relations of inside and outside, smaller and larger, full and empty, upside down and rightside up. How many modern parents would permit their child to experiment this way with their modern electric, automatic coffee maker? Forty years ago, children were surrounded with things which they could take apart and tinker with to their heart's content. If they made a mistake and broke something, Daddy put it together again. The modern child is surrounded with things which are elaborate, fragile, and accident prone and, if he breaks something, Daddy does not know how to put it together.

Not only is there danger of the child destroying the things with which he is surrounded but, even if he could take them apart, they are so technical that he could not understand them anyway. One of the chief amusements of children in past years was taking the alarm clock apart. After many unsuccessful trials, they finally gained some insight into how it worked. In the meantime, they learned much about the mechanics of things in relation to other things—about cog wheels, springs, and levers. Even if modern parents could agree to sacrifice their electric alarm and even if Johnny could succeed in getting it apart, its inner workings would remain a mystery. The most important process is accomplished by electrical currents doing mysterious things inside a sealed unit.

The second reason for restriction of the child's experimentation is the physical danger involved. Not only is it expensive to play with the gadgets, it is dangerous. Virtually the only dangerous thing in homes forty years ago was the fire. The child could see it, feel it, and soon learn to stay away from it. Today the child sticks his finger into an innocent-looking socket and gets electrocuted. If children of the past wanted to experiment with locomotion, they climbed on the family horse and he took care of them. The modern automobile is possessed of no such concern for the safety of our children. If children of the past wanted to see what it was like to run as fast as they could, they ran. But the children of today cannot run far in a modern apartment or even on a city lot, and they cannot run out of the yard because of the traffic.

Modern technology has increased the demands for adaptive behavior. At the same time no similar increase has offered the child greater opportunities for the basic, concrete experimentation on which such adaptive behavior must be based. Higher and higher degrees of skill are demanded and no similar increase is provided in the practice of elementary skills upon which these higher skills are based.

Many children are coming into our schools lacking in basic perceptual-motor skills. As a result of this basic lack, they are less able to participate in the formal educational activities which are arranged for them and they are less able to learn from these activities. They become slow learners in the classroom.

For many of these children, artificial means may have to be devised to provide additional practice in perceptual-motor skills. We may have to arrange for additional experimentation, extending that which we are accustomed to assume has been adequate. We may have to bring the equivalent of ladders to climb, fences to walk, or horses to ride, into the classroom and help the child to build up the sensory-motor skills which are required by the more complex activities of reading, writing, and arithmetic. Later chapters will discuss the nature of these basic skills and the types of practice which can be offered the child in the classroom situation which will help him to develop them.

chapter 2

Skills and Abilities
in Simple Tasks

When a child enters school, certain abilities and certain degrees of skill in various types of activity are assumed. In arranging the prescribed series of experiences which represent the school curriculum, it is necessary that a starting point, a level of ability which can be used as a base, be agreed upon. Since the school is designed primarily for the so-called normal child, it is logical that this base should assume the abilities which the average child displays at the age when he begins his school experience.

This basic assumption of the school is tested and the extent to which each child meets the assumption is examined through the use of readiness tests and similar devices. The skills and abilities represented in the readiness test, however, do not represent the starting point of learning for the child as they do for the school. These abilities are themselves the result of a long series of learnings. They are the culmination of a very extensive and rapid period of learning throughout the pre-school years.

Under normal conditions, the child in our culture can be expected to assimilate these learnings before he reaches school age. However, when conditions are not normal, as when the environment is inadequate or the organism damaged or subjected to extreme emotional disturbances, these assumed learnings may not take place. The child will then enter school with a lesser degree of skill and ability in one or more areas than the educational curriculum assumes. Since later learning is based in large degree upon these earlier learnings, such a child finds himself in ever-increasing difficulty as his school experience continues.

A more fruitful school experience and better school achievement could result if the pre-school learnings in which he is weak could be strengthened so that he would have a more solid base for school learning. Before we can provide this additional help, however, we need to have in mind the nature of the basic learned skills which underlie the school readiness skills. An extended illustration may serve to call attention to some of these more basic learnings.

One of the historically oldest tasks which we demand of a child is that of drawing a reasonably good representation of a square. This task occurs as an item on most standard intelligence tests (Terman and Merrill, 1937; Wechsler, 1949).

It would be interesting to analyze the simple task of drawing a square, a normal accomplishment for five-year-old children, to determine what basic skills are required in this performance. Is this a simple task which can be taken for granted, or is this a complicated task involving many basic learning abilities? What are the types of learned skills which underlie the ability to perform in this simple activity?

GROSS MOTOR

Obviously, certain very basic gross motor activities involving the total musculature of the body or large portions of it, and particularly the large muscle groups, are involved in the task of drawing a square. The first of these gross motor abilities is the ability to sit up. This is a learned skill and we all know how the young infant has to learn to sit up. He has to learn to maintain a certain postural adjustment and to manipulate tensions in various muscle groups as a function of posturing mechanisms in order to maintain a sitting position. He must learn to maintain a muscular adjustment around the center of gravity so that an upright sitting posture can be accomplished. In order to draw a square, he must be able to sit on a chair, at a table, or at a desk. He must therefore maintain the posture appropriate to the chair and appropriate to the desk and must maintain the relationship between these two postures.

Obviously, he must also be able to hold his head erect. Although this is a very basic skill, again we know that it is learned and that the young infant cannot perform this skill without a process of learning.

He must also be able to move his fingers, hand, wrist, and arm in a coordinated fashion. Much of the early behavior of the infant is generalized (Zubek and Solberg, 1954, pp. 133–34). Early movements involve activity of the total organism. Specific movements of isolated parts develop out of this generalized pattern of total movement. In this process of differentiation, the *cephalo-caudal* and *proximo-distal* trends are important. According to the cephalo-caudal principle, development of the head-trunk region precedes that of lower limbs. According to the proximo-distal principle, movements of large muscle groups lying toward the center of the body precede independent movements of parts lying at the extremity. Thus, movements of the total arm precede those of the elbow which, in turn, precede those of the wrist, fingers, and so forth.

In the task of drawing a square, this differentiation of specific movement patterns out of a more generalized total movement must have occurred and must have proceeded to the point where the very specific movements of fingers are possible. It will be seen that this differentiation has already involved much learning and much development before the child reaches the point at which he can pick up the pencil.

Other forms of movement appear to be highly specific from the very beginning. Such responses are in the nature of reflexes; as such, they are very restricted and appear in their initial occurrence very much as they will appear throughout their history. Learning is required in the case of such reflex behavior just as it is required to differentiate specific movement patterns out of generalized movement patterns. These specific responses must be integrated to produce a complete response which can serve some useful purpose in the general behavior of the organism, and this integration must be learned. Munn (1938) believes that certain responses in the child differentiate out of generalized activity, while others are integrated out of specific reflex-like acts. Learning is involved in either case. It is probable that many behavioral responses are the result of the two types of learning (differentiation and integration) which occur simultaneously and in relationship to each other.

Specific movements cannot be random, they must be controlled. Since the drawing of a square is a task in which the product is of small size, the control must be very accurate. The finger, arm, and hand must move differentially yet precisely. Not only must the differentiation discussed above have been completed, but it must have been completed with a considerable precision of control demanded by the size of the copy which he is required to make.

The child must have learned how to innervate the muscles of one arm without innervating in a similar fashion the muscles of the other arm. He must have differentiated one arm from the other and the activities of one side of his body from the activities of the other. He must have differentiated the movements of hand and fingers from the total movement of the organism. All of this learning and all of this development must have occurred before the child attempts the direct task of drawing a square.

EYE-HAND COORDINATION

The problem of eye-hand coordination is often taken very much for granted. It is thought of as a skill involving only accuracy and control and remarkable only when reaching high degrees of precision. However, many physical and psychological skills are involved in making possible any eye-hand activity at all. Before we become concerned with high degrees of eye-hand skill, we should first consider some of these basic abilities.

LATERALITY

Before he can begin to draw a square, the child must be able to distinguish between his left side and his right and to control the two sides of his body separately and simultaneously.

Initial movements in the infant are bilaterally symmetrical. Whatever the child does on one side he does on the other side also. These movements do not have within themselves any right-left consideration but are total symmetrical patterns involving the organism as a whole and not differentiating the two sides. The child has to learn this differentiation.

From a large quantity of experimentation with movement, the child sorts out those pertinent to the right side and those pertinent to the left side. He experiments by comparing right- and left-hand movements with each other and with symmetrical movements. The two-year-old child is actively engaged in this process and we see him using one side and then the other, particularly with respect to the hands. In many cases, we see him definitely experimenting by using one hand after the other to see which one works better and what difference there is in the movement patterns. All of this type of experimentation is involved in learning right and left. Careful observation of older children will show that in many cases this very basic difference between the two sides of the body has not been thoroughly learned. The problem of laterality is discussed in more detail in later chapters.

In order to begin the copying of the square, the child must locate the beginning point. This point must be located with reference to his own body (right side or left side or center), and the kind of movement which will be required to bring his hand to this starting point must be conceived. All of these adjustments are problems of laterality. If he is confused as to which is the right side and which is the left side and if he confuses the movement patterns of these two sides, he will have difficulty beginning the task of drawing the square.

DIRECTIONALITY

Laterality leads to directionality. Our first information about the coordinates of space comes from the kinesthetic awareness of

Many different kinds of skills must be learned before a child can read and write. (Courtesy of Josef Scaylea from A. Devaney, Inc.).

differences in our own body, and chief among these directional differences is the right-left differentiation. At the same time that the child is developing kinesthetic space, he is also receiving visual information which has direction. In a square, for example, he is presented with the horizontal line which forms one side of the figure. The directionality of this line, the right- and left-hand aspect of this visual stimulus, is the result of his matching a visual pattern to a kinesthetic pattern.

Visual stimuli do not have in themselves relationships of directionality nor relationships of space and space coordinates. Horizontal, vertical, and depth dimensions are attributed to visual stimuli on the basis of kinesthetic awareness of these coordinates and subsequent translation through visual clues. If such kinesthetic awareness has not been developed, visual stimuli cannot be matched for directionality with kinesthetic coordinates (since these do not exist) and, as a result, visual stimuli will not have directionality or spatial coordinates. Thus, the very horizontal nature of the line in the square is the result of the development of laterality and associated relationships in the kinesthetic experience of the child.

As mentioned above, the coordinates of space are not given to us in absolute terms. There is no right and left, up and down, fore and aft in objective space, and there are no direct clues to these directions in objective space. We must construct the coordinates of space by projecting these directionalities from the organism out into space. We must develop the coordinates through the kinesthetic experience of our own body; these kinesthetic coordinates must then be matched with observed relationships within the visual stimuli which come to us from outside. Through this matching, directionality and spatial coordinates are projected from the body outward into objective space.

In scribbling or drawing on chalkboards or paper and in similar types of activity, the child experiments with a movement—for example, left to right. As he does so, he leaves a trace of this movement in the form of a pencil mark or a chalk mark. He then experiments with matching this trace which was left with the pattern which he used to initiate this movement. From experimentation of this and similar types, he learns how to match a visual pattern with a kinesthetic pattern and how to transfer the right-left relationships of the kinesthetic pattern onto the visual stimuli. Through extensive experimentation with all types of movement patterns and all types of visual stimuli, he initiates and develops these translations. When the translation has been made, when the matching process has been completed, he begins to develop directionality.

When the child has determined the starting point for his copy of a square, he must next determine the direction in which he must move to produce a line similar to that in the copy. Some of the lines which he draws are right to left, some are left to right, some are up to down, and others are down to up. Unless he can sort out these various directions, he will not be able to complete the drawing of the square in an adequate fashion. He must determine visually the directionality of the line with which he is concerned at the moment, translating this to a kinesthetic movement pattern which will preserve the same directionality, and he must produce this directionally controlled movement.

It is necessary not only that the child initiate a movement in a given direction, but that he change the direction of that movement while a total over-all movement is still in progress. This is the way in which he gets around the corners of the square. At first, such a change in direction appears to be a simple problem and one which would not ordinarily create difficulties. However, we must remember that, to perform this very simple task, the child has to learn how to coordinate the arm, hand, and wrist in order to make a movement in any prescribed direction. This coordination problem itself is difficult, as the clumsiness and awkwardness of many children indicate. The initial problem is further complicated because the direction of the movement must be changed. Such alteration means that not only does a child have the initial problem of coordination of the neurological impulses to muscles, but he must change these coordinations and he must change them *in pattern* as the operation is going on. That is to say, he cannot simply complete one pattern and then start another one; he must modulate over, so to speak, from the first pattern to the second.

In the copying activity, the child has not only the problem of muscular coordination and the neurological innervation to muscles, but also the problem of matching these motor skills to a visual input which is being generated as his pencil moves over the paper. The change in the direction of movement must be controlled by the visual stimuli which come to him from the paper. In order to perform this task, he must have directionality as we have discussed above, and he must also be able to control his motor activities in terms of directional clues which he is receiving from the task itself as the task continues. These clues are visual clues which must be matched to the kinesthetic patterns which dominate his motor behavior.

ABILITY TO STOP

When the child comes to a corner, he must stop a movement in one direction and initiate a movement in another direction. Ordinarily we think of innervating a muscular movement as a positive task, and we pay considerable attention to the ability of the child to perform this task. It is important to remember, however, that stopping a movement is also a positive task. Whenever a movement is stopped before the child reaches the mechanical limits of the movement (length of the arm in this case), a positive act is required which is just as difficult to learn and just as difficult to control as the initiation of movement. As mentioned earlier, the problem of stopping cannot be dealt with independently in the copying task, but must be a part of a total movement pattern which will reproduce the required figure. The pattern of neurological impulses that must be sent down to the muscles to stop a movement is as complicated as the pattern of impulses that must be sent down to start a movement. The same learning is required in both cases. Frequently children are seen who have not solved the problem of stopping. The movements that they initiate will continue until the mechanical structure of the body makes it impossible to go further. Such children have solved the problem of initiating a movement but have failed to solve the equally complicated problem of stopping this movement.

In drawing a square, not only does the child have to learn how to stop the movement, but he has to learn how to stop it on cue.

Here again, he has a visual clue to where the movement should stop, and he must use this visual clue as a stimulus to the positive act of stopping the movement. In this total process, there must be sufficient matching and sufficient accuracy that the movement stops at the corner. The child must match a line, which is developing as his movement proceeds, with the line of the example presented to him, or with its memory image, for length. A direct vision-to-vision match with respect to length cannot be made until the movement is finished. Therefore, in determining where he should turn the corner, he must make a continuing match of a given line against a developing line; he must match a kinesthetic pattern against a visual pattern. Many children start the movement very well but are unable to stop it until the line runs off the edge of the paper—a problem of control of stopping.

In the problem of stopping as in the problem of starting, directionality is important. The production which the child is making must have a directionality as he begins the movement, but it must also continue to have a directionality until the movement stops. As he turns the corner, the directionality changes, but it must change in terms of the coordinates of space which have been discussed earlier. Each change of direction requires the preservation of a consistent set of directional coordinates. The entire problem of matching motor movements to visual inputs, of matching kinesthetic to visual stimuli, is involved anew in the process of stopping and changing directions at every corner in the square.

EYE MOVEMENTS

As mentioned above, directionality in space is projected from the organism outward. The mechanism for such projection in the visual field is the movement of the eyes. Since the child cannot, with his hand, follow direction at a distance greater than arm's length, he must learn how to identify directionality in distant stimuli through some means other than the kinesthetic and tactual impressions from his hands. In effect, he substitutes his eye for his hand. He moves his eye along the stimulus and matches the pattern of eye movement to the kinesthetic pattern in his organism and develops the resulting projection (Hebb, 1949, p. 82).

Such a process means that the child must have accurate control of the eyes, an accurate match between the eye movements and the perceived visual stimulus, and an adequate interrelationship between the movement of the eyes and the movements of other muscle groups in the body. Such matching can become very complicated and must be built up with great accuracy. In the drawing of the square, the child must use his eyes to determine the periphery of the figure and translate this series of eye movements into a series of hand movements which will give him a result in the visual field that matches what he is copying. The problems of ocular control and visual-kinesthetic matching are discussed more fully in a later chapter.

DEXTERITY

It is of course obvious that the drawing of the square requires dexterity of the fingers, wrist, arm and shoulder, and grasp mechanism. These dexterities are learned and the extent of the learning required is obvious whenever one observes the difficulties of young children in drawing and copying.

TEMPORAL-SPATIAL TRANSLATION

The child must go through the processes discussed above to determine what are the parts of a square and where they are located. However, he cannot draw all four of the lines involved in a square at one time. He must put together the parts so that he has a total picture in space. When he is required to reproduce the figure, he must deal with the parts one at a time as a series in time.

In identifying the figure and in perceiving it as a square, the child must deal with the separate lines and angles in an integrated fashion. They must exist for him simultaneously and in relationship to each other. Only in this way can the figure-ground relationship be established and maintained. In studying the copy, therefore, he is required to be aware of all aspects of the form simultaneously and related to each other in space.

When he begins to construct his own square, however, he cannot deal with all of these parts at one time. He must draw first one line and then another. However, in dealing with the separate lines he must not lose the relationships between them or he will not be able to produce a square but will produce four separate lines in some unspecified relationship. For the process of production, he must organize the lines and angles into a series of events in time. He is thus required to deal with the parts of a square under two different conditions of organization: (1) a simultaneous organization in space and (2) a serial organization in time. His product will not be adequate and complete unless he is able to make both of these organizations and to appreciate the relationship of one to the other.

The translation of a simultaneous relationship in space into a serial relationship in time is a factor in many activities which we require of the child. The translation must proceed in both directions. In copying the square, we ask him to translate from a simultaneous series into a temporal series. When presented with a visual form, there is a tendency to move the eyes around the figure, stopping successively on various parts of the contour (Hebb, 1949, p. 82). These visual fixations give successive impressions of sections of the figure. In building up the contour of a figure where more than one such ocular fixation is required, the child must translate the resultant temporal series of impressions into a spatial series. (See Strauss and Kephart, 1955, p. 50.) Many children have difficulty in learning how to make such translations, and their difficulties may occur in either direction. Some children will be able to organize impressions in space but cannot translate them into a temporal series, while other children will be able to organize series in time but will be unable to translate them into simultaneous series in space. In order to achieve in the activities which we set for him, the child must be able to organize his impressions in both of these areas and to shift fluently from one to another as the situation demands.

FORM PERCEPTION

Before the child can adequately copy the square, he must perceive the figure as a form on a background. Since the square is a closed figure, he must be able to develop the contour, maintain the figure-ground relationship, and differentiate the various parts of the figure. The development of an integrated figure-ground relationship also results from a learning process. Many children have particular difficulty learning how to identify the various elements in a perceptual impression and organize and integrate that into a figure or form.

The processes of learning involved in the development of form perception will be discussed at more length in later chapters. Adequate copying of a square is possible only insofar as the child can organize a figure on a ground and can differentiate all the necessary qualities of this figure. Many children will require special help in making this figure-background distinction.

BASIC SKILLS AND ACHIEVEMENT LEVELS

We have discussed above a few of the basic sensory-motor skills involved in the simple process of copying a square. We have not considered such variables as motivation, general intelligence, the establishment of an interpersonal relationship with the examiner, and many other very important but more general aspects of the problem. Our concern here is to point out the vast amount of basic learning required to perform the elementary sensory-motor skills necessary to the completion of this task.

Such activities as copying a square are sometimes considered as though they were in themselves basic performances. We sometimes stop with these simple performances and do not attempt to break them down into more basic skills. In education, most early types of performance, such as copying a square, are subtended under the heading "readiness." Readiness skills are sometimes considered as something which the child acquires either through maturation or through the functioning of innate responses. We have attempted to show in the present discussion that readiness skills can be broken down into more basic types of activity.

In practice, if an attempt is made to develop readiness in a child, it frequently takes the form of providing practice in the simple activities (such as drawing a square) which are considered readiness activities. As we have seen above, however, these activities are already rather complicated combinations of skills. It would seem that if these simple activities were broken down into even more basic skills and teaching techniques were applied to these underlying skills we might be more successful in developing readiness for elementary school tasks.

In this volume we will attempt to identify some of these more basic skills, to suggest methods by which deficiencies in these skills can be detected, and to suggest training procedures which will attack the basic skills more directly. It is felt that with these more elementary types of training certain difficulties in the child can be corrected so that he can increase his achievement in more complex activities. Most of the tasks which we set for the child are complex activities combining many basic sensory-motor skills. If basic skills necessary to this complex of abilities are lacking, the total activity may break down.

Consider the problem of laterality. If laterality is not established in the child and if the directionality resulting from laterality has not been developed, then certain relationships in space will be meaningless. Consider the situation of this child if we attempt to teach him to read. In the first place, many of the letters which are shown him will have no basis for differentiation. Without laterality, there is no difference between a *b* and a *d*. It is not that the child is confused; it is not that he has not learned the difference; it is not that he reverses the letter. The fact is that, for this child, no difference exists at all between these two letters. The only difference between a *b* and a *d* is a difference in direction and, for this child, no directions exist and therefore no differences based on directionality can exist. It is fruitless to attempt to teach this child the complex activities involved in reading as long as he continues to lack this basic skill.

Many of the children who present learning problems in elementary school classrooms appear to suffer from some of the basic difficulties listed above. Since so many of the complex activities which are presented to these children involve these basic skills, the child continues to meet failure and frustration on every hand. The best efforts at teaching often yield discouraging results because the techniques used to teach require of the child complex activities that are impossible for him as a result of his more basic deficiencies.

If these basic deficiencies could be supplied, they might make it possible for him to profit from the teaching activities which are presented to him and hence to increase his achievement. More progress might be made with such children if we went back further in the scale of performance and devoted a portion of the teaching time to activities designed to help him learn these more basic skills.

chapter 3

Motor Bases
of Achievement

THE MUSCULAR BASIS OF BEHAVIOR

The early motor or muscular responses of the child, which are the earliest behavioral responses of the human organism, represent the beginnings of a long process of development and learning. Through these first motor explorations, the child begins to find out about himself and the world around him, and his motor experimentation and his motor learnings become the foundation upon which such knowledge is built. In early childhood, mental and physical activities are closely related (Jersild, 1954), and motor activities play a major role in intellectual development. To a large extent, so-called higher forms of behavior develop out of and have their roots in motor learning.

It is logical to assume that all behavior is basically motor, that the prerequisites of any kind of behavior are muscular and motor responses. Behavior develops out of muscular activity, and so-called higher forms of behavior are dependent upon lower forms of behavior, thus making even these higher activities dependent upon the basic structure of the muscular activity upon which they are built.

The situation is described by Sherrington as follows: "As we look along the scale of life, whether in time or in order of organization, muscle is there before nerve, and nerve is there before mind, 'recognizable mind.' It would seem to be the motor act under 'urge-to-live' which has been the cradle of mind. The motor act, mechanically integrating the individual, would seem to have started mind on its road to recognizability. The great collateral branch of life, the plants, despite all its variety and unexampled profusion of types, has never in any event developed an animal-like locomotory act, nor a muscle nor a nerve; it has likewise remained without recognizable mind. As motor integration proceeds, mind proceeds with it, the servant of an 'urge' seeking satisfaction" (Sherrington, 1951, p. 169).

MOVEMENT AND OVERT BEHAVIOR

In the case of certain gross behaviors where overt muscle activity takes place, the dependence of behavior upon movement can be easily seen. In such activities, the body or parts of the body move through space, and this movement through space can be observed. We can see directly how the behavior is based upon motor movement and how the efficiency of the behavior is conditioned by the efficiency of the motor patterns which are available to the individual.

MOVEMENT AND NON-OVERT BEHAVIOR

In other types of activity, non-overt activities, the relationship between movement and behavior is not so clear. In many activities, the organism is sitting quietly and, to all intents and purposes, not moving overtly while certain behavioral acts are certainly going on. Under this heading fall such processes as thinking and problem-solving where the major portion of the behavior may occur before any overt muscle response is seen.

Muscular activity, however, also plays a significant role in these "pure thought" processes. Experimental evidence suggests that there are at least two kinds of such muscular activity: a general over-all increase in muscular tension involving the whole body, and localized increases in tension limited to particular muscle groups (Krech and Crutchfield, 1958, p. 487). General muscle tension in non-overt activities can be seen by an observable tensing of the postural mechanism, by occasional drumming with the fingers or pacing across the floor. In addition, sensitive electrodes over the major muscle systems of the body will pick up impulses indicating that innervation has been sent to the major muscle systems and that they are under a higher state of tension than would be the case in relaxation. Localized tension during non-overt activity can also be shown by experiments designed to reveal changes in electrical activity of muscles. Sensitive electrodes placed over specific muscle systems will indicate that, during the thinking process, these more limited systems have also been innervated and that tension in particular systems, associated with the problem or its solution, are present (Woodworth and Schlosberg, 1954, p. 178).

Thus, it is logical to suppose that even in "pure thought" activities the muscular basis of behavior is not lost but still provides the foundation for these higher activities. Pure thought activities are based on the ability of the organism to respond muscularly just as the lower responses of simpler experimental tasks are based on motor abilities. There is evidence that the efficiency of the higher thought processes can be no better than the basic motor abilities upon which they are based.

POSTURE

The basic movement pattern out of which all other movement patterns must develop is that of posture. Posture is a positive neuro-muscular act in which a series of muscle groups is innervated in pattern so that the position of the body with reference to its center of gravity is maintained (Dusser de Barenne, 1934). These postural adjustments are very basic and are among the most rigid in the organism.

THE SIGNIFICANCE OF POSTURE

There are perhaps two reasons for the significance of postural adjustment. In the first place, it is through posture that we are able to maintain a constant orientation to the earth's surface and to the environment which surrounds us. The zero point, or point of origin, for all directions and orientations in space is the gravitational axis of the body. If we cannot maintain a consistent relationship to this gravitational force, we cannot maintain a consistent orientation to the world around us. It is therefore essential to consistent relationships with the things around us that we maintain a consistent relationship to our center of gravity. This relationship is maintained through the postural mechanisms.

The second reason for the significance of the postural mechanism is safety. If we cannot maintain our relationship to the center of gravity and our relationship to the earth's surface, we are not in a position to move or to respond quickly and efficiently and therefore we are in danger of harm from external sources. Just as we must have a zero point for the establishment of directions in space, we must have a zero point for movement. This zero point is the posturing mechanism or the upright posture in the case of the human organism.

POSTURE AND BEHAVIOR

The maintenance of postural adjustment is so important that, in the organism, it has been given a dominant place in the scheme of behavior. Posturing mechanisms are largely under the control of the cerebellum. The cerebellum is a mass of brain tissue located below the major mass of the brain and connecting directly with the brain stem and the nerve tracts leading to the major muscle groups. There is a feedback mechanism between the cerebellum and the higher centers of the cerebral cortex. Elaborated behavior patterns are worked out in the cerebral cortex, and the action patterns to muscles resulting from this intellectual problem-solving are sent down through the brain stem. As they pass through the brain stem, the influence of the cerebellum is exerted. If these behavioral patterns would interfere with postural adjustment, a veto is enforced at the brain stem level so that these behaviors are not permitted to eventuate in action. There is a "short-circuiting" mechanism by which these patterns can be returned to the cortex to be re-worked. An interaction of this type between cerebellum and cerebrum can also be seen in the experimental behavior of animals (Fulton, 1949, pp. 525 ff). Thus, nature assures that no behavior will pass through and eventuate in action if it is contrary to the very basic postural mechanisms. In this manner, we are preserved from injuring ourselves, from losing our orientation, and from losing the base or point of origin for our actions, by the dominance which the postural mechanisms exert over our behavior (Strauss and Kephart, 1955, p. 197).

You can observe the veto force of the posturing mechanisms by the following experiment. Stand about five feet away from a table. Now reach out and pick up an object from the table without moving your feet. At first you reach out without difficulty. Then you lean forward as you reach. Soon you are in danger of becoming overbalanced. Do not let this disturb you. Tell yourself how important this experiment is and that you can certainly reach the object since if your entire body were extended laterally toward the table, your arm would surely reach. Now, having intellectualized the problem completely and having assured yourself on an intellectual (cortical) basis of the significance of continuing the forward movement, go right on learning forward until you lose your balance and fall on your face. Such a response is impossible. The normal individual finds it impossible to continue leaning forward beyond the point where balance is threatened. Neurologically and muscularly, there is no reason why you cannot continue to lean forward until you fall. The response of the total organism, however, is such that this dangerous resolve cannot be carried out. The basic postural mechanisms in the so-called lower brain centers have vetoed your fine intellectual solution and their veto stands. No further overt action in the dangerous direction is permitted. As a result, no further action can be performed. Thus, the mechanisms of posture dictate the final decision for action.

It follows from the discussion above that all movement patterns, and consequently all behavior, must develop out of the posturing mechanisms. Movement not in accord with basic posture cannot be performed. Learned movement patterns and learned responses can only result from the elaboration and reorganization of the basic posturing adjustments. This process assures that posture is maintained and that it remains the core of the behavior pattern.

NEED FOR FLEXIBLE POSTURE

It can be seen that since posture forms the core of any behavioral activity it is desirable that the postural adjustments be flexible and operative over a range. If the posturing mechanism is stiff and inflexible, only a limited amount of elaboration can be accomplished without destroying the postural response. On the other hand, if posture is flexible, if it involves all muscle groups or a large proportion of the muscle groups of the body in pattern, a certain range of movement is possible within which posture can be maintained. This flexibility permits much more elaboration and much more manipulation than could a rigid inflexible posture. Such flexibility would thus lead to an increased possibility of motor response and hence to an increased possibility of behavioral response.

The relationship between the flexibility of posture and the elaboration of behavior has been demonstrated by a recent study of Kagerer (1958). In this study, first-grade children were tested to determine their ability in activities involving flexibility of the posturing mechanism. These test scores were then correlated with achievement in school as measured by standardized school achievement tests. Substantial and consistent correlations were found between activities designed to measure ability to move within a posture and achievement in school. Those children whose posture was most flexible and had the widest range did better in first-grade classroom work than those whose posture was rigid and who were unable to perform activities which required flexibility in the posturing mechanism.

The objection may be raised at this point that previous studies comparing physical characteristics and capacities (including posture) with intellectual achievement have shown little relationship (Paterson, 1930). In like manner, the development of high degrees of motor skill through training, as in the sensory motor training of Itard (1932) and Seguin (1907), seems to have had relatively little effect upon intellectual competence.

Although we have been interested for some time in the relationship between motor ability and intellectual activities, only recently have we become concerned with the flexibility of motor activities. Previous studies have for the most part been concerned with the development of motor *skills* and the learning of a high degree of proficiency in a rather limited motor activity. Such studies have not consistently shown significant relationships between motor skills and intellectual activities (see Wellman, 1931). More recent research is beginning to be directed toward the problem of *flexibility* in motor control and the ability to perform a motor task without previous experience or the development of a high degree of skill. Thus, early studies in the area of posture have investigated the postural adjustment of the child while he was not moving. Present studies investigate his posture during processes of movement. The emphasis has swung from highly specific motor skills (which can be learned as "splinter skills" and have limited relationship to the activities of the total organism) to investigations of general movement patterns and the ranges involved in these general patterns.

In like manner, we have been concerned with the existence of the machinery for movement responses and have paid relatively little attention to the learning processes required in operating this machinery. Thus, we have been concerned with problems of muscle pathology and pathology of the skeleton and have largely overlooked the fact that, given a perfect muscle system and a perfect skeleton, the child must still learn to use these parts. The process of innervating a muscle or system of muscles involves the development of a pattern of neurological impulses which can be sent down to this muscle group or muscle groups and result in a controlled and accurate movement. Our problem is not to move single muscles by single impulses, but to move muscles in pattern, by patterns of impulses. Thus, Fulton states "the central nervous system is organized not in terms of anatomical segments, but in movement patterns" (Fulton, 1949, p. 54). We must develop patterns of neurological activity which will produce appropriate muscle movement patterns rather than simply dispensing a single neurological impulse to a single muscle.

This process of innervating muscle groups is learned. It is the result of experience and experimentation with movement and patterns of movement. As Coghill (1929) and others have pointed out, the muscles develop first, the nerves develop second, and the functional activities by which the muscles are moved develop last. We have paid very little attention to this process of learning how to make muscles function. We have not realized to the fullest extent the learning problem involved, and therefore we have in many cases failed to develop the maximum function of muscle groups and movement patterns. Muscles develop function only as a result of use and the concomitant learning.

It is not enough that the functions of muscles be developed per se. Such activity results in the development of isolated skills which have little significance to the organism except as parlor tricks. It *is* desirable that the functions of muscle groups be developed for purposes of an over-all usefulness so that they can contribute to the general behavior adjustment of the organism. For this reason, we are concerned, not with the development of specific skills, but with the development of certain general activities in the organism. Chief among these are the development of laterality and directionality. Both of these functions depend upon movement patterns and the learning of postural and movement adjustments. We will want to foster the motor development of the child, but we will also want to guide it in the direction of these more general activities.

LATERALITY

There are no objective directions in space. The directions which we attribute to space (right, left, up, down, before, behind, etc.) are attributed to external space on the basis of activities which take place within the organism. We do not receive from outside our organism any direct information concerning direction. When a sharp instrument is applied to the skin, there is a direct experience of pain, but there is no similar direct experience of spatial relationships and direction. Spatial clues, visual or auditory, obtain their directionality through learning and through the projection onto external stimuli of internal experiences that result from the movement of the organism.

The first of these directions to develop appears to be that of laterality, right and left. The human organism is anatomically and neurologically designed to be an excellent right-left detector. Our body is bilaterally symmetrical. We have two eyes, two ears, two arms, two legs, etc. Neurologically, the nerve pathways innervating each of the sides of the body remain primarily separate. There is a minimum amount of crossing over, to permit feedback and matching, but essentially there are two relatively independent systems, one for the left and one for the right. All the nerve systems, for example, innervating the left side of the body are kept distinct, pass up through the spinal cord, cross in the brain stem, and enter the right hemisphere of the cortex. This anatomical and neurological differentiation makes of the organism an excellent device for detecting right and left.

LEARNING LATERALITY

Laterality must be learned. It is only by experimenting with the two sides of the body and their relationship to each other that we come to distinguish between the two systems. It is through experimenting with the movement of the two halves of the body, observing the differences between these movements, comparing these differences with differences in sensory impressions, and so forth, that we sort out the right side from the left and ascribe certain differentiating qualities to each (cf. the concept of "reciprocal interweaving," Gesell *et al.*, 1941). The primary pattern out of which this differentiation develops is that of balance. When experimenting with the balancing problem, the child must learn right and left, for he must learn how to innervate one side against the other, how to detect which side has to move, and how it has to move, in order to execute the appropriate compensatory movements as his balance varies from one side to another. Out of these and similar activities, he learns to differentiate the right from the left side.

AVOIDING LATERALITY

It is essential that this type of learning take place and that it be carried through to satisfactory completion. There are several stages in the process at which the child can be stopped and can still make

responses which appear adequate. Two of these stages are of
particular importance. The first is that in which the child learns
that as long as all of his responses are bilaterally symmetrical he
can avoid the problem of laterality. Thus, his movements and his
responses will be organized so that both sides of the body are performing the same act at the same time. In such a child, we will
see both sides of the body brought into play where only one is
necessary, or we will see one side of the body performing while
an abortive performance occurs on the other side. When writing
on the chalkboard, this child uses one hand for the writing activity
while the other hand and arm are noticeably tensed or are making
small movements that are mirror images of those being made by the
dominant side. Such a child has no need to differentiate the sides
because they always perform the same movements. The opposite
problem is one in which the child becomes almost completely one-
sided. In every activity, he performs with one side and merely
drags the other side along. We will see him frequently convert-
ing bilateral activities into unilateral activities. Where he must
use both sides of his body, one side will definitely lead and the other
side will follow without taking a positive part in the performance.
When writing on the chalkboard, this child also writes with his
dominant hand but the opposite hand and arm hang limply at his
side and almost appear paralyzed. This child has no need to differentiate the two sides because, in effect, only one is ever used.

In either of these two cases, the child restricts his movement patterns and restricts his learning. He does not gain an adequate appreciation of right and left and, confronted with problems of laterality in external space, he will reflect his difficulty by confusing the
two directions.

LATERALITY *v.* HANDEDNESS

Laterality must be distinguished from handedness and from the
naming of right and left. Laterality is an internal awareness of
the two sides of the body and their difference. It is probable
that when the child has learned the sides, he still has to solve the
problem of keeping their relationships straight. It seems possible
that he learns to do this by developing one side as the leading side

and consistently leading with this dominant side. Such a learning process may lead to dominance and, among other things, handedness. In this connection, it is significant that studies of young children have shown that handedness *develops*. It is not innate, but appears to develop somewhere around the age of two years. Gesell (1940) and others have noticed this phenomenon. Previous to this time, the child uses his hands alternately and appears to have no consistent choice.

LATERALITY *v.* NAMING OF SIDES

In like manner, laterality must be differentiated from the naming of sides. To ask the child to identify his right hand does not constitute a test of his laterality. The recognition of the right hand as opposed to the left hand can be based on external characteristics of the two parts. Thus, the left hand may be the hand on which I wear a ring. The child's differentiation is then not based on any concept of laterality, but on the observation of specific characteristics of the external parts themselves.

IMPORTANCE OF LATERALITY

The development of laterality is extremely important since it permits us to keep things straight in the world around us. The only difference between a *b* and a *d* is one of laterality. If there is no left and right inside the organism, there can be no projection of this left and right outside the organism, and consequently the directional characteristics of *b* and *d* disappear. In this connection, Lotz pointed out many years ago that if we had *only* visual impressions, the words *up, down, left, right* and so on could have no meaning. The visual field would be circular, but with no position either upright or inverted. It would be lacking anything else in consciousness with which to compare it. One cannot ascribe erectness, inverseness, or slantwise orientation to the universe. Ascription of visual position can derive only from having each field point take its special place in a tactual kinesthetic space image. "Upper" in the visual field is what appears nearer the head and could be reached by a tactile member of the head. "Lower" is what appears nearer the feet and could be reached by lower tactile members. After learning the variable posture of the body, we can give independent meaning to the visual "up" and "down" by reducing our posture to an erect bodily position (Lotz, 1852).

DIRECTIONALITY

When the child has developed laterality within his own organism and is aware of the right and left sides of his own body, he is ready to project these directional concepts into external space. By experimenting with movement patterns directed toward objects in space, he learns that to reach an object he must make a movement, for example, to the right. He then reverses this deduction and develops the concept of an object to the right of himself. Through a number of such experiences, he learns to translate the right-left discrimination within himself into a right-left discrimination among objects outside himself.

Experimenters in the field of child development have consistently noted that spatial relationships and spatial directions develop first in relation to the child himself and only later are objective relations developed between objects. Thus, early in his development a child locates two objects, each independently in relation to himself. This has been called *egocentric localization* or the development of *subjective space*. Later in development, he is able to conceive of one object to the right of another without the intervening step of locating each object with relation to himself. This later development has been called *objective localization* or the development of *objective space*. Piaget (1956), Gesell (1940), and others have outlined this developmental sequence.

DIRECTIONALITY AND EYE CONTROL

One very important factor in the development of directionality is the control of the eyes. Since a great deal of our information concerning space and the location of objects in space comes to us through our eyes, it is necessary for us to develop a series of clues and matches by which this visual information can give us the same directional concept which we formerly received through kinesthetic activity. This is accomplished through the control of the eyes. The child learns that when his eyes are pointed in a given direction, this means that the object lies in that same direction. In order to learn this, he must make a complicated series of matches between the position of his eyes and the position of his hand in contacting an object.

The control of the eyes is very intricate and highly precise. The eyes are moved by six extrinsic ocular muscles which must be innervated in patterns and which must be moved very accurately. The fovea is a narrow area (about two millimeters in diameter) at the back of the eyeball. For most efficient vision, the image must fall on this foveal area. In order to focus the image on this restricted area, the eye must be moved with extreme precision. For this reason, and because of the intricacy of the muscle system by which the eye is moved, the process of learning to control this movement is very difficult. When the child has learned this control, he matches the movement of his eye to a movement of his hand and thus transfers the directionality information from the kinesthetic pattern in his hand and arm to the kinesthetic pattern in his eye. This is, of course, a very precise and very complex matching procedure and a great deal of skill and learning is required to perfect it. When this matching has been perfected, the child can use his eyes as a projection device to determine directionality in space outside the reach of his hand.

DIRECTIONALITY AND THE MIDLINE

One further difficulty is encountered in the matching of kinesthetic information with information from outside which results in directionality. When the child is experimenting with basic movement patterns, he refers all movement to the center of his body as the zero point of origin. Thus, the young infant in his crib first moves his arms in a bilaterally symmetrical fashion toward the center of his body and away in circular motions. As one arm moves in (toward the center), the other moves in also. He therefore learns that this bilateral pattern is an "outside-in" movement. However, with his left hand, it is objectively a left-to-right movement, while with his right hand it is a right-to-left movement.

Thus, one basic symmetrical movement pattern has two opposed objective directions. A little later, when he first moves his hand across the midline of his body, he must learn that the movement remains constant although it has crossed the midline and is now compared with the pattern on the opposite side. Thus, subjectively, the movement is first an "outside-in" pattern and, when it crosses the midline, becomes an "inside-out" pattern. He learns that the objective movement remains "right-to-left" even though it may begin as an "outside-in" movement and, at the midline, become an "inside-out" movement. The subjective direction must be reversed when the midline is crossed in order to maintain the constancy of the objective movement. Young children often show hesitancy and reluctance to move the hand across the midline and display confusion when it is on the opposite side. Many slow-learning children will be seen to show the same hesitancy and confusion at a later age.

The movement of a visual stimulus outside the body derives meaning by being matched to the kinesthetic patterns by which movement was first interpreted. Therefore, when a visual stimulus crosses the midline, the same problems of translation occur as when the hand crosses the midline. Unless the translation can be carried out accurately, confusion results concerning the objective direction of movement of the visual stimulus. Since the child follows the moving visual stimulus with his eyes, the movement of the eyes follows the same pattern as that previously followed by the hand. When the line of sight passes the midline, a reversal of visual-kinesthetic matching must be accomplished.

In order to maintain objective directions of movement without confusion, therefore, the child must learn three procedures and learn them with extreme precision. (1) He must learn where the midline of his body is. (2) He must learn how to reverse the translation at the midline without interrupting the continuous external movement. (3) He must learn to *always* reverse when the midline is crossed. This translation offers some children considerable difficulty. Their problem can be seen in indecision and loss of control when a movement crosses the midline of their bodies. In like manner, it can frequently be seen in eye movements where the child will lose control and following movements will be rough and jerky as the target crosses the midline.

DIRECTIONALITY AND LATERALITY

It can be seen from the discussion above that directionality in space is the projection outside the organism of the laterality which the individual has developed inside the organism. Directionality thus depends upon laterality and, until a good solid laterality has been developed, the elaborations and extensions necessary for the establishment of directionality in space will be limited and inaccurate.

The intermediary step in transferring laterality to directionality is supplied by the eye and its kinesthetic information. We project our visual images into space over the same band of light rays which brought them to our eyes. For this purpose, we must be able to locate accurately that band of light rays. To do so, we must be able to (1) control the eye with accuracy and (2) know accurately where the eye is pointed. Only then can we match the outside relations of space with the inside relations of space which are our only basis for valid projection.

Just as the child establishes the right-left directions by transferring laterality to space surrounding him, so he develops "up" and "down" by transferring the up and down direction within his own body into outside space. He develops a concept of up and down through observing his own body and the relationship of objects to parts of his body, as well as by erecting a perpendicular to the lateral coordinate which he has learned. The fore and aft direction is more complicated and will be discussed in the chapter on spatial relations.

It can now be seen that the primary directions of space and the coordinates of the spatial world are developed within the organism and projected outward into objective space. Orientation in space and the observation of relationships between objects in space becomes difficult if not impossible until these coordinates are established within the body itself. It is through motor activity and the observation of motor activity that these coordinates become established. It is therefore important that the child's motor learning be fostered and that it be directed toward the development of these coordinates. Specially devised activities and training procedures can aid the child in this learning process.

BODY IMAGE

As we have pointed out above, we do not have absolute clues to spatial relationships in the outside world. In all external information, we are dealing with relatives and relationships rather than with absolutes. For this reason, we must have a point of reference around which to organize the relative impressions which we get so that we can impose some kind of order upon them and construct a coherent totality. We use our own bodies as this point of reference. Objects about us are referred to our body and oriented in space with reference to it. For this reason, it is important that the child have a clear, accurate, and complete picture of his own body and its position in space.

As a result of certain sensations which we receive, we form a picture in our minds which represents the way in which the body appears to us. We have tactile, temperature, and pain impressions from the surface of the body. There are sensations which come from the muscles indicating their state of contraction or relaxation. There are visual impressions of parts of the body. There are sensations arising from the viscera. All of these become welded into a unity which represents the body to us. Out of this, we build up a body scheme or *body image*. It is this body image which becomes the point of origin for all the spatial relationships among objects outside our body.

IMPORTANCE OF BODY IMAGE

Schilder (1935) and Bender (1956) have emphasized the importance of the body image. They point out that it is necessary for the initiation of any movement. Thus, Schilder writes: "When the knowledge of our own body is incomplete and faulty, all actions for which this particular knowledge is necessary will be faulty too. We need the body image in order to start movements. We need it especially when actions are directed toward our own body. Every trouble in gnosia and in perception generally, will lead to a change in action. We have again and again emphasized the close relationship between the perceptive (efferent—impressive) side of our psychic life and the motor (afferent—expressive) activities.

Knowing where your body is and how much space it needs are important early learnings. (Courtesy of A. Devaney, Inc.)

Consequently peripheral changes in the sensibility must lead to disturbances in actions. Central disturbances like agnosias will also be disturbances of action" (p. 45).

Schilder has also pointed out that a fault in the body image will be reflected in the perception of outside objects. "Experiences in pathology show clearly that when our orientation concerning left and right is lost, in regard to our own body, there is also a loss of orientation in regard to the bodies of other persons. The postural model of our own body is connected with the postural model of the body of others" (p. 16).

PROBLEMS OF THE BODY IMAGE

As indicated above, the body image is a learned concept resulting from the observation of movements of parts of the body and the relationship of the different parts of the body to each other and to external objects. Many children have difficulty with this learning process and the learning is incomplete. Such a child will display this difficulty when asked to select a space on the floor

among furniture and other obstacles, which is sufficiently large to
permit him to lie down and move his arms and feet freely. He will
select a space that is too small and in which his arms and legs bump
into the furniture when he moves them. On the other hand, he
may demand much more space than he needs for his movements.
Either error indicates an imperfect awareness of the space occupied
by his body in various positions.

Children will also show difficulty in body image in activities
which require them to move various parts of the body upon command. Thus, a child may not be able to move one arm without
moving the other arm as well. When lying on the floor, he may
not be able to move his feet without abortive movements of the
arms. He is not sufficiently aware of the parts of his body and how
to move them or what they can do. Particular difficulty is experienced in activities in which the child is required to move one
member on one side and the other member on the other side, as
when he is requested to move one leg and the opposite arm. Here
he may show his difficulty by starting to move the other two members or by pausing and obviously considering which member is
the one requested. He may have difficulty translating the visual
impression, when you point to a part, into the kinesthetic impression resulting from moving the part. He must learn how to identify the parts of his body on the basis of various sets of clues and
how to control the identified parts independently of other parts.

All of these problems are problems of the body image and indicate that the child has not developed a complete pattern of his own
body and its movements. Since, as we stated above, this body is
the zero point, or point of origin, for all movements and for all interpretations of outside relationships, these movements and relationships will be disturbed if the body image is disturbed.

INFLUENCE ON LATERALITY AND DIRECTIONALITY

We need to mention again the importance of laterality and directionality. These concepts are closely related to the body image
and their development is dependent in large part upon the adequate
development of the image of the child's own body. Only through

a reliable and consistent body image can the child develop a reliable and consistent point of origin for either perceptions or motor responses. We should offer him motor activities and guide his motor development toward an awareness of his body in space and what it can do.

chapter 4

The Perceptual Process

Modern thinking and recent experimentation point toward the conclusion that a closed system, involving a feedback control, is operative in the perceptual process.

Figure 1 will help to make clear the type of system most commonly hypothesized. It should be pointed out that this diagram is not limited to investigations in perception. With minor modifications and additions, it is used extensively in discussions concerning speech pathology, endocrinology, communications, electrical engineering, etc. A model similar to the one used here has been found extremely useful in a large variety of fields.

INPUT

In perceptual theory, the input of the diagram is thought of as activity in the sensory projection areas of the cerebral cortex. Some form of energy impinges upon the exterior of the organism. It strikes certain sensitive cells and (depending upon the nature of the energy and the nature of the cells) sets up a pattern of neural

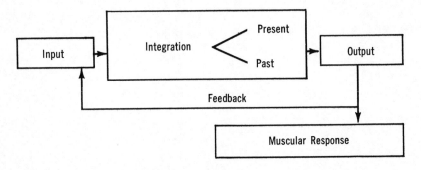

FIGURE 1.   Diagram of Feedback Mechanisms in Perception.

impulses resulting from the firing of a pattern of sensory cells located on the surface of the body.   This pattern of neural impulses
is transmitted to the projection area of the cortex.   There, an
analogous pattern of neural impulses is set up through the action of
internuncial neurones.   It is this pattern of electrical impulses in the
sensory projection areas which constitutes the input.

Bear in mind that the input, as we understand it here, is a pattern of nervous impulses.   These nervous impulses are generated
within the organism as the result of firing by the organism's own
cells.   No outside energy enters the organism for the purpose of
setting up perceptual activity.   Perceptions result from activities
of the organism itself, not from the transmission of outside energy
into or through the organism.   Very often our thinking goes astray
at this point.   We consider that the stimulus enters the organism.
We say, "I put such and such a stimulus into this organism."   From
the point of view of perception, no stimulus ever enters the organism.   The stimulus is effective on sensory cells at or near the surface of the organism.   The stimulation to which the organism responds is the pattern of neural impulses generated by the firing of
these sensitive cells.

The input in our diagram, therefore, is input from the organism
itself.   Other things being equal, the perceptual input corresponds
closely to the energy distribution impinging upon the organism.

This correspondence, however (at least in any one sense field), is never perfect. Neither is the perceptual input a replication of the outside energy pattern. The perceptual input is a translation of outside energy into patterns of neural impulses.

When such an input pattern has been generated in the sensory projection areas, its effects radiate out through internuncial neurones into the surrounding association areas. It is here that the integrative process takes place.

INTEGRATION

The integrative process has proved to be one of the most mysterious of the organism's activities. We still do not know very much about it, and there are many conflicting hypotheses and many alternate theories devised to explain its operation. There is, however, rather general agreement that two basic processes occur.

INTEGRATION OF SIMULTANEOUS INPUTS

In the first place, the integrative process is concerned with all of the sensory inputs operating in the organism at a given moment. Only in the most hypothetical of laboratory experiments is there ever a time when only one sensory input is present in the organism. Normally we are receiving information simultaneously from many sensory sources. Consider the stimulation which you are receiving at this moment. Dominant of course are the visual sensations from the printed page. However, these are by no means all of the sensations you are receiving. Noises of traffic on the street outside, kinesthetic sensations from the postural muscles, temperature sensations from the skin, tactual sensations from those parts of the body in contact with the chair, organic sensations from the digestive tract, all are present as you read. Furthermore, these various sensations do not occur separately; they are welded together into a total "stimulus situation." It is this stimulus situation of which you are aware and to which you are responding at this moment. Any reduction of the total stimulus situation resulting from removing some of these many simultaneous stimuli makes the situation seem unreal, makes you feel uncomfortable, and interferes with your responses. Our normal responses are responses to collections of sensory stimuli, all of which are active in the organism at the same time. We live in a world in which various forms of energy are impinging upon the organism at all times. These various forms of energy are setting up simultaneous input patterns in various sensory fields which are originating in various external areas of the body. The perception which results is based upon the net effect of all of these simultaneous stimulations, not upon one isolated input. It is in the integrative mechanism that all of these simultaneous inputs are integrated and organized so that a single response can be generated which will consider all of the outside energy in one act.

Into the association areas of the cortex, where integration takes place, feed fibers from all the sensory projection areas. As a result of the integrative process, a pattern of neural activity is aroused in the cortex which encompasses the contribution of all the senses into one over-all pattern. Our response is geared to this over-all pattern, not to the pattern in any one sensory area. It is essential that such an integrated pattern be used as the basis of behavior since only then can we efficiently consider all sensory information at one time. Only then can we balance one sense field against another for more complete and more accurate information.

Here again, our thinking frequently goes astray. We attempt to account for a perceptual response as though it were a response to a single stimulus in a single sensory field. Laboratory experimentation, in the interest of rigid scientific control, has frequently attempted to set up situations in which the latter condition held. These attempts have never been completely successful. Even under the most rigid controls yet devised, the organism receives multiple stimulation, not single stimulation. As recent experiments at McGill University (Bexton, Heron, and Scott, 1954) have shown, if the organism comes too close to single stimulation, highly abnormal behavior results. Even under normal laboratory controls, the atypical reactions characteristic of the laboratory are notorious. No matter how interested we may become in a particular sensory stimulus, we must always keep in mind that the stimulus in which we are interested is only a part of the much larger stimulus field involving other sensory avenues and that the response is a response to this total stimulus field. (Compare with Gibson, 1950.) The integration of all of these inputs, so that a total response can obtain, is one of the functions of the integrative mechanism.

INTEGRATION OF PAST AND PRESENT EXPERIENCE

The second part of the integrative process involves the effects of past experiences of the organism. Here we run against the problem of memory and the memory trace. In this area again, there are numerous hypotheses. Modern thinking, however, conceives of at least a large part of the memory process as being a more or less permanent alteration of the organism. Any response of the organism involves not only the present stimulating activities, but effects of past activities as well. The further elaboration of the present stimulus situation by the addition of pertinent data from our past experience invests the present experience with "meaning." It is in the integrative mechanism that this synthesis of present and past experiences occurs.

We therefore find that, as a result of the integrative process, the original pattern of neural impulses which constituted input has been elaborated. This elaboration has involved the addition of all other stimulation present in the organism at the given moment and the alterations and modifications of those input patterns resulting from modifications in the organism produced by its past experiences. As a result, we have a vastly elaborated pattern of neural impulses.

SCANNING

This elaborated pattern is then scanned by a scanning device and translated into an output pattern (Strauss and Kephart, 1955, pp. 9 f). It seems probable that this scanning mechanism is a simple translation from an association pattern to a motor pattern. Just as the scanning beam on a television camera translates the light gradients in the studio into a temporal series of electrical impulses, the scanning mechanism translates the afferent and association pattern in the integrative mechanism into a motor output pattern. Just as the television picture in your living room is an accurate model of the light distribution in the studio, the output pattern is an accurate model of the pattern existing in the integrative mechanism. Thus, we see the scanning mechanism as a simple translation device without alteration. The nature of the scanning device is not fully known. However, it is thought to be related to the alpha rhythm of the cortex. The scanning rhythm appears to be about ten to twelve cycles per second (McCulloch, 1951, p. 100; Wiener, 1948, p. 32).

OUTPUT

As a result of this scanning operation, an output pattern is generated and we enter the output area of our diagram. This output process is again a pattern of neural impulses. However, this time it is a pattern in the motor area of the cortex which can be sent down to muscle and will result in movement. Thus, the output pattern is a pattern of innervation to muscle.

It is generally considered that consciousness first occurs at this point in the perceptual process. We are first conscious of the stimulus when an output pattern has been generated. Thus, we cannot "see," as we think of this process in our everyday speech, until we have an output pattern.

FEEDBACK

When the output pattern has been generated, it is sent down the efferent nerves to muscles and muscular response results. On the way to the muscle groups, however, a portion of the output pattern is drained off and is fed back into the system at the input end. The presence of feedback in the perceptual process makes the system a servomechanism (Brown and Campbell, 1948). Such feedback creates a closed system of control. Information from the output end of the system is oriented toward the input end and used for control. In such a system, the system becomes its own control.

The ordinary traffic light is an illustration of an open system of control. What the traffic does cannot affect the built-in timing mechanism which operates the light. Changes of traffic flow have no effect upon the system. In newer traffic lights, an electric eye senses the flow of traffic in each direction and, on the basis of this information, the timing of the traffic light is altered. These newer systems are closed systems of control. A part of the energy of output (the traffic) is fed back into the system at the input end (traffic light) where it is used to control the system.

The great advantage of closed systems is that they make possible a constant monitoring of the system and continuous alteration in terms of this monitoring. In the older traffic lights, the control was periodic. It was established when an officer checked the system and reset the timing mechanism of the lights. The adequacy of the control was dependent upon how long it had been since the system was checked and what changes in traffic flow had taken place during that time. In the newer traffic lights, the system is constantly checked and the control is altered immediately when the constant check indicates that a change in timing would be more effective in controlling traffic flow. In the perceptual process, this feedback output pattern becomes in itself a part of input. As the feedback re-enters on the input end of the system, it alters the input pattern and thereby calls for a new cycle of the perceptual process. Thus, each alteration of input resulting from the feedback calls for a new integration, a new output, and further feedback. This circular process will continue until the feedback exactly matches the input.

Thus, the perceptual process is not a static affair, not a straight-line process or one-time activity, but a continuing process that remains active until an exact adjustment occurs between feedback and input. Through the feedback mechanism, the process is perpetuated until an adequate response has been generated. The feedback is used as a control in a closed system which becomes self-monitoring.

It is of course apparent that the output pattern need not result in a muscular response on every cycle of the process. It is possible for us to generate an output pattern, drain most of it off in feedback for control purposes, and permit so little to continue to muscle response that no overt movement of the organism occurs. It is in this manner that we can engage in non-overt activities and can try out many possible solutions to a problem before committing ourselves to an overt movement. By this means, the perceptual process can be continued until an adequate matching of output and feedback has been achieved before muscular response occurs. It is of course apparent that much of our more important problem-solving goes on in this fashion.

PERCEPTION AND LEARNING

An appreciation of the feedback mechanism described above will indicate that all of the parts of the perceptual process operate together as a totality. After an input pattern has been elaborated through the integrative process, an output pattern is generated which becomes an additional input pattern because of the feedback. Owing to the cyclical nature of the process, we cannot consider one of these steps without considering all of the others. No area operates independently, but each is influenced by what transpires in the remaining areas and by its own modification of the activities in the remaining areas.

PERCEPTUAL-MOTOR

The fact that we cannot consider any aspect of the perceptual process without considering the total activity becomes particularly significant in the areas of input and output. We are accustomed to think of input as an independent process and output as another independent process. We speak of input activity and output activity as though they could be separated.

In periodicals and in our textbooks, we consistently make a distinction between input (sensory or perceptual activities) and output (motor or muscular activities). If you open a book on child psychology, you will find a chapter devoted to perceptual development and a separate chapter devoted to motor development. The implication is that these are two separate activities which can be studied one apart from the other and which are only very tenuously connected, if at all. Similarly, if you open a book on psychology, you will find a section on sensory activities and a separate section on motor activities. If you are interested in experimental psychology, you will find a chapter on perception and a separate chapter on motor skills. Even in neurology you will find efferent processes discussed separately from afferent processes.

All of these approaches imply, if they do not actually state, that input and output are two separate entities which can be described independently of each other. It is our thesis, of course, that such a division of thinking is impossible and can only lead to error. The input-output functions of the organism occur in a closed cycle. Anything which happens in one area affects all other areas. The input-output system is a closed system, and we cannot stop activities in one area while we investigate the effect of changes in the other. Therefore, we cannot speak of, or think of, input and output as two separate entities; we must think of the hyphenated term *input-output*. In like manner, we cannot think of perceptual activities and motor activities as two different items; we must think of the hyphenated term *perceptual-motor*.

Just as in our thinking we cannot separate what part of the child's activity in any task, such as copying a figure, is motor and what part is perceptual, in our teaching we cannot separate what parts of the activity are perceptual and what parts are motor. Many successful teaching programs have recognized this fact and have trained all aspects of the perceptual process at one time. If we think in these total-process terms, such activities as teaching a child to balance on a walking board in order to improve his perceptual performance no longer strike us as bizarre. In like manner, it will be obvious to us that attempting to teach in terms of input factors alone overlooks many valuable aids. The total perceptual-motor process should be considered in every learning activity which we set up for the child. Learning experiences should be designed for him in terms of this total process in order to obtain the desired results.

Eyes and hands must work together. When eyes give the signals, hands must cooperate. Neither can complete the task alone. (Courtesy of Hibbs from Monkmeyer).

Teaching should be directed toward the total activity of the child in any given task. The total activity includes all four processes: input, integration, output, and feedback. If any of these processes are deficient, the child may be expected to experience difficulty. Classroom teaching, therefore, involves attention to both perception and motor ability, and especially to the very important feedback or matching between them, just as much as it involves attention to integration with its variables of experience and intelligence. Because of the cyclical nature of the process, physical education becomes a part of reading and the too frequent dichotomy between muscular or motor activities and intellectual activities becomes untenable. Since we cannot separate the perceptual and the motor in the processes of the child, we should not attempt to separate them in teaching him.

MEMORY AND LEARNING

Just as we cannot separate input and output in the perceptual process, we cannot separate the integrative process from the total activity. We have pointed out that the integrative process involves the pulling together and organizing of all of the stimuli which are impinging on the organism at a given moment. In addition, it involves the process of tying together with the present stimulation experience variables retained from past activities of the organism. Many past activities are retained in the organism, not as separate pieces of information, not as independent data, but as alterations in the organism itself (Russell, 1959, pp. 25–26).

It seems probable that experiences which the organism undergoes leave more or less permanent alterations in the function of the neural units themselves (*boutons* or *synaptic knobs*, Hebb, 1949; Lorente de No, 1947). It is the effect of the accumulation of these alterations upon present perceptual processes which determines the nature of the elaboration of the input which will occur in the integrative process.[1]

---

[1] Certain learning theories would not admit of memory as an alteration in the organism; others would ascribe to such alterations a minor role in learning. It would appear, however, that the point of view of Russell, Hebb, and others has sufficiently important implications for education to warrant serious attention.

Such a consideration makes of memory or learning something much more dynamic than a mere collection of pieces of information. We can stop thinking of memory as nothing more than a storehouse for ideas and data. Under our present thinking, memory and learning are dynamic processes as a result of which all future activities of the organism are modified. As Koffka (1951, p. 227) has pointed out, learning is a true development, not a mechanical addition of performances.

ROTE MEMORY

It is true that we have a type of learning which seems to result in mere storing of isolated pieces of information. We call this *rote memory*. It is the thorn in the flesh of every educator. It is possible, under certain conditions, to make a very restricted modification in the organism influencing only very specific activities which are themselves as restricted as the modification itself. Thus, these rote memory items can exist in the organism and are called forth only by very specific stimulation. Their effect upon the total activities of the organism is extremely limited.

This rote memory type of learning, however, is inefficient and minimally useful. Any teacher can describe its problems in detail. Children who learn in this manner are the type of pupils who will sit in the class, read the textbook, pass back the information word for word on the tests and examinations, and then, when asked to solve a problem using this identical information, will be completely lost and have no idea of how to proceed.

LEARNING AS A DYNAMIC PROCESS

Opposed to the rote memory type of learning is the much more dynamic learning process which all teachers try to achieve. In this situation, much broader modifications of the organism result. Such learning results in usable knowledge in which large areas of the organism's activity are influenced. Such learning results, not in isolated bits of information, but in major alterations in the approach of the child to the solution of his problems.

It should be pointed out that all learning does not represent the dynamic process described above. Isolated facts are important and their learning by a rote memory process is often necessary. Remembering your telephone number and street address are important items although they cannot be expected to produce any major change in over-all response. In like manner, many basic pieces of information must be "committed to memory" and a rote memory process must be used. Many more learnings, however, are more generalized and are maximally useful when they contribute to a large number of behaviors. For example, the quantitative principles of arithmetic are general and, when learned, enter into and influence large areas of the individual's thinking. The basic addition and subtraction facts, on the other hand, are isolated bits of information best learned by rote memory processes. They accomplish their purpose when they are integrated with and serve the general quantitative system. They have little use when they exist for themselves alone.

It should be obvious that the type of learning which results in broader modifications of the organism cannot be considered independently of the other activities in the perceptual cycle. Such learning is a very definite part of perceptual activity and every perceptual activity results, to some extent, in learning of this kind. We cannot think of learning as something which is turned on or turned off at specific times, as in a school classroom. Learning is a dynamic factor in every activity of the organism. Whenever the integrative mechanism is activated and whenever the feedback demands an alteration in this integrative process, learning occurs. Such learning will then influence subsequent activities of the organism. We cannot, therefore, separate learning and experience from the total perceptual cycle.

NEED FOR CONSISTENCY OF INPUT

It follows from this point of view regarding learning that the experiences of the child must occur in some kind of order. They must be integrated and capable of being combined in such a way that the structuring of the organism which results will produce a total pattern and will give rise to a logical output. From what

we have already said, it is apparent that the output pattern can be
no more adequate and can be no more generalized in its effective-
ness than is the integrative pattern from which it is derived. Essential to the building up of a sound workable structure in the integrative mechanism is consistency of input. Experiences which are
similar in nature must come into the organism through the input
channel in a similar form. Two identical experiences must not
leave different alterations in the organism. If the experiences are
similar, their alterations must reinforce each other and not conflict
with each other.

Illustrative of this problem are those conditions in which inconsistent or transient deficiencies involving the input mechanisms occur. Thus, one slow-learning child was found to have a problem
in keeping the two eyes working together. When he looked at
an object which was beyond arm's length away, the eyes worked
together properly. As the object was moved in toward his face,
somewhere near arm's length, the eyes would break apart and he
would see a double image of the object. The distance at which
the breakdown occurred was not always the same but depended
upon fatigue and the general condition of his organism at the time.
As a result, he sometimes saw singly and sometimes saw double.
There was little predictability and he could not know which condition would hold in a given situation or, when the breakdown
occurred, which of the two images was the valid one. The result
was continuous confusion particularly in near-point tasks such as
school work.

The problem in this case was not so much the defect itself as
the inconsistency of the resulting information. Had the eyes been
uncoordinated all the time, he could merely have learned to sup-
press vision in one eye and relatively less trouble would have re-
sulted. It was the confusion resulting from the inconsistency which
interfered most seriously with his performance. It is probably for
this reason that clinicians have so frequently noted that minor defects of the input apparatus give the individual more trouble than
a much more major defect appears to cause. The interference
caused by the minor defect is transient and interferes with the consistency of the information. The interference from the major defect is always present and therefore can be compensated.

When we consider such a problem, it becomes apparent that one of the very important variables involved is the input pattern itself. The external sense organ and the control exerted by the child over the external sense organ must be such that they give consistent input for similar experiential situations. Here lies one of the most important considerations in the area of perception. How consistent is the input into this organism and how is the organism manipulating its sensory receptors to maintain this consistency? How is information from various sense fields collected and how is it matched with the fed-back data of output? Such questions are essential to readiness for school work. They may be of extreme importance in the case of the slow-learning child.

chapter 5

Development of Form Perception

GLOBULAR FORM

We adults are thoroughly accustomed to seeing the world around us as a collection of distinguishable objects and shapes occupying positions in space relative to each other. We therefore find it difficult to imagine that the ability to perceive our surroundings in this fashion represents a very long and very complicated process of learning. In all probability, the infant organism does not see the world in this way. What the infant sees are primarily vague masses without distinct contour, without recognizable shape, and without definite location in space. In this connection, Harlow (1951) writes, "We would hazard that the only basic perceptual factors are size of differential brightness-hue areas in the perceptual field, steepness of gradients between the parts of the visual fields containing the differential areas, and total boundary extents."

71

What Harlow is suggesting here is that the only things which the newborn infant sees are ill-defined masses which differ from one another only in area, intensity, and perhaps color. None of the aspects of objects which we as adults are so accustomed to dealing with (form, detail, shape, contour, etc.) are as yet a part of his perception.

It is this vague, ill-defined mass which has been called by Werner (Werner and Strauss, 1939) *globular* form. These masses are characterized by cohesiveness; that is to say, they hold together and appear different from their surroundings. They are not, however, sharply distinguished from the surroundings and do not stand out against it in the manner of a figure on a ground. Their chief characteristic is their cohesiveness. They are primarily undifferentiated and amorphous.

They are characterized by qualities of the whole, by which we mean that their wholeness, or cohesiveness, is their important characteristic. Individual aspects and details are not differentiated or sorted out, and the total form exists only as a totality with no parts or no relationships of parts. As a result, these forms can operate in one way and one way only. The quality of the whole is the only characteristic which they possess.

We have often likened this globular form to a "blob," which is the most descriptive term we have found. What a young child sees when he looks out on the world is probably nothing more than a series of ill-defined blobs having no qualities in and of themselves except their extension and intensity.

Gelb and Goldstein (1938) have recorded the case of an adult who suffered a severe brain damage. In describing the perceptual activity of this patient, they suggested that his visual impressions lacked all specific characteristic structure such as the normal individual is accustomed to experiencing. Instead, this patient's visual experiences were "blobs" from which he obtained only crude impressions, such as vague evidences of heighth, width, and their relationship. It would appear that the perceptual problems of this patient, who, as an adult, could give more direct evidence of his condition than could an infant, are in many respects similar to the visual impressions of the young infant before perceptual development and learning have taken place. Gelb and Goldstein agree with

Harlow that such undifferentiated, primitive perceptions do occur. It is reasonable to assume that initial perceptions are thus undifferentiated and that more refined perceptual impressions must wait upon learning and development.

SIGNAL QUALITIES

One can imagine how the child, looking about him, sees a series of these ill-defined "blobs." Perceptual learning with regard to these blobs begins very early, probably within the first few days of life. The child discovers that one of these blobs is such that the gradients of light which represent it present some characteristic aspect or element (perhaps a bright spot near the top which he will later know as a face or a moving protrusion which he will later know as an arm). The blob possessing this characteristic aspect can be expected to behave in certain ways. It will increase in size and the steepness of the gradient between it and the surrounding area will increase. When the size and steepness of the gradient have reached a maximum, suddenly food will appear in his mouth, certain pleasant sensations will occur from stroking the skin, and certain unpleasant sensations from wetness on portions of the anatomy will disappear. Thus, he learns to identify a characteristic detail in one of these blobs which he finds behaves in a characteristic manner and which is somewhat predictable. As a matter of fact, when he sees this characteristic detail, he can, to a certain extent, control the accompanying blob. If he makes certain noises, the blob can be expected to go through this characteristic set of stages, and all the pleasant sensations will result. He learns to exert this control very quickly, as all parents know.

He soon discovers that other blobs do not behave in this characteristic manner. He can scream his little lungs out, and nothing happens. He therefore differentiates from one of the masses certain characteristic elements which he recognizes as different and which can be used to identify one of these blobs.

Werner (1948) calls the undifferentiated mass *syncretic form.* He refers to that detail which the child differentiates and which

he uses for recognition as a *signal quality*. In early stages of learning, these signal qualities may be very limited and may represent
only one or a limited number of the many details which we as
adults perceive in the object. Shinn (1900) describes the behavior
of a six-months-old infant who was given a round rattle one day
after he had become accustomed to a square one. The infant accepted the toy and then tried in vain to find the corners on which
he was accustomed to chew. The signal quality for "rattle" was
present when the toy was handed him but the additional details
which would permit him to distinguish this object from other similar objects had not yet been differentiated out of the primitive
mass.

The element or elements used as signals for recognition may be
any distinguishing characteristic of the mass, such as dark or light
spots, sharp changes in contour, or protuberances. Hebb (1949)
believes that the most characteristic elements for this purpose are
lines and angles. At first, probably only one such element is distinguished, the remainder of the object being still only a blob.
Later, more elements will be distinguished by the same process used
in distinguishing the former until a large number of single elements
characterizing the object have been distinguished. At this stage, we
can imagine that these elements are not held together in an integrated fashion but are merely combined additively because of their
proximity in the amorphous mass.

Gesell (1940) shows how the child in his early copying behavior
reveals with pencil and paper how he is differentiating details one
at a time out of a formless mass. Thus, when he attempts to copy
a square, the three-year-old makes roughly circular marks which
may or may not close. At four years, he may draw a circle or
may produce a roughly circular form one side of which is straight,
like a *D*. He may also execute one corner correctly, the remainder
of the form being vague. At five years, he may draw three corners adequately, and at six years his square has four adequate sides
and four adequate corners. He has been identifying and differentiating the details of the form little by little out of what was
initially a vague mass.

This process of identifying characteristics of globular masses continues very rapidly. The child probably differentiates one element

after another out of the globular form until he has built up a large number of elements characterizing a particular form. This differentiation of elements, or dimensions, or qualities, or characteristics, of globular forms does not occur suddenly but is acquired gradually as individual characteristics are attended to and differentiated out of the mass. It is this type of differentiation which has been stressed by Gibson and Gibson (Gibson, 1953; Gibson and Gibson, 1955). They have pointed out to us the importance of this differentiation process and the extent of learning involved. This type of differentiation continues well into adult life and becomes increasingly intense as interest is settled on certain forms or on certain areas of forms.

CONSTRUCTIVE FORM

Since the number of details involved in any form may be immense and since the importance of the form involves not only the details themselves but the relationship between these details, the differentiation process which we have described above becomes somewhat complicated. The child winds up with a mass of details about a particular form. To identify the form, he has in effect to sort through all of these details and check them off (present or absent) before he can make a valid judgment regarding the form. This is confusing, uneconomical, and time-consuming. For this reason, he learns to put together those elements which he has differentiated out of the globular mass into a new type of form. We have called this new product *integrated form* or *constructive form,* and it is the type of form perception discussed by Strauss and Lehtinen (1947) and later by Strauss and Kephart (1955). This constructive form is characterized by the organization of the details previously differentiated out of the globular form into an integrated, coordinated unit. When such an integration has been made, there emerges from the mass of detail a new quality which is characteristic of this form and this form only.

Thus, if we are presented with a figure made up of four equal sides and four right angles, we call this a square. The squareness is a very definite quality of the figure which we can recognize at once and which we are very much aware of as a quality. It is unique to this particular set of elements and especially to the relationships between these elements. There is, however, no squareness in any one of the parts. We have four equal lines and in no one of these lines is there any quality of squareness. We have four right angles and in no one of these angles is there any quality of squareness. The quality of squareness is inherent in the relationship between these eight basic elements. As such, it is emergent when the elements are integrated in such a way that the relationships are preserved. Squareness is a unique and emergent quality of this figure. In the words of the Gestalt psychologist, it is "something more than the sum of the parts."

Similar stages in the development of perception have been stressed by Werner (1957), who lists (1) global, (2) analytic, and (3) synthetic. Russell (1956) speaks of perceptions as changing from "(1) a general, vague impression to (2) differentiation of parts, followed by (3) some sort of integration of the whole again."

If the child is able to put together the elements of a figure in such an integrated and coordinated fashion, he has a much more economical tool with which to manipulate the vast number of elements which he finds in the world about him. Since this emergent quality, this "something more than the sum of the parts," is unique to the figure square and is a single quality, it can be used to stand for the total figure and all of its parts. Thus, if we can identify a figure as square, this very identification presupposes four equal sides and four right angles. The unique quality of squareness presupposes the parts. Since squareness is a unitary quality, it can be handled psychologically as easily as can any one of the elements. Since it presupposes the direct number and relationship of elements, it can be used as a single act to handle all of the elements involved in this complex. Thus, integrated or constructive form is a highly economical method of dealing with large numbers of elements in our environment at one time.

LEARNING FORM PERCEPTION

Although the globular form characteristic of the initial stage of perception is innate, the constructive form characteristic of the final stage must be learned. We can obtain some information concerning this perceptual learning process from the studies of Senden (1932) and Riesen (1947). Senden compiled reports of a number of cases of individuals born blind who were given sight by surgical operation in early adulthood. Although these individuals had had contact with familiar objects and had probably built up certain concepts of form through tactual and kinesthetic information, their visual impressions of form were new. Some of these cases were able to see differences between two figures seen together, but in a number of instances, even this ability to identify differences was not possible. Thus, sometimes a patient saw the difference between a sphere and a cube and sometimes he did not. The use of single elements as identifying characteristics is illustrated by the patient who had been trained for a period of thirteen days in discriminating between a square and a triangle. At the end of this extensive learning program, he still could not report the form of these two objects without counting their corners one after another. He had to pay attention specifically to the "signal qualities" he was using before he could identify the object.

Any alteration in the stimulus situation could destroy the recognition of form. Thus, a patient who had learned to discriminate between an egg, a potato, and a cube of sugar and promptly to name these objects could not recognize them when they were put into colored light. The cube of sugar could be named when it was seen on the table but would not be recognized when it was suspended by a thread with a change in the background.

These adult patients were experiencing the same type of learning in the area of form perception which we have described in the young child. Their difficulties in the learning process illustrate the learning stages which we can hypothesize are necessary for the young child. It should be pointed out, however, that Senden's studies cannot be accepted uncritically. Adequate controls were not used in all cases and certain relevant observations were not made in a controlled fashion. Nevertheless, in spite of these weaknesses in the study, we can gain from Senden's observations some hints regarding the probable development of the perception of form.

Riesen's study is a report of the visual responses of chimpanzees who were raised in total darkness until an age when the normal animal would have definite visual response patterns. The results of Riesen's observations were very similar to those of Senden and tend to confirm the hypotheses of the former work. Here again, we cannot accept this study uncritically. There are many problems involved in reasoning from the performance of animals to the performance of human beings, and we must be very careful how we attribute characteristics observed in animals to human behavior. However, the study of Riesen also can give us some hints regarding the probable course of perceptual development.

As mentioned earlier, the quality of the whole stressed by Gestalt psychology attaches to both the globular form and the constructive form. In the case of globular form, however, the wholeness derives from its cohesiveness, the fact that it holds together in space. The emergent quality of constructive form derives from the articulation which the child has been able to make among the details. Globular form is characterized by lack of differentiation. Constructive form is characterized by maximum differentiation plus integration between the elements which have been differentiated.

We might be able to understand the difference between these two types of form perception if we use an analogy. Globular form is like a concrete wall. There is no differentiation of parts; it is a total homogeneous mass, possessing no internal characteristics except its cohesiveness. Constructive form is like a brick wall. It is composed of a large number of recognizable units articulated closely together. The concrete wall can be thought of only as a mass; its strength derives from its cohesiveness. The brick wall can either be thought of as a mass or can be analyzed into its units which can be manipulated individually or in groups. Its strength derives from its articulation. Both possess qualities of the whole: "wallness." In the concrete wall, however, this quality is limited to the totality. If we break up the wall, we have only a mass of rubble which cannot be reclaimed. If we break up the brick wall, however, we have a series of units which can be recombined either into the same wall again or into a different structure. The "wallness" emerges from the articulation or integration of the units, the bricks. Obviously, if we have need to construct and reconstruct (as we do in perception), the brick wall is more flexible.

Pieces fit together to form figures, but only if you have learned how to see a form, which is more than the sum of its parts. (Courtesy of H. Armstrong Roberts).

PROBLEMS IN LEARNING FORM PERCEPTION

The construction of an integrated or constructive form, as has been suggested, is a learning task and a very difficult learning task. Many children experience difficulty at the early stage of differentiating elements from the initial globular mass. They either do not or cannot attend to the details of this mass; hence, these details remain unrecognized. Many more children break down at the higher level where the details, having been differentiated, must be integrated into a constructive form. If this integration fails to take place, the child is unable to deal with a coherent figure in the manner in which we are accustomed to deal with it; instead, he is left with a mere mass of elements which he can manipulate only one at a time or in very small groups. Since he cannot perceive an integrated form, he does not respond to the totality of the elements in a figure but responds to only one or a limited number.

An illustration may make this procedure more clear. We once observed a sixteen-year-old brain-injured child at a summer camp. In connection with the camp activities, the children attended a campfire in the evening. This youngster announced that he would come to the campfire in disguise so that no one would know who he was. At the appropriate time, he appeared in his disguise. This consisted of an old felt hat pulled down over his forehead and a red bandana tied around the lower part of his face. Of course all of the children recognized him at once. He, however, failed to understand why the rest of the children could recognize him when he was disguised in this manner.

On the following evening, another campfire activity was scheduled. During the afternoon, this youngster announced that he was going to be disguised again and that this time no one would be able to recognize him. The time for the campfire arrived and the boy came in his disguise. It now consisted of an old felt hat pulled down over his forehead and a blue bandana across the lower part of his face. This night the children not only recognized him but perceived that this was the same disguise which he had worn the previous night and taunted him with the fact. The youngster was very disturbed. How could they recognize him and why did they think that this was the same disguise that he had worn last night?

He later discussed this problem with one of the staff members. "Why," the adult said, "would you think that the children would not recognize you when you wore the same hat and the same bandana tonight that you wore last night?" The child said, "Oh, no. I wore a red bandana last night and tonight I wore a blue bandana."

This child thought that whenever he changed an element in the situation, he changed the total situation. Unfortunately, in his case this was exactly true. He had not been able to construct an integrated form. He was therefore bound by the elements of a figure, and for him, if you changed one of the elements, you did, in fact, change the whole. He could not deal with all of the elements in a complicated form, such as the human figure, all at one time. He had to deal with them element by element. He became confused when an element was changed and he could not encompass the variation of minor elements within the total cluster of elements.

The chief characteristic of the child who has been unable to construct an integrated form is his response to elements in a situation rather than to the situation as a whole. We are apt to speak of him as impulsive. In any given situation, he is apt to respond to one item where we would respond on the basis of a collection of items. We must not forget that for him this collection of items does not exist as it exists for us; only one item exists and to this he responds. Since many of the items in the situation may be necessary to the solution to the problem, he will come out with the wrong answer. The modifications of his behavior which should be dictated by other elements in the situation do not take place. We describe him as distractable, impulsive, or uninhibited. All of these behaviors can well be the result of his inability to construct an adequate figure.

THE PROBLEM OF CONSTRUCTIVE FORM

It is very difficult for us as adults to realize the nature of the world in which such a child lives. Form for us is so compulsive and so universal that we cannot imagine what the situation would be if it did not exist. We deal with figure constantly. There is never any situation where we are not aware of a figure on a ground, or where we are not aware of numerous figures on numerous grounds. We constantly shift our figure-ground relationship as we change our attention from one point in the situation to another. We cannot imagine seeing four equal lines and four angles without seeing a square. This is why teaching is so difficult with such children. We cannot see what they see; we cannot imagine the situation in which they are operating, and therefore, we have difficulty in constructing adequate learning situations to help them.

We can gain some insight into the problems of the child with inadequate form perception if we observe what happens to our own perceptions when the process of form is deliberately interfered with. Figure 2 is similar to items of the Street Gestalt Completion Test (Street, 1931). It presents the silhouette of a common figure.

FIGURE 2. Incomplete Silhouette. Missing parts must be filled in perceptually and integrated with the parts presented before the form can be detected.

However, certain parts of the total form have been randomly removed. As a result, it is difficult for us to generate perceptually the missing parts, integrate them with the existing parts, and "see" a dog. If the child has not adequately differentiated the parts of a figure and if the parts do not articulate closely together, he may have much the same type of difficulty with *all* forms which we have with this experimental form.

Note how, before you had the solution to Figure 2, you gave undue attention to the parts. You tried to "make something" out of one or more of the more predominant black areas by themselves. We have said that the child with poor form perception tends to respond to details. You next tried to use one of the predominant areas as a single clue to the whole figure (signal quality). The most difficult task of all was to integrate *all* the areas (plus what had been omitted) into a total form. Yet it was only from this total form that a *meaningful* figure emerged.

Figure 2 is only an exaggeration of a problem which confronts us continually. Seldom do we have the time and opportunity to see *all* the elements in a figure. Consider your behavior in reading this page. You do not take time to see every letter, much less the parts of each letter. Yet you construct the words from the relatively small number of elements which you do see. It is similar with most of our perceptions. We see pieces, as in Figure 2, which we integrate to produce meaningful forms. We can do this quickly and efficiently because we have learned how to do it. For the child who has trouble learning form perception, constructing the figure of the chair across the room or the word on the page may be as difficult as constructing Figure 2 was for you.

Another method of showing the problem of constructive form is the "Hidden Figures" technique of Gottschaldt (1926). In Figure 3, the dollar sign with which we are all familiar has been hidden by the addition of a number of irrelevant details. It is difficult for us to hold together those elements which pertain to the familiar sign and keep them separated from the additional elements. The figure does not stand out from the background.

Here again, we have merely increased the difficulty of a problem which is always present. Figures do not exist in a vacuum, nor are they conveniently presented on homogeneous backgrounds. They are embedded in backgrounds which are themselves collections of elements. We must perform constantly the same task required in Figure 3 to keep forms separated from their backgrounds. The child who has had difficulty in learning form perception may well have as much trouble with common everyday figure-ground problems as we have with Figure 3. For this child, the elements of perceptual figures, whether these be objects or printed symbols, become confused with the elements of the background and a meaningful figure cannot be held. Of course it is only by holding the figure, well integrated and solid, that any of us keep it separated from the surrounding ground. Any weakness in the figure lets it slip easily and become confused with the ground. It is often noticeable how frequently the slow-learning child is disturbed by flaws or spots in the paper on which he is working—minor background features which are not even noticed by other children.

FIGURE 3. Hidden Figure. The addition of distracting elements makes it difficult to see a common figure within the pattern.

If we disturb the grouping of elements, we can create a difficulty in our own perception. In the sentence "se eSpo trun," it is difficult for us to recognize the all too familiar "see Spot run" of primer fame. Here we have merely regrouped the phonic elements. For the child, however, in whom difficulty has occurred in forming proper integration of phonic elements in the first place, we may in ordinary written or oral material all too frequently present him unsuspectingly with "se eSpo trun" and wonder why he does not respond. For us, the proper grouping of elements is compulsive; for him, it may frequently be only a matter of chance.

CONSTRUCTIVE FORM AND READING

Let us consider as an illustration the problem confronting such a child when he begins to learn to read. In the kindergarten or first grade, he will probably be taught to read by the so-called "look and say" method. This method consists of having the child identify the word as a whole. Certain characteristics of the total word are discovered by the child or, if he has difficulty, may be pointed out to him by the teacher. Frequently, we draw a frame around the word so that these characteristics are shown up more forcefully. Thus, the word *toot* has an element which sticks up at the front of the word and another element which sticks up at the back of the word. By the "look and say" method, the child can identify this word by merely recognizing these characteristic elements. Actually, it is not necessary for him to see the remainder of the word at all. If he can recognize these characteristic elements, he can call the word adequately and pass the reading test.

This kind of task offers little difficulty for the child who is deficient in form perception. He has merely to differentiate out of the globular mass those particular elements which are characteristic of this word. He can then call the word off and nobody is aware that these particular elements are the only elements in the situation to which he has paid any attention. As a matter of fact, he is apt to be better at this type of activity than the child who has constructed an integrated form. He is not distracted or misled by any of the intervening elements in this word. Since the characteristic elements are the only ones he perceives, he is never confused by any of the other elements in the word.

A little later on, however, he is going to be taught to read by the "word analysis" method. In this method, he is taught to break the word down into its parts and to sound out the characteristic phonetic elements of each of the individual parts. But how can he break this word down into its parts if it does not have any parts to begin with? Since there is no integration between these elements, if he pays attention to one, he loses all the rest. Thus, difficulty begins. In order to learn satisfactorily by the word analysis method, it is necessary that the child hold together in a pattern all of the elements of the word, that he pay attention to these elements in serial order but not lose the total pattern. Now our child who is weak in form perception has real difficulty. He is asked to break down into a serial order of parts a globular whole which for him has no parts. He is asked to integrate in time a series of elements which were presented to him integrated in space. But for him they had no integration in space, and therefore he cannot integrate them in time. He is in the predicament described by Vernon (1957, p. 15): "the implications of these studies for reading are that children (or, at least, some children) are less likely to see words as wholes than as meaningless jumbles of details with no apparent relationship between these. On the other hand, letters may perhaps be seen as unanalyzable wholes, and hence there is difficulty in differentiating their structure." Again, Vernon writes, "The one universal characteristic of nonreaders suffering from specific reading disability is their complete failure to analyze word shapes and sounds systematically and associate them together correctly" (*op. cit.*, p. 74).

Not only must the child analyze the word form on the page into its parts, but he must associate these parts with the appropriate phonetic sound. Again, Vernon says, "We have no definite evidence as to the incapacity of such cases to perceive and analyze printed words, but it is quite clear that they often fail to recognize that a certain spatial orientation of the letters is essential, and also a particular order and arrangement of the letters within the word. Again, we have no definite evidence that they *cannot* hear the sounds of letters and words, though this may occur in some cases of mild hearing loss and high frequency deafness; but it is probable that many of them do not listen to, and hence do not hear, the separate phonetic units in the total word sound, and do not remember them in their exact order. This may often be due merely to inattention and lack of interest; but sometimes it seems as if they 'are like the deaf adder that stoppeth her ears, which refused to hear the voice of the charmer, charm he never so wisely!' The result is that they are unable to associate the visual and auditory units, because they are uncertain which correspond with which" (*op. cit.*, p. 188).

SENSORY-MOTOR SKILLS AND FORM PERCEPTION

The development of adequate form perception depends upon the adequate learning of basic sensory-motor skills such as we have discussed in earlier chapters. It is obvious from what we have said that constructive form is dependent in large part upon the relationship between elements. In visual perception, at least, these relationships are relationships in space. As we have pointed out earlier, the coordinates of space and hence the coordinates upon which the relationships of form must be built are learned. This learning begins with the development of laterality.

Our first information about form and about the spatial relationships involved in form is kinesthetic and tactual. We must learn kinesthetic laterality before we can proceed to visual form. This laterality must be projected outside of the body in terms of directionality before we have a basis for maintaining the relationships involved in form. We have already discussed in this connection the importance of the control of ocular movements and the use of the eyes as a mediator of the projection of directionality into visual stimuli. These basic skills are necessary in order to ensure that the relationships involved in a form are presented to the child and are responded to by him in a consistent manner.

His problem is to build up an integrated pattern which will represent the relationships within this figure. If those relationships do not come to him in a consistent fashion, if they vary from one presentation to another, it is obvious that he will experience difficulty

in constructing a pattern within himself that will represent a consistent set of relationships. Such consistency in input is ensured by
the basic sensory-motor skills which we have discussed in previous
chapters.

RELATION OF FORM PERCEPTION TO ACHIEVEMENT

When we can be sure that the child has adequate basic sensory-
motor skills, we will need to give him additional help in the development of form itself. It is at this level that such activities as pegboards, drawing, copying, coloring, paper cutting and pasting, etc.,
become important.

In a recent study of some 1500 public school children in the first
three grades, Lowder (1956) compared the ability to copy simple
forms with achievement in school. He obtained a correlation of
.52. This correlation takes on considerable significance when we
consider that it is almost identical to the co-efficient usually found
when we correlate I.Q. against school achievement in the early
grades.

Numerous other workers have observed a correlation between
copying ability and achievement. Potter (1949) reported a correlation of .60 between a task of copying forms and reading achievement. When mental age was held constant, this value dropped to
.18. Robinson *et al.* (1958) found correlations ranging from .38 to
.44 when the Visual Achievement Forms described below (see p.
150) were compared with the Chicago Reading Tests in first-grade
children. Interestingly enough, her data revealed the correlation
between the Kuhlmann-Anderson test of intelligence and the Chicago Reading Tests to be only .54. Small (1958) compared the
developmental drawing performance of kindergarten children with
their scores on the Metropolitan Readiness Test. His correlations
ranged from .51 to .61. On the basis of these independent studies,
it would appear that there is a significant relationship between form
perception, insofar as this function is measured by copying performance, and reading achievement.

In addition to these statistical studies, the work of Strauss and
Lehtinen (1947) with brain-injured children has shown the importance of form perception. Their clinical studies as well as those

of Strauss and Kephart (1955) reveal the relation of form perception to achievement in these children. Clinical evidence from these and other sources indicates that training programs designed to increase form perception ability can aid the child in increasing his achievement level.

chapter 6

Space is therefore essentially a concept developed in the brain (Craik, 1952, p. 61). It is not like brightness or color which are given to us through direct sensory activities. It is always a second-order sensory datum. Although we think of space or a space world as a substantial, existent reality and although we behave as though we had direct information concerning it, we had in fact to build up this space world for ourselves through the interpretation of a myriad of sensory data none of which was directly connected with space itself.

This entails a serious difficulty. At one and the same time, we must learn to interpret sensory information in terms of space and build up the spatial concepts which make interpretations of these sensory data in spatial terms possible. Thus we have a circular problem. We cannot develop a stable space world until we learn to interpret the information from our senses in terms of space. However, we can build up this space world only upon the basis of the spatial interpretations of sensory data. If either of these two poles were stable and given, we could use it to form the basis of a calibration for the other. Such, however, is not the case. We are required to build both ends simultaneously and in relationship to each other. It is not surprising, therefore, that spatial localization and the development of a stable space world prove difficult for many children and even for many adults.

One of the clues to distance is size of the retinal image. The farther away an object lies, the smaller its image on the retina of the eye and, until we can make a spatial interpretation, the smaller it looks. Through learning, we develop, as it were, a scale by which apparent size of the image is translated into distance of the object from the eye. If we knew how far away the object was to begin with, we could calibrate the scale of image size with little difficulty. However, the only way we can know how far away the object is (if we consider, for illustrative purposes, that image size is our only clue to distance), is to observe the apparent size of the image. Thus, we are reduced to making a series of approximations in which the exact interpretation of neither the image size scale nor the distance scale is known. By repeating these approximations many times, we achieve a reasonable collation of the two scales. Both scales vary concomitantly. If one scale could be stabilized, the other could be compared to it and exact translations made. Since neither can be stabilized, only through a complicated observation of co-variance can they be equated. What is true of image size is true of all other clues to distance. The problem is further complicated by the fact that different clues must be matched to each other as well as to objective distance.

IMPORTANCE OF A STABLE SPACE WORLD

The importance of a stable space world can scarcely be overestimated. It is through space and spatial relationships that we observe the relationship between things or objects in our environment. We can only observe these relationships between things insofar as we can locate them in space and hold them in this spatial relationship while we make our observations. We cannot compare two objects unless we have an adequate space in which to put them while we make comparisons.

In an earlier chapter, we discussed the importance of form perception and the manner in which it serves to hold together the elements of a figure so that we can deal with them en masse and can observe the details within the figure for purposes of recognition or comparison. All of the relationships in which we are interested, however, do not occur within figures or objects. More of them occur between figures or objects. This latter type of observation is possible only if we have a space world in which we can place the figures in such a way that the relationships are maintained and can be adequately observed. Thus, space becomes as important as form and for the same reasons. It is through the preservation of relationships between objects in an adequate space world that we are able to observe similarities and differences and to handle the myriad of elements within groups of objects.

IMPORTANCE OF SPACE IN ARITHMETIC

The importance of space is particularly obvious in numbers or arithmetic. Arithmetic, as Strauss and Lehtinen (1947) have indicated, is a visual-spatial problem. Stern (1949) has devised a method of teaching arithmetic based in large part on the spatial concepts involved. Mathematics deals with groups of objects and the characteristics of groups and grouping phenomena. If the child has not developed an adequate space world, he will have difficulty in dealing with grouping phenomena, since groups can only exist in space. It is not surprising, therefore, that we find so many children who achieve adequately in school until they approach the problem of numbers. Here they fail miserably. Since stabilizing the space world is the most complicated of our readiness skills and since it develops last in the series of skills, we may expect to see many children who develop adequately until they reach this final stage and then, for some reason, fail to complete this most highly developed skill. It seems probable that this group of children represents many of the apparently specific arithmetic disabilities which we find in our schools. If Strauss and Lehtinen (1947) are correct, it seems likely that these children have developed adequately until they arrived at the problem of space. Here development failed to continue satisfactorily. They achieve adequately until they arrive at arithmetic where spatial knowledge is at a premium.

IMPORTANCE OF SPACE IN CONCEPTUALIZATION

Most writers are agreed that concept formation rests upon a foundation of percept formation. Thus, Zuk (1958) states that we must recognize the close association between perceptualization and proper conceptualization. Perception and learning are not independent phenomena but must go hand in hand. Piaget (1956) points out how the abstractions of space (Euclidean geometry) grow upon the perception of space. Hurlock (1942, p. 285) relates the formation of concepts to the ability to perceive relationships between new and old situations. These are but a few examples of a rather general agreement concerning the importance of adequately organized percepts for the development of concepts and higher orders of thought. The observation of relationships is vital to more advanced thinking. In like manner, a space world in which these relationships between experiences can be preserved is vital to their observation.

The child who has difficulty with space is likely to have similar difficulties in thinking. As we have pointed out above, we observe similarities and differences between objects by locating them firmly in space and then observing these characteristics. Such similarities and differences are very important to advanced thinking. Concepts, categorization, grouping on the basis of characteristics, and the like, all involve primarily dealing with similarities and differences. The importance of such categorizing in the thinking process has been repeatedly pointed out by various researchers (e.g., Vinacke, 1956; Welch, 1947). Unless we can compare the characteristics of different objects, we cannot make the judgments upon which categorization is based.

Concepts, of which we make so much in education, are in effect categorizations in which the common factors are elements within the objects. To develop such concepts, we need to compare many objects, selecting those in which the characteristic forming the basis of the concept is present, grouping these together, and extracting from the group the common characteristic which then becomes the concept. It is such categorization which leads to generalization and abstraction. Unless comparisons between objects can be made accurately, precisely, and in detail, the resulting concept will be weak. To make comparisons between objects, we need a stable and sufficiently extensive space world so that objects for comparison can be held in mind and observed while the relationships between them remain stable.

IMPORTANCE OF SPACE IN ORGANIZING TIME

Someone will object that we have forgotten the concept of time as an organizer of objects or events. He will say that it is possible to do all the things we have discussed under space above in the time dimension without using space at all. As Einstein and others have pointed out, however, time and space are but different dimensions of the same reality. In order to respond optimally to our environment, we need to be able to deal adequately with both of these dimensions. Bühler (1930) states that rhythm and melody in time perception stand on the same level as spatial forms, thus indicating the close psychological relationship between space and time.

Because of the dominance of vision in our sensory repertory and because vision is a dominantly spatial sense, we tend to attach greater significance to space than to time in our behavior. Our very measurement of time is an example. The clock is an instrument which translates time into changes in space. The hand moves around the face of the clock, and from an observation of the extent of this movement, we deduce the passage of time and the amount of time which has elapsed. Thus, in order to stabilize time and deal with it on more than a transient basis, we must translate it into spatial terms. We find it difficult to think in terms of time without some such translation, without reducing time to space. When such a reduction has been made, we feel more secure and our thinking becomes easier and more definite.

Translations from time to space and back again are demanded of us every day. When we read a word, we have a simultaneous impression of the letters organized in space. When we are asked to spell the word, we must take this simultaneous presentation and reduce it to a series of elements (separate letters) in time. Thus, spelling becomes a temporal series whereas reading is a simultaneous series.

Likewise, in developing an idea of the room in which we sit, we are required to translate from a temporal series to a simultaneous series in space. The angle of vision provided by the eye is limited: the visual image subtends what lies within about 180 degrees as you look straight ahead and do not move your eyes or head. Obviously, this angle is not adequate to let you see all the things in the room, and you must therefore move your eyes or head and shift this visual angle to another direction. You now see some of what you saw before and some new material. This process has given you two presentations separated in time. You repeat this process as many times as necessary to cover the extent of the room. The result is a series of impressions in time. However, you do not think of the room in which you sit as a series in time but as a complete presentation in space. You know that what is behind you is there, and you are able to respond to it although you cannot see it. You have put together all the pieces which you obtained in a temporal series as you looked around the room into one single, complete presentation, simultaneous in space. Thus, all the room exists for you at one time although you have never seen it all at once. You have translated a temporal series into a simultaneous series.

For many children who have had difficulty in developing a space world, such a construction of the physical environment around them is impossible. For them, what they do not see at this particular moment ceases, very literally, to exist. Thus, many children have no operative space behind them. When they are looking ahead, the only existence, for them, is straight ahead. Anyone who has worked with retarded children has seen many examples of this inability to realize surrounding space.

One example is the boy who for many years had had difficulty in developing a space world surrounding himself. One day he was playing a game in which a ball tied to a string and hanging from a tree limb was set swinging. As the ball swung toward him, the boy was attempting to hit it with a ball bat. He frequently missed and the ball swung around behind his head. On these occasions, he would look to the right and left, up and down, wondering where the ball had gone. Suddenly, it would appear out of nowhere in front of him again. When it swung behind his head, it was, for him, completely gone. He had no space world behind him and nothing occurred there. One day when he missed the ball and was looking around for it, it swung back, hitting him on the head from behind. He turned around to another youngster who was standing near and upbraided him unmercifully for hitting him in the head with the ball.

A complete space world surrounding us is possible only insofar as we can translate a temporal series of impressions into a simultaneous impression in space. We see many children whose point of breakdown seems to be this problem of translation. They behave as though they could perform if their performance could be limited to either time or space. Thus, the child who was asked to draw a square and who went around the contour as rapidly as possible, was having trouble translating. He gave the impression that he could draw a very good square if he only had four hands and four pencils so that he could draw all the lines at one time. If he could deal throughout with the simultaneous presentation, he could succeed. However, when he had to translate from one to another, he fell apart. In like manner, in everything he did, he performed as fast as he could. If he started to walk across the room, he would begin at an adequate gait. As he progressed, however, he would walk faster and faster until, when he arrived, he would be running as fast as he could. He was trying to perform without time. At first, he would talk normally but would go faster and faster as he progressed until the words ran together incoherently. Again, he was trying to rule out time so that he would not have to translate from a simultaneous presentation in space to a temporal series in time. It can easily be seen how important such translations are in our everyday life. We have mentioned spelling, but these translations are also used in copying, drawing, writing, talking, or any activity which takes place in time but where the major idea lies in the total response rather than any of the temporal elements.

CLUES TO SPACE

Since the ability to manipulate space is so essential to learning, it is desirable that we look at the clues by which we locate objects in space and see how these are used to develop a space world. As we have said, the most direct clue to space is movement (see Bartley, 1958, p. 207). We move our hand until it comes in contact with an object. Through kinesthesis, we estimate how far we had to move and, from this estimate, determine how far away the object is. For greater distances, we move our entire body. Thus, we walk to an object and, from the amount of movement involved, estimate how far away the object was.

Vision, however, is our most efficient indicator of space. Movement is too slow and, in many cases, too difficult to be depended upon for the many and precise estimates which we must make in our everyday experience. If we had to make all our estimates of distance through the more direct data from overt movement, time would be too short for us to gather the information on which our behavior must be based. Vision, however, can give us rapid estimates of space and, if we have learned to use it, accurate estimates which we may substitute for those acquired more slowly through movement. Furthermore, vision can give us numerous estimates at once. We can look at a number of objects and can locate them all in space simultaneously, whereas, if we depended upon kinesthesis, we would have to locate each object independently. Here again, time would be consumed and accuracy sacrificed to the magnitude of the task. As we will see later, this problem of locating a large number of objects simultaneously in space is a very important consideration in achievement. Vision, alone among the senses, is uniquely fitted for such space structuring.

As we have pointed out above, there is no direct information concerning space. Vision, however, gives us a number of clues which can be used to interpret distance and location in space.

PERSPECTIVE

Perhaps the most commonly considered visual clue to space is that of perspective. We encounter this clue in artists' products and photographs. Those who work with representational objects become adept at creating impressions of distance and depth through the use of this clue. There are certain characteristics of visual data which are related to distance. If an object appears to lie above another, the higher object is probably farther away. If an object overlaps another, the overlapping object is closer. Parallel lines continued into the distance appear to approach each other, and shadow and light distribution indicate depth and position. Any elementary text on sketching or drawing will outline in detail the rules of perspective (Abbott, 1950).

Through observation of these apparently impossible aspects of our visual picture, we come to ascribe different positions in space to the different objects involved. Thus, we learn to interpret perspective in terms of space and to assign each object its proper location in space in such a way that the perspective makes sense.

ACCOMMODATION

The lens of the eye is a marvelous organ. It has the power of changing its shape and thereby changing its refractive power when we are looking at objects at different distances. When you shift your gaze from a distant object to a close one, the lens of your eye changes its shape and its power so that the new object of regard is as accurately focused on the back of the eyeball as was the former. You know that when you take a photograph, you have to adjust the camera lens for the distance to your subject. If you do not, the photograph will be out of focus. The same kind of adjustment must take place within your eye. But in the eye the adjustment is automatic. You have merely to shift your gaze and the new adjustment is made for you without your conscious effort.

This change in the power of the lens is accomplished by the action of the ciliary muscle which holds the lens in a sort of an elastic bundle. By relaxing and contracting, the ciliary muscle can squeeze the lens into a thick, stubby shape or let it stretch to a long, flat shape. The thicker the lens, the more its power and, as a result, objects at a nearer distance come into focus.

In the ciliary muscle are sensitive end organs, called *proprioceptors*, which tell us how much tension there is in the muscle. The amount of tension on the ciliary muscle is (with certain exceptions in the case of refractive error) directly related to the distance of the object which is in focus. By observing the tension in the ciliary, therefore, we can estimate the distance of the object. The process by which an object is brought into focus is called *accommodation*. We have, through the proprioceptive end organs in the ciliary muscle, an estimate of the amount of accommodation we are using. This information can therefore give us some idea of the distance to the object. Thus, we get a clue to space through accommodation (Woodworth and Schlosberg, 1954, p. 451).

CONVERGENCE

If we look at an object with both eyes, we must get the same picture in each eye. To do this, we must point each eye at the object. Since the eyes are set apart in the head, each eye must be pointed differently from the other if it is to center on the object of regard. The object, as it were, becomes the apex of a triangle of which the line between the right eye and the left eye is the base. The line of sight of each eye then becomes one of the sides of the triangle.

If an object is far away, the apex of the triangle will be far removed from the base. The sides of the triangle will be nearly parallel and the two eyes will have to point in a nearly parallel fashion to give us a single image of the object. However, if the object is near, the apex will be near the base of the triangle and the sides of the triangle will form a sharper angle with the base. The two eyes will have to point in toward each other to triangulate upon the object and give us a single image. Thus, the parallelism between the two eyes alters with the distance of the object of regard.

The eyes are controlled by six muscles attached to the outside of the eyeball. It is through the operation of these muscles that we are able to move our eyes about in our head. In these extrinsic ocular muscles, as they are called, are sensitive end organs (more proprioceptors) which tell us how much tension is being placed on each of the muscles. Through the operation of these proprioceptors, we can tell the position of our eyes from the condition of the muscles controlling them. You know that this is true because, if you shut your eyes and move them about, you know where they are pointed even though there is no image to tell you. You are receiving this information through the proprioceptive end organs in the extrinsic muscles. Just as we can know where the eyes as a team are pointed, we can know where each eye separately is pointed. Thus, we can tell whether they are nearly parallel or whether they are pointed in toward each other. In this way, we can estimate through these proprioceptive clues the distance of the object of regard.

The process by which we triangulate the two eyes upon an object is called *convergence*. Since we have information concerning the amount of convergence present at any time, we have through convergence a clue to the distance or location in space of an object (Woodworth and Schlosberg, 1954, p. 457).

IMAGE SIZE

The image of an object on the back of the eyeball varies in size with the distance of the object. The further away an object is the smaller the size of its image on the retina. This is the same phenomenon we see in a camera. You know that when you take a picture things which are close are large on the photograph while

things which are far away are small. The size of the image is a
function of the size of the object and of its distance.

Here we have another clue to distance. We learn to interpret
the size of the image as a function of distance. If we did not, the
man standing on the other side of the street would appear to be
a small pigmy while the man standing on this side of the street
would appear to be a giant. So completely do we learn to make
these adjustments that we reach the point where we are no longer
aware of differences in the sizes of the images on the back of our
eyeballs. Never do we see the man on the other side of the street
as unusually small because we immediately correct his apparent size
for the distance at which we see him. We must have our attention
called to the difference in image sizes before we notice it. However, originally we had to learn this correction. Originally, things
which were far away looked small and things which were near
looked large. By experimentation and manipulation, we had to discover the relationship between apparent size and distance and to
learn to correct size in terms of distance. We have become so
adept at this that we omit the intermediate steps and automatically
make the translation. We become so interested in keeping our images constant that we forget that what we are doing is using image
size as a clue to distance and are estimating distance from the apparent image size.

This phenomenon has been discussed in psychology as *constancy
of image size* or *size constancy*. It is through the interpretation of
inconsistent image sizes that we estimate distance, and thus image
size becomes a clue to distance and to location of an object in
space (see Bartley, 1958, pp. 215–16).

STEREOPSIS

As we pointed out above, when the eyes are focused upon an object they are not parallel in the head but are turned in toward each
other. The further away the object the less they are turned in
and the nearer an object the more they are turned in. Such relative
postures are necessary to give a single image of the object because
the eyes are separated in the head by the nose. In a previous section, we discussed this posture under the term convergence and

we saw how awareness of eye posture or convergence could give us a clue to distance.

There is, however, another effect of this posture of the two eyes. If the eyes are not strictly parallel, the image on the back of one eyeball falls at a slightly different position relative to the center of that eyeball than is the case in the other eye. When the eyes are exactly parallel, the image falls on the exact center of each eyeball. (Because of the shape of the eyeball, which is not a perfect sphere, this is not strictly true. However, the results of the phenomenon are the same although a correction must be made for the shape of the orb.) When the eyes are not strictly parallel, the image in each eye is displaced slightly toward the outside of center. The more the eyes are turned in, the more this displacement will occur; the more nearly parallel, the less it will occur. As we have seen, the eyes are turned farther in when we are looking at a near object. It follows that, when we look at a near object, the displacement of the two images on the back of the two eyeballs will be greater also. We can interpret this displacement of images between the two eyes as a clue to the distance of the object. This phenomenon is called *stereopsis* (see Bartley, 1958, pp. 229–32).

Stereopsis is the clue to distance (or depth) which is manipulated in stereo photographs. Here two pictures are presented, one to each eye. Neither eye can see the picture meant for the other eye. The two eyes are kept separate either mechanically by a septum (as in the old hand stereoscope) or by polaroid or colored filters (as in stereo movies where the viewer wears special glasses). The two pictures are taken in such a way that the angle of photographing is changed in the way in which the images to the two eyes would be changed. In other words, the two pictures are taken on the sides of a triangle of which the object is the apex. When they are shown separately to each eye, the same type of image displacement is produced which we obtain normally from the triangulation of the two eyes. As a result, the composite single picture which we see appears to have depth.

Stereopsis as a clue to space has been given a great deal of attention experimentally. Tests have been devised, designed on the same basis as the stereoscope or depth photographs, to determine the accuracy of an individual's ability to interpret this phenomenon as a clue to distance. It is this type of test which is frequently referred to as a *depth test* in visual examinations. You may have encountered this kind of test in examinations given by the armed services or even in drivers license testing. Examples of these tests can be found in the common testing instruments, such as the Keystone Telebinocular, the Bausch and Lomb Orthorater, or the American Optical Company Sitescreener.

Stereopsis is a very important clue to distance and to relative location in space. If you have looked through a stereoscope, you know the difference which the addition of this clue makes in viewing a picture. Surfaces and elements of figures stand out sharply in depth and the consciousness of three dimensions in space is greatly increased.

MOVEMENT PARALLAX

Another clue to distance which is of great importance has to do with the apparent movement of objects at different distances. Hold two pencils up before your eyes, one at twelve inches and the other at arm's length. Now move your head from side to side. Notice how the nearer pencil appears to move farther and faster than the pencil held at arm's length. This is the phenomenon called *movement parallax*. Whenever we move our head or the position of our eyes, the apparent speed and extent of the movement of objects in our field of vision vary with the distance of the objects. Near objects seem to move far and fast; distant objects seem to move slow and little.

You may have noticed this phenomenon when driving in a car. As you watch a line of telephone poles down the road ahead of you, you can see that they seem to approach very slowly. As they come closer, they seem to move faster and faster until they rush by the side of the car. We can observe the phenomenon more extensively if, while riding in a car, we detach ourselves from the movement of the car itself and only pay attention to the movements of objects in our visual field. We will then see that a whole world of movement is taking place. Some objects are moving slowly, some are moving rapidly, some are moving to the right, some to the left, some up, and some down. An extremely complicated pattern of movements differing in speed and direction is taking place. If we can attend to the movement patterns only and forget about our own movement, the entire scene becomes unbelievably complicated and confusing. However, when we turn our attention to our own movement again, everything falls into place and makes perfect sense. We have learned to interpret this complicated series of movement patterns in outside objects as a clue to distance, and we use this complicated scheme to help us locate objects in space. For a further discussion of this topic, the reader is referred to Graham (1939) pages 877–82.

TEXTURE GRADIENT

Gibson (1950) has pointed out that any surface which displays texture shows a gradient of size among the texture elements as distance increases. Thus, in a brick sidewalk, the apparent size of the individual bricks decreases as the distance increases. The texture of the surface appears coarse when we look at the near portion and fine when we look at the distant portion. Since nearly all surfaces have some kind of texture, this phenomenon, which Gibson has called the *texture gradient,* becomes an important factor in perception. We can use observations of this texture gradient to estimate distance. It becomes a very important factor since it provides us with a sort of a scale on which we can locate a number of objects at once. As we shall see later, the problem of simultaneous location of numerous objects is of great concern in space perception.

These are only a few of the clues to distance which we can obtain through our sense of vision. Many more could be mentioned: atmospheric haze, interpretation of known contours, etc. However, the clues discussed above will serve to illustrate our point. For a more complete discussion of space clues, the reader is referred to Graham (1951). There are three important points to note concerning all of these clues as well as those others which we have not mentioned.

LEARNED CLUES

As we have repeatedly stressed, the relationship between any of these clues and distance is a function of learning. Initially, we do not get information about distance directly from the clue; we had to learn to interpret the clue in terms of distance. Each of the clues is a variable in the visual data. That is to say, something in the visual datum changes, something is altered. It is this alteration or change which gives us the information about distance. Since space does not come to us directly but is inferred from changes in visual impressions which we must learn to interpret, any clue to distance or space is the result of a process of learning—learning to see changes in visual data as distances.

MULTIPLE CLUES

The second point of importance is the fact that no one of these clues is adequate in itself to give us accurate information about distance. Woodworth and Schlosberg (1954, p. 464) point out that any actual experience of depth involves several of these factors. The data from several clues are, so to speak, fed into a depth-perception computing machine. The final judgment is the result of a process in which the single factors are not merely added together but are weighed and balanced against each other. If we try to make our spatial judgments on the basis of only one clue, regardless of which one, we will be limited and inaccurate in our estimates. Any one clue suffers from two difficulties: it is limited in its extent, and it includes certain distortions over parts of its range. If we depend solely on a single clue or a simple addition of clues for our spatial judgment, we are at the mercy of these limitations and distortions.

We can see this fact most clearly perhaps in the case of perspective. We all know how artists and others trick us with false perspectives. Short objects can be made to look tall and wide objects to look thin by manipulating perspective. We can change the apparent distances of objects by changing the perspective and, in the case of illusions, we can even confuse the spatial relations by confusing the perspective. This perspective clue to space can be distorted, not only by outside manipulation, but in the natural course of events in our everyday life. If we depend on it alone for our estimates of space, we will often be deceived into making false judgments.

What is true of perspective is also true of all the other clues. Accommodation and convergence are limited. When an object lies somewhere beyond fourteen to twenty feet, our accommodative mechanism is completely relaxed and no more clues from this phenomenon occur. In like manner, our convergence mechanism is so nearly parallel beyond fourteen to twenty feet that no further observable changes are present. Therefore, these clues are operative only over a limited distance. Image size is variable. It does not follow a straight line curve but the apparent changes alter at different distances. Furthermore, the interpretation of image size is dependent upon knowledge of the object at which we are looking. After all, the man on the other side of the street *may be* a pigmy. Used alone, this clue can therefore distort our judgment and give us false impressions. Stereopsis is another phenomenon which is operative only over a limited distance (fourteen to twenty feet). Furthermore, it is a phenomenon of two eyes and is useless whenever, for any reason, one eye cannot see the target.

No one clue to distance is adequate in itself. We must combine all these clues into one complicated total impression from which we make our judgments. Through learning, we come to know how to depend more on one clue in one situation and on another in another situation. We discount the evidence of one clue at one time and discount the evidence of another clue at another time. We emphasize one clue now and discount it later. We *integrate* all this information, sorting out the limitations and inaccuracies by weighing one clue against another and, from the total impression, form a judgment. Our final judgment is based on a set of corrections and summations resulting from all this evaluating and re-evaluating. The accuracy of our final estimate depends on how well we can complete this complicated process of integration of data.

EXTRAPOLATED CURVES

As we have mentioned earlier, our most direct clue to space is movement, particularly that of the hand. In the process of learning all the complicated relations between visual changes and distance which we have been discussing, we can make direct comparisons through that distance within which we can reach. In the case of image size, for example, we can compare the apparent size of the object with its known distance when we are holding it in our hand and moving it away from us. When we reach arm's length, however, we can no longer obtain direct information about distance. We can observe directly that the image gets smaller at a given rate as we move it further away until we reach arm's length. But we see another image of the same object and it is smaller than any we have seen before. We assume that this is because it is still further away than the distance through which we can reach. However, we can have no direct evidence, and we can get no direct

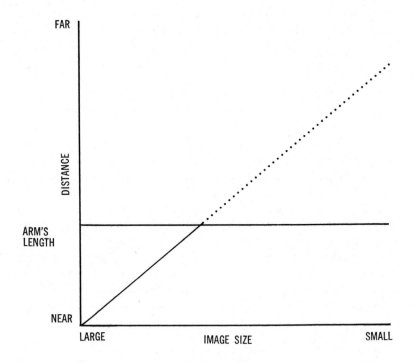

FIGURE 4. Extrapolation of a curve required to evaluate image size as a spatial clue beyond arm's length.

confirmatory information. All we can do is project the curve of change in image size with distance, as we have been able to observe it directly within arm's length, to points beyond where direct investigation is possible.

In Figure 4, which is a schematic representation of this task, we can obtain the values on the vertical axis through hand activity up to arm's length. Beyond that point, we have no information about the values on the vertical axis. We can obtain the values on the horizontal axis through a much greater distance, but we cannot compare the two values beyond arm's length. What we must do, in effect, is to draw the curve through the distances where we have all the values (both vertical and horizontal axes) and then project the curve (dotted line of Figure 4) beyond this point. Mathematically, we call this *extrapolating a curve*. On the basis of complete knowledge over a part of the area, we construct the relationship and then project it beyond the point where information is complete.

Obviously, this process of extrapolation is relatively simple as long as the curve is a straight line as in Figure 4. However, as we have seen, many of the curves representing the relationship between visual changes and distance are not straight lines. As a result, a very extensive and exacting process of learning is necessary to make the proper extrapolations. Furthermore, in many of these clues there are other factors which enter the picture to distort the curves under certain circumstances. We are therefore faced with the necessity of making more than one extrapolation, using one under certain circumstances, another under other circumstances. Also remember what we have said about combinations of clues. It is necessary to evaluate the curves representing each of the clues together, since we must integrate all the information before making a final judgment.

The process of learning space localization is a very complicated one. It begins early in life and continues through adulthood. Even as adults we are still revising and re-evaluating our spatial judgments. Many of us give up and live in a limited spatial world. Our achievement is adversely affected as a result. It is not surprising that the young child has so much trouble with this complicated learning problem. He begins sorting out these clues as soon as he becomes mobile and can experiment with his hands. He continues to elaborate this learning actively for the rest of his life. There is evidence that one of the major learning problems of the kindergarten child has to do with this process of developing spatial localization for the objects and things around him.

SPACE STRUCTURE

The problem of spatial localization is further complicated by the fact that in our daily life we are not confronted with a single object, but with a multiplicity of objects. Our space concept depends upon our ability to locate these many objects in space simultaneously in such a way as to preserve the relationships between them. In this manner, we develop for ourselves a space structure or *space lattice* in which we spot each of these objects in its proper relationship to ourselves and to each of the other objects. All of the complicated processes which we have described above must be carried out a large number of times, but it is not sufficient that we locate a single object and then forget it. To preserve the space structure, we must retain in the central nervous system the results of a given localization while we add to it additional localizations of other objects existing in our spatial milieu. None can be omitted, none can be added, and none can be replaced. If such errors occur, we will make similar errors in our behavior.

Bartley (1958, pp. 205–6) makes a similar point when he distinguishes two types of behavior in space. The first of these is encountered in animal behavior where the animal has to deal with items in space one at a time or in sequence. He must move about in space and find his way from place to place but does not need to react to all the items in his space world at once. This type of behavior deals only with restricted portions of space at any given time. The second type of behavior is that in which the organism responds to space as a whole. Bartley refers to such space perception as a *space domain*. The organism responds to space as a whole, to the extensional space domain as a domain, rather than to single bits of it.

DEVELOPING A SPACE STRUCTURE

Many slow-learning children reveal by their behavior an inability to respond on the basis of this total space domain. The young child arrives at a space structure through a process of development. First, he locates objects singly with reference to himself and only later develops a system of objective coordinates by which he can handle numerous objects in space through a system of fixed directions (see Piaget and Inhelder, 1956). In estimating spatial relations, the child may be able to tell you how many steps it will take him to walk over to an object *a* and how many to walk over to an object *b*. However, he may have no idea of how many steps it would take to walk from *a* to *b* when he himself is located at a point removed from the two objects. Furthermore, he may have no idea of how to begin such an estimate except by walking over to one of the objects and thus putting himself in its position. In this manner, he changes the problem to the more simple one of estimating the distance from himself to the object. Such children have learned space localization but not space structure. They have not attained the space domain of which Bartley speaks.

Freeman (1916) suggests that the child first locates objects in space with reference to himself, then later with reference to a second object with whose location he is familiar, and finally by means of a system of fixed directions. It is only in the last stage that a space structure becomes possible. Many slow-learning children have found their development blocked before this last stage was reached. Their behavior, particularly in the area of abstraction and generalization, suffers as a result. They require special assistance to permit them to develop a stable space structure with which to stabilize the relationships which surround them.

If it is to be maximally useful, this space structure must be comprehensive and complete. It is not enough that we preserve localizations for the particular objects to which our attention is directed, but we must at the same time retain impressions of the localization of objects which are not at the moment in the focus of our attention. Thus, as I sit here in this room and direct my attention to the table on the far wall, I must be able to localize this table with reference to myself, with reference to the far wall of the room, and with reference to the side walls, the ceiling, the floor, etc. At the same time, I must retain impressions of the desk before me and its location with reference to myself and with reference to the table which at the moment is the center of my attention. If now I shift my attention from the table to the desk itself, I cannot permit my previous localization of the table to disappear and be finished. I must retain an impression of the table and its location while my attention is concerned with the desk and the objects upon it. Thus, in order to develop an operative spatial structure, we must be able to shift the focus of sharp localization from one point to another as our attention is directed to one object after another, but it is very important that as our attention shifts in this manner, the localization of the remaining objects does not completely disappear. In other words, we must set up a complete spatial structure for any environment in which we find ourselves, simultaneously locating each object in relation to ourselves and in relation to every other object.

SPACE STRUCTURE AND FORM PERCEPTION

It can be seen that the problem of a space structure is similar to the earlier problem of form perception. Just as we had to learn to put the elements of a figure together into a constructive form, we must learn to put the objects around us together into a space structure. In this sense, space structure is a highly elaborated form. Just as we could deal more easily with elements by the use of form, we can deal more easily with objects through the use of space. Just as we use form to observe similarities and differences *within* objects, we use space to observe similarities and differences *between* objects.

PROBLEM OF COMPLETE SPACE STRUCTURE

This problem of spatial structure becomes particularly significant in respect to objects which lie behind us. In our everyday life, we are aware of the objects behind us and of their relationship to us and to each other, just as we are aware of the objects in front of us and their relative locations. We cannot, of course, see the objects behind us. We have very little information concerning their spatial relationships or even their existence. However, we know they are there and our space structure exists behind us in the same fashion that it exists in front of us. Through the use of this structure, we are able to turn around and still respond immediately to the objects behind us which we cannot see.

The young child, however, finds it difficult to build up this space structure behind him. If you have ever seen the toddler attempting to sit down on a footstool, you have seen the problem illustrated. He is not sure that there is anything behind him nor is he sure of its exact location. He cannot behave with certainty until he can feel the object on which he is attempting to sit. He also has difficulty in bringing his body into proper contact with this object after he has located it with his hands. The space behind him is not structured yet and he cannot respond to objects and information behind him in the manner in which we adults, who have developed such a complete spatial structure, can respond. We see this problem very clearly in the case of certain retarded children who, at a later age and at a higher stage of general development, experience the same sorts of problems as the toddler trying to sit on the stool. Space behind them does not exist. When they turn their backs, objects and situations go out of existence for them. Thus, the retarded child who was struck from behind by the swinging ball reveals a problem of space structure. His structure is incomplete. It exists only in a direct line in front of him. Space far out to the sides or behind does not exist for this child.

IMPORTANCE OF SPACE STRUCTURE

Obviously, the development of a spatial structure is a particularly difficult and complicated problem. In proportion to its difficulty and its complication, however, is its importance. As philosophers and scientists have pointed out, the only information which we get from the outside world is relative. We do not get absolute information through our sense organs about objects or events occurring outside us. Our only information is in terms of relationship (see Vernon, 1952, pp. 3 ff). We see and respond to objects in relation to other objects. We do not respond in terms of absolute values. For this reason, it is absolutely essential to the accuracy of our information about the physical universe that we be able to maintain at all times, and with great precision, the *relationships* between objects. These relationships are maintained through the development of a space structure and through the use of space structure to maintain stable relationships between the objects which lie around us. Without such a space structure, we lose or distort many of these relationships and our behavior suffers from inadequate information.

OCULAR MECHANISMS

We have suggested in the discussions above that our localization of objects in space is the result of input signals on the basis of which an image of the object is generated in the cortex. This image is then projected out into space. In effect, we, ourselves, are putting things into space where they belong. Information concerning spatial localization is not direct information but is derived from the manipulation of sensory signals which come to us. The only way in which we can create impressions of objects in space is to project the elaborations of these sensory inputs into the space surrounding us. Most important in this process is the visual avenue. We do not, of course, get all of our sensory information through vision, but, as stated earlier, vision gives us the most efficient set of clues for spatial information and therefore the normal individual depends to a very great degree upon visual information for his spatial judgments.

The only way in which we can accurately project the visual images into space is to project the image along the same line of sight by which the input signals came to us. Visual input is carried along a light ray. We know that light rays travel in straight lines. We therefore determine the angle of the ray which brought the information to us and project the image along that same light ray. In this manner, we place the image accurately in space. Obviously, it is very important that we know with great accuracy the angle of the incident light which has brought us the visual information. As indicated earlier, the only zero point for localization of anything in space is our own body as the point of origin of the spatial coordinates. Unless we can know with accuracy the angle of incidence, with reference to our own body, along which the information came to us, we will be unable to project the image into its proper position since we will not be sure of the angle of projection.

This information concerning the source of incident light is given to us through the external ocular muscles. As we know, these muscles control the position of the eye in its socket and, through sensitive end organs in the muscles themselves, return to us information concerning the relative position of the eyeball. Through the operation of these muscles and their proprioceptive end organs, we know in what direction our eye is pointed. We have stressed earlier that learning to control these eyes is a very complicated and very exacting task. The degree of accuracy required is extreme. The young child has difficulty in learning to control the movements of his eyes. He is not able accurately to move the eyes to a position where he wants them. He does not have complete information concerning the direction in which they are pointed. He is not able to direct them accurately toward an object which has attracted his attention, nor is he able to keep them focused on a moving object. Instead of being smoothly and constantly under control, his eyes move in a jerky and uncontrolled fashion. The infant frequently displays a condition in which the eyes "wander about." This is not only true with reference to two eyes together, but may be true of either eye separately. We call this condition *strabismus.* In the infant, it is due to the fact that he has not yet learned how to direct his eyes purposefully toward an object or how to use these eyes to maintain an object in the focus of his vision. Slightly older children have learned to keep the eyes together and do not show such extreme deviations. However, many of these older children show inaccuracies and inadequate control when the visual demands are increased.

One result of inaccurate control of the eyes is insecurity in space. The child is not sure where his eye is pointed, and he is not confident of the location of an object in space, because he is not confident of the line of sight along which he is to project this image.

Therefore, accurate and precise control of the extra-ocular muscles is essential to the development of spatial localization and particularly to the development of the space structure which we discussed earlier.

LEARNING OCULAR CONTROL

We frequently need to provide the child with additional help in the problem of learning ocular control. He must learn first to control the eyes themselves as an organ. He must learn to control each eye separately, and he must learn to put the two eyes together as a team. He must also learn to match the information about changes of eye position with the information which he gets from his hand about changes in motor movements. He must arrive at the point where he can substitute the movement of an eye for the movement of a hand and, because these are accurately matched, where he can obtain the same information from the eye movement that he previously obtained from the hand movement. As distances increase, he must learn to calculate the lateral distance subtended by a given angular movement of the eye and must be able to calculate this as a projection on the lateral movement of the hand in angular separations of lesser distance. He must learn to do with his eyes alone what formerly he did with his hand and arms and total body. This is possible only insofar as he matches precisely and accurately changes in the location of the eyes with changes resulting from movement of all of the other parts of his body. Obviously basic to this precise type of matching is highly accurate, highly precise, and highly efficient control of the eyes as an organ.

It must be stressed that the problem with which we are dealing here is one of learning to control a mechanism which is in perfect working order. There are certain pathological conditions in the eye and in the musculature of the eye which make it difficult or impossible for the child to make necessary eye movements. These conditions are medical problems and should be treated by medical techniques. Neither are we concerned here with weaknesses in eye muscles. These, too, are problems for the professional eye man. Our concern is with the child who has adequate ocular machinery but who has not learned to use it efficiently. The eye and its muscular attachments work adequately; what the child must learn is how to generate a pattern of neurological impulses which will control this mechanism with precision. This latter type of learning is a skill and can be taught in the same way as any other skill.

In like manner, we are not interested in teaching a neuromuscular skill for the sake of highly skilled performance alone. We are interested in ocular skills only in terms of the perceptual information which they can provide us. We must therefore teach, not control for the sake of control, but control by perceptual information for the sake of elaborating and standardizing this information. Methods for testing the accuracy of this control and methods for aiding the child in establishing this control will be discussed in later parts of this volume.

INTRODUCTION

BREAKDOWNS IN PERCEPTUAL-MOTOR DEVELOPMENT

In the preceding section, we have traced the development of perceptual-motor abilities in the child from the stage of initial motor performance through perceptual-motor matching to the development of form perception and space structure. Normally, the child develops through these various stages during the pre-school years and by the age of six or seven has achieved a space structure. In many children, however, the developmental process has broken down; at one of the earlier stages, the child either failed to develop further or developed in an atypical or distorted manner. Such breakdowns in the developmental sequence may be the result of environmental deprivations, injuries or defects in the organism, or emotional pressures with which the child has been unable to cope. Many of these breakdowns reveal themselves in the early elementary grades through difficulties in learning and low academic achievement.

If the child's learning difficulties are related to a deficiency in perceptual-motor readiness, it is necessary to identify the point at which the breakdown occurred. A child's development may be blocked at any of the stages described in Section 1. One child may fail to learn the basic motor patterns themselves. Another may complete this learning but fail to make perceptual-motor matches. Still another may progress through these stages but break down at the level of form perception or space structuring. As we have noted earlier, a breakdown at any stage will influence the child's performance and development at later stages. In order to help the child who is in difficulty, it is necessary to identify the stage at which learning failed, to supply the necessary learning, and to assist him in more advanced stages of development which now become feasible on the basis of the new learning. It is necessary, as it were, to "get the child back on the track" and to help him integrate and complete his readiness skills.

OTHER DEVELOPMENTAL AREAS

It should be pointed out that we have been concerned with only one area of development. Paralleling in many respects the perceptual-motor development which we have discussed is the development of verbal and symbolic abilities. Because of the scope of the problem, it has not been possible to discuss verbal development in detail. It should be borne in mind, however, that verbal development parallels perceptual-motor development, and breakdowns in the development of verbal abilities may also occur. Therefore, some children will be found whose perceptual-motor abilities are adequate but whose verbal development has been restricted. Children from low social and economic levels and from foreign-language homes will frequently show this deficiency in verbal facility. Their low academic achievement is predominantly the result of inadequate verbal development.

By the same token, the problem of concept development could not be discussed in detail in the present volume. It is felt that the development of concepts represents a higher level of performance than any which we have discussed (see Strauss and Kephart, 1955, pp. 112–27; Piaget, 1952). A child may therefore display adequate development through the stages which we have discussed but break down at the higher level of concept formation.

It will be found, however, that many of the children who show difficulty in school learning at grades one to three will also show difficulties in perceptual-motor development and that these perceptual-motor difficulties are related to the problem of school achievement. In such cases, the first problem is to identify the point of breakdown. When this point has been discovered, training techniques can be applied which will aid the child in overcoming his difficulty and will permit him to continue his development.

PURPOSE OF THIS SECTION

This section is devoted to a description of a series of performances designed to permit the observation of a child's perceptual-motor behavior. On the basis of the stages in development presented in the previous section, a series of tasks has been devised.

These performances are designed to reveal the perceptual-motor performance of the child at each developmental stage. The examiner observes the performance of the child and attends to certain evidences in his behavior which indicate his perceptual-motor status.

For each task, inadequate performance is described. These evaluations are discussed, on the one hand, with relation to the developmental stages which have been described and, on the other, with relation to training techniques which will be described in Part III and which can be useful in assisting the child who displays the developmental problems indicated by inadequate performance of the observational task. These tasks are designed to permit observation of the child in a relatively short period of time and without the use of complicated devices and apparatus. A close observation of the child's performance will permit the teacher to identify his level of development and to make a preliminary selection of training methods which will aid him.

It is felt that the teacher will find this series of observations helpful in evaluating children's ability and performance. It provides a somewhat new way of looking at the child and can serve as a guide to a re-evaluation. The observations presented here are somewhat different from the customary evaluations through readiness and achievement tests. The present observations can therefore provide valuable additional information as a guide for dealing with the problems of the child.

LEARNING PROBLEMS *v.* DISABILITIES

It will be noted that many of the tasks in this series require motor performances of the child. It is obvious, of course, that the crippled child or the child with a specific motor disability should not be asked to perform such tasks. The problem which this series of tasks and the subsequent training activities are designed to deal with is the problem of inadequate motor *learning*. It is assumed, in both this section and the next, that the child does *not* show a specific motor disability. It is assumed that no medical or physiological reason for his problem exists. In cases where specific defects are present, the child should be referred for medical treatment before readiness training is undertaken. Subsequent training should therefore be modified as indicated by the medical report. Many of the problems which are encountered in the classroom, however, do not represent specific disabilities but general lack of motor learning. It is these perceptual-motor learning problems which are investigated in this section and in Part III.

The tasks have been designed for and clinically investigated with children six to nine years of age. Although they will be found useful with retarded children at older age levels, some of the tasks will be found too simple for older groups. By the same token, some will be found too difficult for children below age six. Since the identification of the readiness problems in which we are interested is most critical when the child begins school, tasks at the six- to nine-year level have been selected.

1. WALKING BOARD

The walking board is a modification of the childhood game of walking a rail fence or walking along the rails of a railroad track. Techniques similar to this have been used extensively in kindergarten and elementary school grades (Jones, Morgan, and Stevens, 1957, p. 64). Commercial models of a walking beam will be found in many school systems.

The primary function to be observed with the walking board is that of balance. We can also observe postural flexibility since the balance problem also creates a situation in which movements which cannot be predicted far ahead of time must be performed without losing basic postural adjustment. Laterality is involved in maintaining balance itself and is approached more specifically when we ask the child to walk the board in the sidewise directions. When we introduce the backward direction, we require difficult spatial orientation and spatial projections.

FORWARD

The walking beam is a section of two-by-four measuring eight to twelve feet long and laid along the floor with its wider edge down. The child walks on the two-by-four as he would walk on a fence rail.

Start the child at one end of the beam. Ask him to walk to the other end. Give no further instructions. Observe the manner in which he is able to balance himself on the beam. Is he able to catch his balance and correct himself when he is in danger of falling off?

Some children will be found who attempt to solve the problem by avoiding the requirement for balance. Thus, they will run across the beam or take very long strides in an effort to reduce the number of times that they have to come to balance. In these cases, instruct the child that he is to walk slowly and use normal strides. Other children will attempt to place their feet crosswise on the beam and thus increase the extent of the surface in order to decrease the demand for balance. Such children should be instructed to place their feet straight along the board. After the examiner has observed the child's initial attempt, he may demonstrate the proper method.

Evaluation. Inadequate performance in this task is indicated by failure to maintain balance. The child who steps off the board more than once or who pauses frequently when he is out of balance and has trouble regaining his balance is showing difficulty. His performance would indicate that he could profit from training procedures designed to aid general postural adjustment, such as the walking board training and the balance board and trampoline training, described in Part III.

Watch the manner in which the child maintains his balance. Does he use one side of the body much more consistently than the other? For example, does he use one arm almost exclusively as a counterbalance? If so, walking board or balance board training can be modified to help him learn to use both sides together. Ask him to walk the walking board or balance on the balance board while holding a broomstick or long pole in the manner in which a tightrope walker holds a balancing pole. Set his hands wide apart on the pole. When he makes a balancing movement with one side, a compensatory movement of the opposite side is forced upon him by the pole. In this manner, he can be given practice in bilateral activity.

On the other hand, the child may appear too bilateral on the walking board. Does he use his two arms symmetrically during too much of his performance? Does he appear to have trouble when balance requires a response on one side only? If so, the walking board and balance board training described in Part III can be modified again. In this case, give the child two objects to carry in his hands as he balances. One of these objects should be markedly heavier than the other. With the weights in his hands, bilaterally symmetrical responses become impossible. The same extent of movement on both sides requires more effort on one side than on the other. In like manner, the counterbalancing effect of a movement on one side is greater than that of a movement of the same extent on the other side. Similar training can be provided for the feet and legs by tying sandbags onto the child's ankles.

BACKWARD

Start the child at one end of the beam with his back toward it and the board extending out behind him. Ask him to step up on the beam and walk backward to the other end. The same avoidance behaviors discussed above may be encountered here and are dealt with in the same manner. In addition, in the backward task, the child may twist his body so that he is able to look behind him to see where he is going. If this occurs, ask the child if he can walk the beam backwards without looking. Stand in front of him and ask him to keep looking at you while he walks the beam.

Evaluation. Inadequate performance is indicated by frequent loss of balance and by stepping off the board more than twice. If the child cannot perform without watching his feet or hesitates excessively in stepping back, he may be having trouble with the backward direction. Such children can be helped by training in posture and balance (walking board, balance board, trampoline). For the child who has trouble with the backward direction, the "stunts" described in Part III may be useful, particularly the crab walk and the elephant walk. Also highly useful are the two trampoline stunts, seat drop (see p. 228) and back drop (see p. 229).

SIDEWISE

Start the child at one end of the beam facing at right angles to it so that the beam extends to his right. Ask him to step up on the beam and walk sidewise to the other end. Observe whether the child is able to shift his weight from one foot to the other. He should move his right foot to the right and bring his left foot up to it. Notice any hesitation or confusion when movement must change from one foot to the other. Some children will try to cross one leg over the other. After the examiner has observed this difficulty, he may demonstrate the correct method. If the child takes unusually large strides, ask him to step normally. When he has progressed to the end of the beam, ask him to walk back sidewise, moving to his left. Some children will be found who can walk the board in one direction but not in the other. It is felt that these children are accustomed to avoiding the laterality and directionality problem by using only one side as a leading side. When asked to lead with the opposite side, they cannot perform. In walking the beam from right to left, the child must lead with his left foot. In walking from left to right, he must lead with his right foot.

Evaluation. This activity is designed to provide additional information regarding the use of the two sides of the body. It is particularly useful in identifying the child who is too one-sided. Watch for the child who has particular difficulty in one direction (stepping off the board more than twice) and for the child who obviously performs more easily in one direction than in the other. Such children are probably having trouble with laterality and are solving the problem by using excessive dominance of one side.

Modifications of the balance board and walking board training described above will be found useful. One of the best devices for such children is the trampoline since it emphasizes the importance of symmetrical activities. Angels-in-the-snow (page 230) may be needed to help the child identify and control the parts of his body on the non-dominant side.

2. JUMPING

We can gain further information concerning the child's ability to maintain balance and posture if we ask him to perform against the pull of gravity. The easiest method of controlling such activities is through the use of hopping, skipping, and jumping performances. The present techniques are designed to indicate how well the child can maintain control of his body when he is asked to behave symmetrically, to behave with each side alone, and to behave alternately between sides. Many of the activities suggested here have been included in the curriculum of physical education for many years (Cowell and Hazelton, 1955). Through careful observation, they can also be used to give us insight into the level upon which the child is behaving.

The series is designed to present first bilateral activities (item A), then unilateral activities (items B and C), then alternating activities—regular alternation (items D, E, and F) and irregular alternation (items G and H). In order to perform at an acceptable level, the child must demonstrate laterality, body image, rhythm, and the neurological controls related to each of these factors.

On alternating activities, the examiner should observe very carefully to see whether the alternation is a true flow of activity from one side to the other or whether it is two separate activities. Skipping is a good example. Skipping has been used extensively in classrooms and many children have been listed as able to skip when the activity did not flow smoothly from one side to the other. Such children, in effect, hop once on the right foot, stop, and then hop once on the left foot. They have treated each side separately and have set up a separate task on each side of the body. The performance which we would like to see is one in which the movement flows smoothly and uninterruptedly from one side to the other and back again. The latter type of performance is indicative of much better laterality and body image than is the former.

A. BOTH FEET

Stand the child at the side of the room where he has a clear space measuring the length of the room in front of him. Ask him to put both feet together and to jump forward one step. The child must hold his feet together while he jumps and must not step forward as in walking. Observe whether he can use both sides of his body in this parallel fashion.

B. RIGHT FOOT

Ask the child to stand on his right foot with his left off the floor. Now ask him to jump forward one step using his right foot only. Observe whether he can shift his posture in order to operate with one side of his body only. During the task, the left foot must not touch the floor.

C. LEFT FOOT

Ask the child to stand on his left foot and jump one step forward with his left foot only. Some children will be found who can perform this task with one foot but not with the other. Observe the same behavior as in the right-foot task.

D. SKIP

Ask the child to skip across the room using the feet alternately. Observe whether this is good free movement. Does the child alternate sides with ease or does he, in effect, have to stop after each step and determine which side he must use next?

E. HOP 1/1

Ask the child to stand with his feet together. Now ask him to hop on the right foot, lifting the left. Next ask him to hop on the left foot, lifting the right. Now ask him to alternate, hopping first on the right and then on the left. The child's body should remain in one spot during the hopping performance. Observe whether he is able to shift easily from one side to the other and whether his behavior is smooth and rhythmical or stiff and jerky. The latter type of behavior is evidence that he cannot readily shift from one postural orientation to another in a lateral direction.

F. HOP 2/2

This task is the same as the foregoing except that the child hops twice on the right foot, twice on the left, etc. This task is more difficult since the rhythm patterns and alternations are not as regular. Observe the performance for rhythm and smoothness.

G. HOP 2/1

Ask the child to hop twice on the right foot, once on the left, twice on the right, etc. This task is still more difficult since the alternation patterns are more complicated. Observe the performance for rhythm and smoothness.

H. HOP 1/2

Ask the child to hop once on the right foot, twice on the left, etc. This task is the same as the preceding except that the sides are reversed.

EVALUATION

Items A through E are related to the child's ability to control his gross musculature and to alternate activities across the center of gravity of his body. Failure on any of these items would suggest that the child could profit from training techniques concerned with gross body control, such as angels-in-the-snow, trampoline exercises, and some of the stunts described in Part III.

Items F through H introduce in addition to body control a factor of rhythm. The child who fails only on the latter items can be expected to profit from rhythm training (see page 235) and from trampoline training where special attention is paid to the establishment of a rhythm in body movement which is matched to an outside rhythm, the movement of the bed of the trampoline (see page 224).

The following five techniques are designed to reveal the child's knowledge of his own body and how to control its parts. In the Identification of Body Parts, he is asked to indicate parts on the basis of a verbal clue, thus showing that he knows what the parts are. In the Imitation of Movement, he is asked to display knowledge of how to move the upper extremities on the basis of a visual clue and to demonstrate that he knows where these parts are and their position. In the Obstacle Course, he is asked to display knowledge of where the parts of his body are with reference to outside objects and the amount of space occupied by his body or its parts. In angels-in-the-snow, he must be able to control both upper and lower extremities in all combinations. He must have sorted out the neurological patterns of innervation so that he can voluntarily move combinations of parts without interference from other parts. He must know where the parts are and their position at all times and in various combinations of movement. In Stepping Stones, he must demonstrate control of the parts on the basis of interpretation of an outside stimulus. He must know how to make the parts behave according to the demands of a concrete situation.

Combined with the major factor of body image in these techniques are such variables as laterality, directionality, control, and rhythm.

3. IDENTIFICATION OF BODY PARTS

Ask the child to stand facing you at a distance of about ten feet. Say to the child:
1. Touch your shoulders.
2. Touch your hips.
3. Touch your head.
4. Touch your ankles.
5. Touch your ears.
6. Touch your feet.
7. Touch your eyes.
8. Touch your elbows.
9. Touch your mouth.

Observe whether there is hesitancy in any response or whether the child is decisive in obeying each command. Observe whether in the paired parts he touches both members of the pair. In the case of the command "touch your elbows," it is necessary for him to cross his arms over each other. A slight hesitancy here is permissible since many children are startled at the change in posture required. When he has started a movement toward a part, can he move accurately to that part or does he start in the general direction and then "feel around" for the final target?

EVALUATION

This performance is related to the problem of body image. There are two general areas of knowledge involved. The first is awareness of the existence of the parts and their names. Recognition and naming of parts of the body is routinely taught in nursery and kindergarten programs and these methods are adequate for this purpose.

The second area is awareness of the precise location of parts. Difficulty in this area is shown by the child who can start in the general direction of the part but must experiment or "feel around" to make final contact. He is not aware of the exact location in space of the part.

Such a child may be aided by training techniques designed to call attention to the parts of his body and their location or control. Such activities as angels-in-the-snow and the stunts and games described in Part III will be found helpful.

4. IMITATION OF MOVEMENTS

Ask the child to stand facing you at about eight to ten feet and far enough away from walls and other obstructions that when he extends his arms he will not strike some object. With his hands loose at his sides, ask him to do whatever you do. Beginning with pattern No. 1, move through each of the patterns in Figure 5 in order. Observe the child's movements in going from one pattern to the next. These patterns are so designed that unilateral, bilateral, and cross-lateral movements are required.

Observe the following:

(1) It is desirable that the child reverse the laterality of the examiner's movements. That is to say, when you move your right hand, he should move his right hand. A great many children will be found who parallel the movement which they see. Thus, when you move your right arm, they will move their left. Do not instruct the child regarding this translation. If he does not spontaneously reverse the pattern, allow him to go on paralleling it. Most children will continue to parallel the examiner's movement. This performance is acceptable as long as it is consistent. However, the child who sometimes parallels and sometimes reverses is indicating trouble.

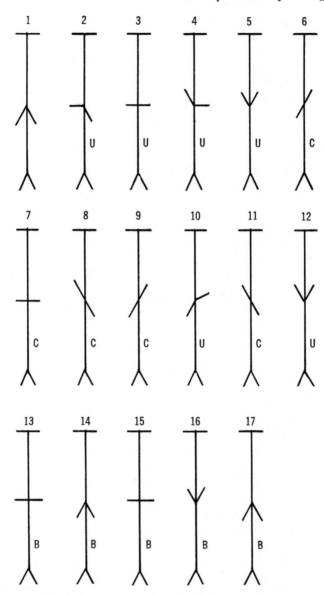

FIGURE 5. Positions of the arms for 17 items of the Imitation of Movements task. To move from each position to the next requires one of the following types of movement: **u**=unilateral movement, **b**=bilateral movement, **c**=crosslateral movement.

(2) Movements should be made promptly and with definiteness. Observe any hesitation or lack of certainty in the child's response. Look especially for abortive movements either in the arm which should not move or toward a different direction in the arm or arms which should move.

(3) The child may fail to reproduce the movement pattern on the first attempt. Some children will become confused. They will move both arms when only one is required to move. If the movement is completed before the child appears to recognize that he has made a mistake, pay special attention to this fact. Sometimes a child may take the wrong position and not recognize this fact until it is called to his attention. In this case, point out his error and be sure that he achieves the correct position before proceeding, since the next pattern of movement will be altered if he does not start from the correct position. Observe the child who reverses his patterning. He may reverse the pattern for a time, then parallel it for a time. This child is showing confusion in laterality and in body image.

EVALUATION

This activity is related to the child's ability to control his upper limbs independently and in combination. It also requires the translation of a visual pattern into a motor pattern which will reproduce it. Difficulty is shown whenever the child displays hesitancy, lack of certainty, or error in executing the patterns.

The child who displays difficulty can be aided by training procedures designed to help him with identification and control of individual parts. The angels-in-the-snow and rhythm techniques described in Part III will be found useful. To aid with the translation of the visual pattern into a motor pattern (and the reverse), this same examination procedure can be used as a training device. Repeat the movements a number of times and ask the child to attempt to reproduce them. Pay particular attention to those patterns with which he shows particular problems.

The visual-motor translation ability can be further aided by use of chalkboard training activities described under "Directionality" (page 169), "Orientation" (page 180), "The Clock Game" (page 171). These latter activities are particularly useful in bridging the gap between the visual-motor translation in a free situation and the more precise translation required for performance on paper-and-pencil tasks.

5. OBSTACLE COURSE

(1) Ask the child to step over an obstacle, about as high as his knee, without touching it. An adequate obstacle can be constructed by laying a yardstick or some other narrow board across the seat of two chairs. Observe whether he can step over the obstacle with adequate estimation of its height. Does he knock off the board or does he step too high to clear the board?

(2) Ask the child to duck under an obstacle about two inches lower than his shoulders without touching it. A suitable obstacle can be provided by laying the yardstick across the backs of the chairs. Observe whether he can estimate the height of the board. Does he knock it off or does he bend much too far forward to clear it?

(3) Ask the child to squeeze through a narrow opening without touching it. A suitable opening can be provided by placing the chairs back to back and close enough together that the child must turn his body in order to squeeze through. Observe whether he can estimate the space and can manipulate his body to fit it. Does he touch either chair?

EVALUATION

This task is related to the child's awareness of the space occupied by the parts of his body in various positions. Items 2 and 3 are related particularly to awareness of those parts which are behind him and cannot be seen directly. Difficulty is shown when the child either overestimates or underestimates by more than approximately one and one-half inches.

For the child who experiences difficulty with this task, the stunts and games described in Part III will be found useful. One of the best training devices for such children is a trampoline (page 224). On this device, the child must maintain awareness of his body and its position in space in relation to an outside object (bed of the trampoline) while his body is in an unusual position with respect to the force of gravity. The seat-drop and back-drop exercises are particularly useful in aiding the child's awareness of those parts of his body which are behind him.

6. ANGELS-IN-THE-SNOW

Ask the child to lie on his back on the floor with his arms at his side and his feet together. Ask him to move his arms up over his head. Be sure he moves them along the floor. Ask him to feel the floor with his wrists as his arms move. Be sure he gets his arms completely above his head until his two hands touch.

Next ask him to move his feet apart. Be sure he moves them wide apart and keeps his heels on the floor during the movement. The examiner may demonstrate the movement of arms and legs. These preliminary exercises are used to acquaint the child with the technique. When he has learned what you want him to do, say:

1. Move just this arm (pointing to the right arm). Now put it back.

2. Move just this arm (pointing to the left arm). Now back.

3. Move just this leg (pointing to right leg). Now back.

4. Move just this leg (pointing to left leg). Now back.

5. Move both arms. Now back.

6. Move both legs. Now back.

7. Move this arm and this leg (pointing to left arm and left leg). Now back.

8. Move this arm and this leg (pointing to right arm and right leg). Now back.

9. Move this arm and this leg (pointing to right arm and left leg). Now back.

10. Move this arm and this leg (pointing to left arm and right leg). Now back.

Do not give the child any clue to the limb which you ask him to move other than pointing to it. Some children will be found who are unable to identify the limb by this visual clue alone. Note that he was unable to identify visually.

Observe whether or not the child's movements are smooth and decisive. Note any jerky movements and any hesitation in beginning a movement. The latter probably indicates a difficulty in initiating a movement in a prescribed limb. Note whether all movements reach their maximum extension. Many times the child will restrict the movement of one or more limbs when he is required to control the entire movement sequence. Frequently the movements will be adequate when they are bilaterally symmetrical (as in the pre-test exercises) but will become restricted when unilateral or cross-lateral patterns are called for.

Observe whether the child starts his movement promptly and whether his first movement is a definite part of the prescribed pattern. Frequently a child will identify the innervational pattern necessary to begin the movement by abortive trial movements. Such lack of complete knowledge will often be revealed in false starts, moving the limb up and down on the floor a fraction of an inch to identify it, asking for repetition of instructions, looking from one limb to another before beginning, and so forth.

Observe carefully whether there is overflow into other limbs whose movement is not called for. Thus, when the child is asked to move the left arm and right leg, is there also movement in the right arm or left leg? Often the prescribed movement will be translated into bilaterally symmetrical patterns and both arms or both legs will move.

EVALUATION

Difficulty with this task indicates that the child is experiencing problems in controlling the parts of his body individually or in prescribed combinations. Inadequate performance is shown by (1) marked hesitancy in beginning the movements; (2) restriction of the extent of movement in any of the patterns; (3) overflow of movements to limbs not required in the pattern; (4) inability to initiate movement or identify a limb on the basis of visual clues alone (developing tactual information by pressing against the floor or kinesthetic information by abortive movements); or (5) inability to carry out any of the patterns.

For the child who has difficulty with this task, the task can be used as a training activity (Part III, page 230). In cases of severe failure, simpler techniques such as the walking board, imitation of movement, stunts, etc., may need to be used first to develop more adequate control of limbs and laterality concepts before the child can perform successfully in the present activity. In cases of paralysis or spastic conditions, medical assistance will be required and special attention may need to be given to specific limbs.

7. STEPPING STONES

Stepping stones are six-inch squares of cardboard. Ten of these are black and ten are red. The squares are placed around the room according to the pattern in Figure 6. The black squares represent the left foot and the red squares the right foot. The arrangement of squares is such that the child is required to take steps of different lengths and in different directions. The attempt is to examine his ability to change control of the legs and trunk under conditions which demand irregular performances.

A black ribbon is tied around the shoe of the child's left foot and a red ribbon around the shoe of his right foot. These ribbons offer clues to which foot he should use. Since the verbal concept of "right" and "left" is not being examined here, we offer these clues so that the performance will not be influenced by this factor.

Say to the child, "Put the foot with the black ribbon on this first square." Help him until his foot is properly placed to begin. "Now put your red foot on the next square. Now walk around all the squares, putting your black foot on the black ones and your red foot on the red ones. You must always step on the very next square. Don't skip any and do not back up. Do not step on the floor, only on the squares." If the child does not understand the instructions, the examiner may demonstrate for the first six squares only. Instruct the child to place the *ball* of his foot on the squares.

Notice that the length of step demanded varies. Watch the child closely to observe whether he has difficulty in adjusting his length of stride. Such difficulty will usually be displayed in hesitation or "false starts." Notice that along the back wall, the child is

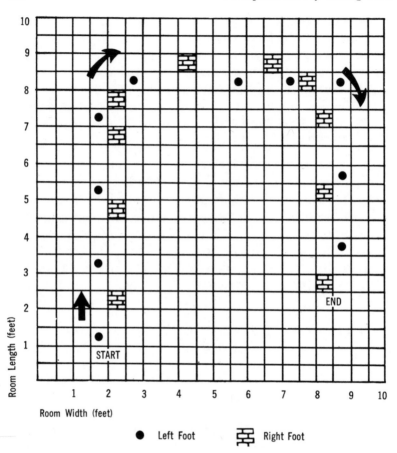

FIGURE 6. Diagram for placement of "Stepping Stones" in a room ten by ten feet.

required to cross one foot over the other to follow the stones. Watch closely to determine whether he has special difficulty here. Some children will be unable to make this adjustment and will give up or change the prescribed foot placement. The examiner is not to demonstrate the method for these stones since we want to know whether the child can determine what he has to do to solve the problem. Notice that the stones are placed in such a way as to demand sometimes a right-foot lead and sometimes a left-foot lead. Careful observation can reveal whether the child is too symmetrical and has difficulty when one side or the other is called upon to lead.

When testing large groups of children, it will be found convenient to fasten the squares to the floor or draw them on the floor in a more permanent fashion.

EVALUATION

This task is related to the problem of eye-foot coordination. Can the child determine, on the basis of a visual stimulus, the direction of movement required for his foot and can he make the necessary body adjustment to bring his foot in contact with the visual stimulus? Also involved are problems of laterality and directionality. Difficulty is shown by the child who fails in any of the steps or who steps off the stones or alters the prescribed foot placement in order to solve the task.

The child who is having difficulty may need fundamental training in laterality ("Walking Board," page 217). He may need special help in the control of the legs ("Angels-in-the-Snow," page 230). Or he may need help with the visual-motor translation involved in the task. In the latter case, the examination technique can be repeated as a training activity. Lay out a series of patterns of steps similar to the one described above. Vary the size of stride, the lead foot, and require at times that the feet be crossed. Provide the child with practice in a number of different patterns of steps. Additional aid can be given through training activities in which specific movement patterns are prescribed for the legs and feet— kick-ball and similar games, drawing in the sand (page 230), or rhythms with the feet (page 235).

8. CHALKBOARD

One of the most direct methods of testing the child's adequacy in directionality is through observation of his performance on a chalkboard. In such activity, we ask him to produce a movement which will leave a trace in the form of a line on the chalkboard which will possess certain characteristics of shape and size. The child is required to develop a memory (visual) image of a given shape in response to our instructions, translate this into a movement pattern, and produce the required movements. The projections characteristic of directionality go on twice: once indirectly when the memory image is translated into motor patterns, and once directly when these patterns are externalized and the child uses the developing trace to control the performance.

By comparing performance on either side of the body, particularly when both sides are required to perform simultaneously, we can frequently see evidence of problems with laterality. The child who is avoiding the laterality problem by becoming too symmetrical will reveal this difficulty by his inability to regulate one side of the body to accommodate what is occurring on the other side. Frequently, in his unimanual performance, we will see his other hand tense or even perform abortive movements imaging those of the active hand. The child who is too asymmetrical will display his problem when simultaneous performance of two hands is required. He will tend to neglect one hand and observable distortions in performance between the two hands can be seen.

Problems of the midline are raised whenever the performance must cross this line. In extreme cases of midline difficulty, the child will be observed to split his performance, performing that part lying to the left of the midline with his left hand and that part lying to the right with his right hand. In less severe cases, the child will, by distorting the position of his body or the position of the drawing with relation to his body, throw all the activity to one side of the midline and thus avoid the problem of crossing.

Thus, the chalkboard can provide us with an excellent opportunity to observe the child's motor patterns and their projection into outside space. By selecting the activities we require of him, we can see the extent to which the two sides of his body work together and complement each other. He can show us what effect this coordination of sides is having upon his external actions and his perceptual interpretation of external events. As is frequently true in all such performances, we can learn more if we pay particular attention to *how* he performs rather than concentrating all our attention on the product which he achieves.

A. CIRCLE

Ask the child to step up to the chalkboard and draw a circle. Give no other instructions concerning size or other characteristics of the drawing. Allow the child to use his preferred hand and do not suggest which hand he should use. Allow him to select the position of his drawing with reference to the total space of the board and do not suggest where he should place it. Should the child ask about any of these characteristics, tell him to "make it like you think it should be."

Observe: Preferred Hand
Size of Drawing
Position of Drawing with Reference to Midline of Body
Accuracy of Production
Direction

Preferred Hand. We are interested in whether he prefers the same hand for this type of activity which he prefers for other types of activity, especially bimanual activities and writing.

Size. Many children will be found who with these instructions will produce a circle which is only two or three inches in diameter. (In this activity, we would like to see a circle eighteen to twenty-four inches in diameter.) These children will usually be found to be using the wrist and fingers in the drawing performance but not the forearm and shoulder. These are the types of children in whom we suspect a restriction in gross-motor movement patterns when these are applied to purposive activities. If the child draws a circle which is markedly too small, ask him to make a bigger one. Continue to repeat this instruction after each trial until he produces a drawing eighteen to twenty-four inches in diameter. It may be necessary in some cases for the examiner to demonstrate the size by drawing a circle of the desired size himself. If this is done, the examiner should erase his circle before the child begins his.

Position. Many children will be found who draw their circle markedly toward the side of the body represented by the preferred hand. It is felt that these children are avoiding the problem of crossing the midline because they have not mastered the translation of movement patterns which occurs there. They keep their performance entirely to one side to avoid the necessity of making this translation. Should the child position his drawing in this fashion, stand him in the center of the board space, ask him to look straight ahead and make his circle with this spot as its center. In some cases, the child will be unable to perform under these conditions. The following difficulties have been observed in such children. (1) One side of the circle becomes flat (usually on the side away from the direction of the preferred hand). (2) The child may draw half the circle with the right hand and the other half with the left. (3) The child may display confusion in finding the starting point for the drawing. (4) The circle may be reduced in size.

Accuracy. Particularly in children who have not developed free movement of the wrist and forearm, we are apt to see distortions of the circular figure. The circle requires the rotation of the wrist if a smooth drawing is to result. The child may lose direction and produce "dog ears" or he may stop and "think out" the directional problem before proceeding. These difficulties usually occur at the bottom of the drawing and at the side opposite to the preferred hand. The examiner should observe whether the wrist is stiff or whether the child is having difficulty in controlling it.

Direction. The circle should be drawn in a counterclockwise direction if the child uses the right hand and in a clockwise direction if he uses the left.

Evaluation. If the child shows difficulty in achieving the proper size in his drawing, it is probable that he is displaying a "splinter skill" and that his performance with chalk, paper and pencil, and similar media is not related properly to total motor performance. Such restricted motor performance may be a general pattern in large areas of the child's performance or it may be specific to the copying or reproducing tasks. Look carefully at his performance on the previous tasks. Does he show restricted and cramped gross motor performance on such tasks as the walking board, jumping, and angels-in-the-snow? If so, his chalkboard performance is probably a reflection of general motor inability. In this case, he will need gross motor help (walking board, balance board, trampoline) before, or along with, help in the drawing task itself. On the other hand, if the child's general motor performance is adequate but his chalkboard performance is cramped, it is likely that his "splinter skill" is limited to drawing activities. Such a child would profit from training designed to free his motor approach to paper and pencil and to similar activities (see Part III: "Scribbling," "Finger-Painting," page 161—168).

If the child shows difficulty in positioning his drawing, it is likely that he is having difficulty mastering the midline problem. His difficulty may be due to a basic lack of laterality. If so, he should be given help with his basic laterality before, or simultaneous with, help in the drawing performance (see "Walking Board," "Balance Board"). On the other hand, his difficulty may be only in directionality and in the projection of his laterality onto outside objects with its accompanying problem of midline translation. In this latter case, he can be given chalkboard training in directionality (see "Chalkboard-Directionality," "Clock Game," "Chalkboard-Orientation").

If the child shows difficulty only in the accuracy of the drawing, it is probable that he is having difficulty with form perception. In this case, he can be helped by means of the chalkboard-drawing and copying activities described in Part III.

B. DOUBLE CIRCLES

Ask the child to take a piece of chalk in each hand and to draw two circles simultaneously, one with the right hand and one with the left. If the drawings are markedly small, ask the child to draw them larger. Repeat this direction until diameters of eighteen to twenty-four inches are achieved. Allow him to take his own position at the board and to draw the circles wherever he wishes on the board surface. Do not demonstrate the performance or describe how the movements are to be made.

Observe: Relative Size of Drawings
Position of Drawings with Reference to Each Other
Direction of Movement of Two Hands
Relative Accuracy of Two Drawings
Attention

Size. In this bimanual performance, children will be found who draw circles of very different sizes with the two hands. Thus, the right circle may be eighteen to twenty-four inches in diameter and the left circle only three or four inches. In such children, the movement patterns of the two sides are felt to be inadequately correlated with each other.

Position. Many children will produce small circles wide apart on the board. These children usually display the inadequate patterns of wrist and forearm described above. Other children will begin circles so large that they overlap in the center. Occasionally, a child will be found who draws one circle on top of the other. Such a child is probably avoiding the problem of bimanual activity.

Direction. In right-handed children, the right circle should be drawn counterclockwise while the left is being drawn clockwise. These directions are reversed in left-handed children.

Accuracy. The most common distortion of shape is that in which both circles become flat on the inside. This difficulty is thought to be related to the problem of laterality and especially to the problem of the midline and the location of the midline. It is this characteristic distortion which we especially look for in this performance. In some cases, one circle will be accurate and the other will be highly inaccurate. The distortions in the two circles will not be parallel, but it is as though the child were performing two entirely separate tasks at the same time. Such children are thought to have inadequate correlation between the sides of the body.

Attention. In some children, all attention is given to one circle, while the other is left to take care of itself. Their visual guidance is all given to the performance of one hand, while the other has little or no guidance. This procedure can be observed by watching the child as he performs. Does he watch the performance of one hand closely and pay little or no attention (rarely looking toward it) to the other? Does he show concern over the performance of one hand and not over the performance of the other? Does he definitely lead with one hand while the other trails along inaccurately? It is thought that these children have avoided the problem of laterality by making one hand so dominant that the other merely follows along. They behave as though they were one-sided organisms merely dragging the other side along because they cannot get rid of it.

Evaluation. If one circle is noticeably smaller than the other, the child is probably having difficulty matching activities on the two sides of the body and/or in matching these motor activities to perceptual data. If the problem is motor, he can profit from bilateral activities such as the walking board. If the problem is primarily the perceptual-motor match, he can be helped by chalkboard activities of a bimanual nature (see page 180).

If the child has difficulty positioning the circles or if he shows the common distortion of shape by which the two circles are flattened toward the center, he is probably having difficulty with the perceptual-motor translation at the midline. Such a child shows the same problems described above under positioning of a single circle. His problem may be basic laterality or visual-motor translation or both. When difficulties exist in positioning the double circles, the same training considerations hold as when difficulties exist in positioning the single circle.

If the child shows inconsistency or indecision in determining the direction of movement of the two circles or if he draws them with parallel movements, he will need help in identifying and executing movements in various directions. Orientation training (see page 180) would then be indicated.

If the child directs all his attention to one hand in this bimanual task, it is probable that the perceptual-motor match is too restricted. He guides only a restricted part of his motor behavior by perceptual data rather than his total motor pattern. Such a child could profit from bimanual training procedures such as the clock game and orientation portions of the chalkboard training described in Part III.

C. LINES: LATERAL

Ask the child to turn around so that he cannot see you. Place an *x* about eighteen inches to the left of the center of the board and a second *x* a similar distance to the right. Ask the child to turn around and draw a straight line from one *x* to the other. Do not point or show by gesture how the task is to be performed. Allow him to select his preferred hand and give no other instructions.

Observe: Use of Body
             Use of Hand

Body. Many children will place the chalk on the left hand *x* and walk across to the right hand *x* without moving their hand or arm. It is felt that these children are having difficulty in crossing the midline and are avoiding the problem by this type of performance.

Hand. When the child has difficulty crossing the midline, he will display his problem through the manner of controlling his hand. When the hand is across the midline, directional information will be inadequate. He will make false starts, either in aiming at the *x* or in the drawing itself. He will pause before he starts and may pause during the drawing performance. His production will be in-accurate on the side away from his preferred hand. Occasionally a child will be found who draws the left half of the line with the left hand and the right half with the right hand.

D. LINES: VERTICAL

Ask the child to take a piece of chalk in each hand and, beginning at the top of the board, draw two parallel vertical lines simultane-ously. Children who have difficulty in laterality will frequently show distortions of the two lines. Most characteristically, this dis-tortion involves a "bowing" of the lines. Sometimes one hand will receive all the attention and the other merely follow along or cease to function altogether.

Evaluation. These two tasks are directed toward the child's method of handling the midline problem. As in some of the earlier tasks, his problem may stem from a difficulty in basic laterality or it may be confined to a problem of perceptual-motor translation. An observation of the earlier tasks concerned with basic laterality will reveal the extent to which this factor may be contributing to the present problem. If basic laterality is poor, training in this area should precede or be integrated with training in the perceptual-motor translation. Where basic laterality is adequate, the child can profit from training in which the midline problem is stressed, such as chalkboard orientation and the lazy eight (see page 182).

9. OCULAR PURSUITS

The technique of *ocular pursuit* attempts to investigate the abil-ity of the child to control ocular movements. This control is ob-served in a perceptual situation. The child is given a target to fol-low and is required to perform the perceptual act of keeping the target in view. For this operation, adequate control of the eyes is necessary. It should be noted that this technique is not designed to indicate *why* control is not present. Lack of control may be caused by a malfunction of the muscular system of the eye and may be a medical problem. On the other hand, the difficulty may be in matching perceptual data with motor data and may be a prob-lem of learning within the perceptual area. The present technique will not reveal which of these two explanations is the correct one but will only indicate that the child does not have adequate control of the external ocular muscles to permit him to perform in complex perceptual tasks.

We have already stressed the importance of ocular control to the problems of achievement. The examiner should remember the precision of control required by such complex tasks as reading. Therefore, he is looking for minimal problems in the child. Gross lack of control is the exception. Most of the slow-learning children who will be encountered in the classroom situation will evidence only minor difficulties revealed by slight irregularities in the ocular pursuit task. Such minor irregularities are less likely to be due to physiological causes and more likely to be due to problems of perceptual learning.

A. LATERAL

Obtain a common lead pencil with an eraser. Drive a thumb tack through the eraser so that the head of the tack is parallel to the length of the pencil. Hold the pencil upright before the child's eyes and about twenty inches before his face. Ask him if he sees the head of the tack. Then say, "Now watch it, wherever it goes." Move the pencil about eighteen inches to his right, following an arc of a circle of which the child is the center and with a radius of twenty inches. Next move the pencil laterally to the child's left until it is eighteen inches to his left.

By following the arc of a circle, the target is kept at a constant distance from the eye. If it were moved on a straight line, the distance to the eye would be greater at the extreme left and right extent of the movement and less in the center. Since a change of distance involves a change in accommodation of the eye in which we are not interested, we can eliminate this problem by moving the target in an arc, keeping the eye-target distance constant.

If the child moves his head instead of moving his eyes, ask him to hold his head still. If he is unable to do so, lightly hold his head with your hand. Repeat the lateral movement of the pencil until he follows with his eyes, holding his head still. Watch closely the movements of his eyes as he follows the pencil. Observe whether the movements are smooth or jerky. Since control of eye movements is an extremely precise task, the examiner must watch very closely; lack of control may be shown by extremely small spasms. The eyes should move as smoothly as ice cubes in a glass of water. Any jerking or unevenness is an indication of lack of complete control.

Watch the two eyes working together. Observe whether they maintain their relationship to each other or whether one wanders off from the target. The loss of relationship may be apparent only at the extremes of the movement or may come and go during the movement. Observe whether both eyes are following or whether one eye is leading and the other is simply being pulled along. This relationship can usually be observed by watching the timing of the two eyes. Does one get ahead of the other or do they stay together? In some cases, one eye will move but not the other.

Observe whether the child is always on target or whether he loses it from time to time. If he loses the target, can he regain it promptly or does he have to "look around" for it? Does he overshoot the target and have to wait for it to catch up?

Pay particular attention to the performance when the target crosses the midline of the child's body. Many children have trouble in crossing the midline and will reveal this fact by a slight jerk in the movement at this point.

Evaluation. This task is designed to identify the child who needs help in establishing ocular control. The child who cannot follow the target, who loses the target easily, or who cannot follow without turning his head has not established ocular control. The child whose pursuit movements are jerky, lack smoothness, or are not well coordinated needs additional help in establishing such control. These children can be assisted by the use of the training procedures for ocular control described in Part III.

B. VERTICAL

Move the pencil in a vertical direction until it is in a position about eighteen inches above the child's eye level. Move it in the arc of a circle as in *A* above. Move the pencil downward until it is eighteen inches below the child's eye level. Make the same observations as in *A* above.

Evaluation. Same as *A* above.

C. DIAGONAL

Move the pencil to the left until it is eighteen inches from the center and downward until it is eighteen inches below the line of vision. Move it in a diagonal direction until it is in a similar position in the upper right corner. Make the same observations and same scoring as above. Move the target in the opposite direction (upper right to lower left). Evaluate the poorer of the two performances.

D. ROTARY

Move the pencil in a circle directly facing the child and having a radius of eighteen inches. Make the same observations and same evaluation as above.

E. MONOCULAR—RIGHT EYE

Place an occluder or cover before the child's left eye. Repeat tasks *A* to *D* above. Make the same observations except for those pertaining to the relationship between the two eyes. Often children will display adequate movements when both eyes are seeing the target but will not be able to do so when one eye only is seeing the target. The evaluation for these four tasks is the same as that for tasks *A* to *D* above except that no attention is paid to the relationship between the two eyes.

F. MONOCULAR—LEFT EYE

Move the occluder in front of the child's right eye. Repeat tasks *A* to *D* above. Make the same observations and same evaluation as in *E* above.

NOTE

Particular care should be taken in observations when the target is moved in a diagonal direction. These diagonal movements are the last to appear developmentally and are the most difficult for the child. Difficulty is often shown in a "stair-stepping" movement. The eyes move laterally until they lose the target, then vertically to catch up, then laterally again, etc. In this way, the child can "follow" the target without making a diagonal movement of the eyes. This stair-stepping may be apparent over only a part of the total range of movement. It is most frequent in the neighborhood of the midline.

10. VISUAL ACHIEVEMENT FORMS

This technique is designed to permit observation of the child's perception of form and the adequacy of his figure-ground relationships. The problem is approached through the copying of simple geometric forms (see Figure 7). Copying tests of this type have been a part of school readiness tests for some time and have proved to differentiate between higher achieving children and lower achieving children in the classroom situation.

Note that in this technique the manner by which the copy is produced is as important as the child's production itself, if not more important. Carefully observe the manner in which the child approaches each drawing and the steps by which he reaches his production. In many cases, difficulties will be revealed by the child's process of solution which will be hidden and overlooked when only the end product is considered. Breaking up of the forms, segmenting of the figures, reorientation of the page to alter the problem, and similar evidences of difficulty can be best observed by watching the child while he is at work on the task. Therefore, pay close attention while the child is working and do not base your judgments solely upon the final product.

Seat the child comfortably at table or desk. Sit directly across from the child and present the forms (Figure 7) to the child one at a time in a straight vertical and horizontal orientation. Furnish the child with an eight and a half by eleven sheet of plain paper. Say, "I want you to copy these seven drawings (flip through the pages) on this sheet of paper." Present the drawings one at a time, beginning with the circle. The instructions are, "Make one like this," pointing to the form. Should the child ask, "How should I make it?" or "Where should I make it?" the examiner should reply, "Make it any way you think you should" or "Make it wherever you think it should go." Do not give the child any specific information concerning the nature of the task or the position on the page.

Many children will turn the paper during the drawing performance in order to change a line or lines into an easier orientation. The examiner should note this shifting but should not comment on it to the child. Do not allow the child to use a ruler or other drawing aid.

Children should be able to copy the forms at the chronological age of seven years. For children six years of age, present only the first five forms. For five-year-old children, present only the first four forms; for four-year-olds, the first three. Do not present this material to children below four years of age.

Note the form of the drawings. This technique is designed to investigate the child's concept of figure and ground. Observe whether he completes the form as a whole or whether he completes a piece at a time. The child should complete each form with one continuous line. In the case of older or more advanced children, the form may be broken down into elements in the interest of increased accuracy (Werner's [1944] constructive approach). In such cases, the child usually indicates this approach by measuring or estimating. Pay special attention to the divided rectangle. The child must see the diagonals and the bisecting lines as parts of the total figure. Many children will segment this form and will break up the internal lines. Such children have not seen the internal lines as dividers of the total figure. The diamond presents special difficulty. The child frequently reveals his trouble by the presence of "ears" on the diamond form. This form is presented in two orientations: one with the wide dimension horizontal and one with the wide dimension vertical.

The forms should be drawn in a size approximating that of the material presented. Many children will draw very small figures which they crowd together in one section of the page. Forms should be oriented on the page in a right to left direction and in rows from top to bottom.

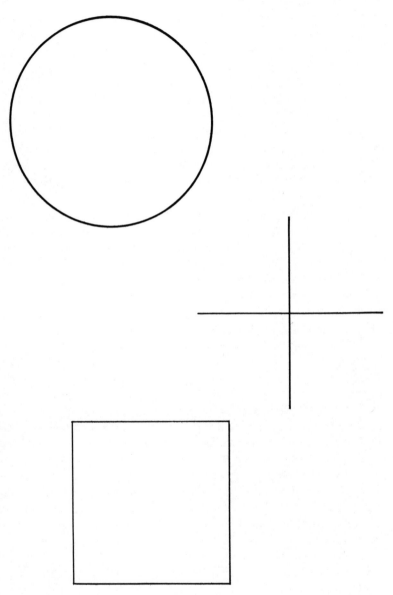

FIGURE 7.

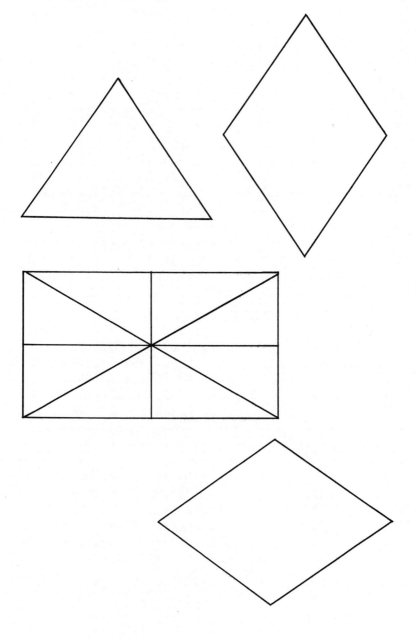

EVALUATION

The child's ability to perceive and manipulate forms is revealed by this task. The child who cannot produce recognizable form in one or more of the drawings or who shows gross segmenting in his productions shows a weakness in form perception. He could profit from the chalkboard activities in drawing and copying (page 183). The child who shows minor segmenting on a number of the forms (particularly the divided rectangle), or who shows "dog ears" on any of the forms, is probably having difficulty maintaining constructive form during the task. Such a child could profit by additional help from activities in which form perception must be maintained under difficult conditions. Activities of this type are described in Part III, "Training Form Perception."

The child who draws the figures markedly too small and cramps his productions into a very restricted area of the sheet would suggest the "splinter skill" discussed above.

11. KRAUS-WEBER TESTS

The Kraus-Weber Test is a series of performances designed to measure minimum muscular fitness. The standardization and use of the tests are described by Kraus and Hirschland (1954). They have been further investigated, and a series of training activities designed to assist children whose test performance is below average have been designed by Prudden (1956). Certain items in this series were found by Kagerer to be related to school achievement in the early grades (1958).

Test 1. Child lies flat on back, hands behind head, legs outstretched. Examiner holds his feet to the floor. He then pulls up into a sitting position without using hands.

Scored *passed* if child can achieve sitting position.

Test 2. Child lies on back, hands behind head and knees bent. Examiner holds his feet to the floor. He pulls himself up into sitting position without using hands.

Scored *passed* if child can achieve sitting position.

Test 3.   Child lies on back, hands behind head, legs out straight. He raises feet ten inches from the floor while keeping legs straight and holds this position for ten seconds.

Scored *passed* if child can raise legs without bending knees and hold this position for ten seconds.

Test 4.   Child lies face down, hands clasped behind neck, a small pillow under his hips. Examiner holds his feet to the floor. He is asked to raise his head, shoulders and chest off the floor and hold the position for ten seconds.

Scored *passed* if child can raise himself and hold this position for ten seconds.

Test 5.   Child lies face down, his head resting on his hands and a pillow under his hips. He raises his legs off the floor without bending the knees and with the feet ten inches off the floor. He holds this position for at least ten seconds.

Scored *passed* if the child can achieve the described position and hold it for ten seconds.

Test 6.   Child (without shoes) bends from the hips, keeping his knees straight and feet together and touches the floor with his finger tips. He should hold the position for three seconds.

Scored *passed* if child can touch floor without bending knees or "bouncing" and hold position for three seconds.

EVALUATION

Items 4 and 5 of the Kraus-Weber series have been shown to be related to school achievement in the early grades (Kagerer, 1958). The child who has difficulty with these two items would appear to lack general postural and gross motor coordination. He can be helped through the sensory-motor training techniques described in Part III.

INTRODUCTION

The observations described in the previous section can point up areas of weakness in the child's perceptual-motor development. The present section describes certain training activities which may be used to strengthen these weaknesses. The particular training techniques to be used with any given child will depend upon his particular needs as revealed by his performance on the observational tasks or by other methods of assessing his abilities.

In general, the following descriptions of training activities are presented in relation to the major areas of development which have been discussed earlier: sensory-motor learning, ocular control, and form perception. The chief exception to this pattern is the description of chalkboard training. The chalkboard will be found a useful device in many areas. Therefore, all chalkboard activities have been grouped together for convenience in description.

It will be discovered that training is easier if it is begun with the most basic area of performance in which the child is weak. Thus, ocular-motor training will be easier if the child can be given a certain amount of basic laterality and directionality before the ocular-motor training is begun. Training in form perception will be easier if the child has sensory-motor skill and ocular control beforehand. This is not to say that these previous skills must be completely trained before a higher skill is attacked. However, a minimum amount of the more basic skills will greatly aid learning of the higher skills.

Throughout the following presentation, the description of simplified training activities for the child who is markedly deficient in the area being discussed will be followed by the description of more difficult performances for the child with greater proficiency. It is not anticipated that these very simplified, early approaches will be necessary in all cases or in all areas with any one child.

Each child will vary in his ability in each task. It is probable, however, that some children will be very deficient in an individual task and will require the additional, simplified methods described. Therefore, these lower level tasks have been included. When the child's level of performance has been established, training should begin on this level and move up to succeeding levels as rapidly as possible, excluding the levels which are below the child's initial ability. In general, it is better to begin below the child's level and move more rapidly than to begin above his level and risk frustration on his part. In like manner, when the child has mastered a given level of performance, he should be moved to higher levels as soon as possible in order to avoid boredom.

It must constantly be kept in mind that no training technique is a goal in itself. The purpose of any activity used for training is to teach the child certain *generalized* skills and abilities. Thus, the walking board is used, not to teach the child how to walk along a rail, but to teach body balance and laterality. Performance on the specific task is secondary; teaching the generalization is primary. For this reason, attention must always be focused upon the generalization, and frequent variations of the specific task which will promote generalization should be introduced.

For the most part, the activities described here are not new but have been used in education and similar areas for a long time. In the past, however, they have been used largely to teach specific skills; here, their use is advocated for the purpose of aiding the development of more generalized skills. It is this new setting for older techniques which is the key to success. Emphasis is shifted from the training task itself to the contribution which this task can make to a general skill. With this new emphasis, familiar tasks take on new meaning and are used in new ways.

chapter 7

Chalkboard Training

SCRIBBLING

The earliest activity of the young child in any copying or drawing performance is that of scribbling. The very young child experiments with movement patterns and observes the traces which are left by these patterns on the paper, chalkboard, or whatever medium is being used. In the early stages, these movements are quite random and grow out of the child's experimentation with the basic movement patterns of his organism (Russell, 1956, p. 87; Gesell, 1940, p. 169; Bender, 1938, p. 7). He enjoys this new experience since it permits him to observe these movement patterns more accurately than he can when he moves merely for the sake of movement. Thus, his first approach to paper and pencil or any other writing or drawing medium is one of continued experimentation with the movement patterns which he has been carrying on for a long time. From this new experimentation he obtains two things: (1) additional experimentation with movement patterns and (2) observation of the pattern in the trace left by the activity.

PROBLEMS FOR THE SLOW LEARNER

In the slow-learning child, experimentation with these basic movement patterns has frequently been restricted. Being less quick in
learning and less extensive in experimentation, he has failed to develop some of the basic patterns of the organism and, among those
which he has developed, he has failed to complete the learning
process. As a result, his knowledge of and ability with the kinds
of movement which we find most useful in our culture are less
adequate than in the case of other children. With this inadequate
background, he is often forced into specific kinds of movement
patterns by the school or by educational requirements of his culture. Thus, when he reaches the age of five or six, we set him
down at a desk with a pencil and paper and require him to produce rather specific and highly skilled motor movements.

Such paper and pencil activities present difficulty to this child
for two reasons: (1) because the size of the product is restricted
and (2) because the patterns required are complicated. As we know
from developmental psychology (Zubek and Solberg, 1954, p. 133),
movement patterns begin in gross form using extensive muscle systems and, by a process of differentiation, are refined so that they
can be produced in smaller size and with a less extensive musculature. This process of development requires time and careful learning. The slow-learning child has been restricted in this learning
process and, as a result, when we set him down to the small-size
task required in the paper and pencil activities of the early grades,
he is not ready to produce this refined and this specific a motor
movement pattern. However, we insist that he perform in activities of this type. As a result, he very frequently breaks off a pattern of movement from his total movement pattern and develops
this "splintered" pattern specifically for the purpose of solving the
problem at hand. We frequently see a subsystem of movements
designed for the paper and pencil task but unrelated to the total
movement patterns of the child.

Adding to the problems created by size, the complexity of the
movement pattern which we require of the child is greatly increased
during early school experience. This complexity of movement, like
the problem of size, puts the slow learner at a disadvantage. He

has not absorbed these movement patterns as rapidly as other children have and he has not experimented as extensively. As a result, those patterns which he does possess are the simpler and less complicated ones. Now we throw him into a situation where extremely complicated patterns are required and, here again, he solves the problem in the only way he can. As far as possible, he reduces the complicated patterns which we require to simpler systems, distorting the tasks which we set for him in the interest of simplification.

Therefore, with slow-learning children, we frequently have the problem of returning to basic motor movement patterns and permitting the child to recapitulate the process of development by which finer and more complex patterns are achieved. A difficulty, however, arises immediately. Because we have forced him to make certain adaptations in order to adjust to the situations in which we have placed him, these adaptations have become fixed and the uninhibited type of experimentation by which the normal child develops these higher degrees of skill becomes impossible for the slow-learning child. We must break down these adaptations and find some method of getting the child back into the uninhibited experimentation which he requires to strengthen the basic skills needed in the learning process.

As an approach to this problem, chalkboard scribbling has been found a useful procedure. In this activity, the child is presented with a chalkboard and a piece of chalk. He is told to scribble, to make any sort of lines on the board which he would like to make. No restrictions are placed on the product which he is to produce but he is encouraged to experiment as broadly as he is willing to do.

"SPLINTER" MOVEMENTS

Very frequently we find these children, even on the chalkboard, maintaining the adaptations which they have learned in the paper and pencil situation. Thus, it is not infrequent to find a child who will rest his wrist against the chalkboard and make all of his movements with the fingers and hands.

It is felt that this kind of behavior is a transition to the chalkboard of specific techniques developed to solve the problem of paper and pencil work in the early grades. It is felt that such children have developed a restricted motor approach in relation to a specific problem and that this motor pattern exists in isolation, "splintered off" from the remainder of their motor activity. As such, it has limited usefulness, being adequate for only one type of activity. More important, this isolated response confuses the child since he is required to live with two basic sets of motor approaches. Since there is little or no connection between his two motor approaches, the complications of the environment to which the child is required to adjust are increased.

Our first attempts on the chalkboard will be to break down this limited approach and to encourage the child to approach the chalkboard task in terms of his total motor pattern rather than these specific patterns of hand and fingers. Therefore, we will want to move him away from the board so that he cannot rest his wrist against it. We will encourage him to move with his shoulder and elbow as opposed to his hand and fingers. We will also encourage him to make his productions larger and to fill a larger space at the board.

TIGHT MOVEMENTS

We may find many children whose movements in the scribbling activity are tight and jerky. These children give the impression of being overcontrolled. It seems as though they were paying so much attention to the problem of controlling the movement that they had no attention left over for initiating the movement. Here again, it seems possible that many children of this type have been forced into conditions requiring precise control of a movement before they have had sufficient experimentation to understand the movement thoroughly.

With children whose movements are tight and jerky, our aim is to free the movement patterns. Encourage the child to move freely, not to be restricted, not to worry about where he is going or the form of the pattern which he is producing. We want his movements to be free-flowing and smooth.

In order to assist the child in freeing his movement patterns, it is often desirable to ask him to come away from the chalkboard so that his hand does not touch it. In this position, we ask him to make free-flowing movements without reference to direction or form. When he has achieved a smooth, free-flowing movement without the resistance of the chalk on the chalkboard, we can then move him up to the board and ask him to do the same thing on the chalkboard.

We can also aid him by using the auditory and tactual clues to smooth-flowing movement that are produced by the friction of the chalk as it moves over the surface of the chalkboard. We encourage him to observe the rhythmical sounds which result from smooth-flowing curved movements and the rhythmical feel of such movements. We may even take a piece of chalk ourselves and point out these rhythms, asking him to imitate our rhythm as he produces his pattern.

In all chalkboard training that features scribbling, the teacher should be alert for jerky, rough, or tight movement patterns. Do not permit the child to persist in these patterns, to practice the errors which he is already making. Encourage him to smooth out and free these movement patterns. The first and perhaps most important value of this training procedure is that it teaches the child free-flowing movement.

OBSERVING THE "TRACE"

The chalkboard permits us to observe the movement patterns of the child and the freedom with which they are being produced. By observing the marks which he leaves on the board, we can see irregularities and tensions in his performance. By adding this information to our direct observations of his movements, we can help him learn initiation and control of major movement patterns.

However, in addition to what the chalkboard shows us, it also shows something to the child. Through the marks which he leaves on the board, he can observe the movement pattern which he has produced in a manner in which he is not able to observe it otherwise. When he simply makes a smooth movement in free space, this movement remains a series of activities in time. He progresses through the movement pattern and, as one phase is completed, the next phase is begun. At no point can he observe the total pattern all at one time. He must be content with the portion of the pattern which he is negotiating at any given instant in time. When the chalk leaves a mark on the board, however, this mark becomes a trace of the movement pattern itself. The trace remains permanent through time. By observing the trace, the child is able to observe the total movement pattern at one time. By this method, he has translated a movement pattern which was a series of activities in time into a simultaneous presentation in space. By observing this trace, the child can see the whole process of the movement pattern instead of being concerned with only fragments of it as it progresses through time.

This observation of the trace left by a motor movement pattern is very important in the development of the young child. He uses it for the purposes described above, to observe a pattern in a more permanent fashion. Such observation is one of the reasons for the young child's fascination with scribbling as a play activity. Just as it is important to the development of the normal young child, it is important to the development of the slow-learning child. With his confusion among movement patterns and his inadequate elaboration of movement patterns, it is particularly important that the slow-learning child be able to observe these patterns as total processes.

Therefore, in this scribbling performance we will want to call the child's attention to the trace left as a result of his movement. We will want to make sure that he carefully observes this trace and that he identifies it as a permanent record of a movement. When he has produced a pattern and when we know that he is aware of the movement which produced the pattern, we will ask him to stand off from the board and look at the mark which he has made. We may even ask him to trace over portions of his pattern so that he can observe the manner in which a pattern on a chalkboard can "stand for" a pattern of motor movement.

In this manner, he can be taught that marks on a piece of paper or a chalkboard symbolize movement patterns. Such knowledge increases the richness of the symbolic information conveyed by such marks and helps him to gear the whole symbolic field into his total pattern of activity. We can therefore use the activity of scribbling on a chalkboard for two basic purposes: (1) to help the child smooth out and free motor patterns and (2) to help the child stabilize these movement patterns in time and recognize symbolic visual patterns as permanentized motor movement patterns.

THE MOTIVATIONAL PROBLEM

Of course, with older children we will find difficulty in obtaining free scribbling movements because of the motivational problem. Many of these children will consider this type of activity "baby stuff." The ingenious teacher will be able to find many methods of motivating the child and modifying the activity in the interest of motivation while still ensuring that the two basic results to be obtained from this training procedure are retained.

FINGER PAINTING

Finger painting can frequently be used as a substitute for chalkboard scribbling in cases where motivation is a problem. In this use of finger paints, we must direct our attention away from the product which the child achieves and toward the process by which he manipulates the materials. We will therefore use the finger paints as a scribbling technique. We will be interested in how the child moves his hands and fingers and how he observes the results of these movements.

Finger paints, like the chalkboard, can be used to free the movement patterns and to produce smooth-flowing, free movements. Here again, we must pay attention to the activities of the child rather than to the product. We encourage the child to experiment with all kinds of movements placing emphasis on smooth movements *vs.* unsmooth movements. We also encourage him to observe the differences in the traces resulting from these movement patterns. In this manner, we do the same thing with finger paints that we were able to accomplish with chalkboard scribbling. It is essential that the finger paints be an experimental medium in which the child can experiment freely with his movement patterns without relation to any product which might result.

Through constant experimentation and observation, marks (which are the traces of movement) come to stand for the movement which produced them. (Courtesy of Nothman from Monkmeyer).

One definite advantage of finger paints in this connection is the possibility of the use of two hands. Since he can get both hands into the paint, he can experiment with movement patterns of the two hands simultaneously. This permits him to observe the difference between the same movement in both hands and the opposite movements in both hands. He can observe the difference between parallel movements on the two sides and contrary movements on the two sides. Here again, we are interested in experimentation. Encourage the child to make smooth, flowing movements simultaneously with both hands. Point out any differences between the patterns in the two hands (such as size, shape, smoothness of movement, etc.) and help him to experiment with these patterns until they are matched. The possibility of observing both hands operating simultaneously is a marked advantage of the finger painting medium.

CHALKBOARD (DIRECTIONALITY)

The teacher stands at the chalkboard beside the child. He places a dot at random on the board. The child places his chalk on the dot. The teacher then places another dot at random on the board and the child draws from the first to the second dot. The teacher then makes another dot and, without lifting his chalk from the board, the child draws from the second dot to the third. The game is continued in this same manner, the teacher always waiting until the child has drawn his line before placing the next dot.

PURPOSE

The purpose of this technique is to aid the child in establishing and maintaining directionality and changes of direction. For this reason, the dots are placed at random and in such a fashion that the child must change the direction of his movement each time.

This technique is somewhat similar to the connect-the-dot puzzles commonly encountered in which the dots are numbered and the child connects them in series. The present method is felt to be superior for training purposes since it can be used with children who have not yet learned to count and also because the presence of so many dots is often distracting to the child and he cannot perform the task.

SPECIAL PROBLEMS

For children who have difficulty with this activity, use shorter lines and permit the child to pause after drawing each line before he is given the new direction. Some children will have difficulty in establishing the direction in which they should draw and will start off in the wrong direction. Aid the child by calling his attention back to the target dot, as by calling "here" and tapping the dot with the chalk. If necessary, guide his hand to help him get started.

Other children will start in the right direction but will be unable to maintain this directionality until they reach the target dot. As a result, their line will "wander" toward the target. Encourage the child at all times to "draw nice straight lines." Shorter distances do not require the child to maintain his directionality for so long a period and hence are easier. If he has trouble, start with short distances and increase their length as the child's skill increases.

Some children can initiate a movement successfully but then have difficulty stopping. Such a problem will result in the child's "overshooting" the target dot. We can aid him by guiding his hand with ours or by providing a cardboard stop at the target dot against which he can bump his chalk. We can give him a stronger stimulus for the stopping response by using larger dots or colored chalk which will produce a dot of a contrasting color to the line he is drawing. We can also help him with the anticipation of his stop by chanting a rhythmic phrase such as "Hit the *dot*." This phrase should be spoken with distinct rhythm and with a marked accent on the last word. The child can then move in rhythm with the chant and by following the rhythm anticipate when he is to stop. Rhythm also helps him maintain his attention on the problem of stopping during the entire act.

The technique should start with short lines and a marked pause at each target dot. As the child gains skill, the teacher should place his dots at greater distances and increase the tempo of the game. Be sure, however, that the child comes to a full stop on each dot.

At first the child will be distracted if he must cross a line that he has already drawn to reach the next target dot. Therefore, at first, we will place our dots so that he is never required to cross a line he has previously drawn. When he becomes more skillful, we can cross and re-cross previously drawn lines. Do not attempt to produce a meaningful drawing as an end product of this game but use the technique only to aid the child with the problem of changing the direction of lines. At all levels of difficulty of this task, we should work toward a smooth, continuous movement.

CROSSING THE MIDLINE

As we have discussed in earlier chapters, the problem of maintaining direction while crossing the midline may give some children difficulty. For this reason, at early stages of the game, the dots should be kept on one side of the midline, preferably the side of the dominant hand. As the child increases in skill, we can begin to cross the midline. These crossings should be limited in the early sessions. Thus, the child will be asked to cross the midline only for an inch or two. As he gains skill with the specific problem of crossing, we can increase the extent of the movement across the midline so that eventually we can ask him to draw from full arm's length in one direction to full arm's length in the opposite direction. Watch the child closely during these activities. Be sure that he does not avoid the midline problem by walking back and forth in front of the chalkboard (thus moving his midline with him and avoiding crossing) or by pivoting his body at the hips so that the midline is thrown at various angles in such a way that he is not required to cross it (see Part II, "Chalkboard Tests").

THE CLOCK GAME

In the directionality training described previously, we have required the child to orient on one point in space and perform a motor movement which will bring his hand to that point. In this simple activity, it was only necessary that he determine the direction of a single point. This he could accomplish by a sighting or aiming type of activity. When he had determined a single direction, it was only necessary for him to move his hand in this predetermined direction.

As we have seen before, the child must learn to orient his whole organism toward the concept of direction. Since the two sides of the organism are in some respects opposite to each other, the directional orientation required by each side is somewhat different from that required by the other. It is therefore desirable that some training procedure be used in which the child is required to orient

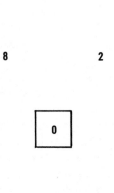

FIGURE 8. Chalkboard positions used in the Clock Game.

both sides of his body simultaneously in a given direction or toward a given set of directional commands. We would like him to be able to orient directionally with both sides simultaneously. Therefore, we would like an activity in which both sides must be oriented independently and must perform a directional movement simultaneously. In this manner, we can be assured that the child is orienting directionally with his organism and not with a single part or group of parts. He must also learn to control the interaction of the two sides of his body toward a common goal or toward separate but predetermined goals. In this manner, he can learn to use his two sides in an integrated fashion. The "reciprocal interweaving" of Gesell (Gesell, 1928) can be perfected and its results observed.

On the chalkboard locate eight numbered points equally spaced around the circumference of a circle approximately eighteen inches in diameter (see Figure 8). The points should be so arranged that points 1 and 5 determine a vertical axis, points 7 and 3 determine a horizontal axis, and points 6 and 2, 8 and 4 determine two diagonal axes. The diagram is presented in Figure 8. In the center of the imaginary circle, place a square box labeled *O*. This box is the goal for all movements terminating in the center of the circle.

Instruct the child to place the right hand on one of the numbers and the left hand on a second. Then ask him to move the left hand to a prescribed number and the right hand to another prescribed number which you call out for him. He should move both hands simultaneously and they should arrive at their respective goals at the same time.

There are a number of combinations of movements which we will want to investigate with this procedure.

1. OPPOSED MOVEMENT

a. *Toward the Center.* In this pattern of movement, the child is started with his two hands on the circumference of the circle and asked to bring them both toward the center. Thus, in the simplest movement we start him with his left hand on the number 7 and his right hand on the number 3. He is then asked to bring both hands to the center box *O* simultaneously. Watch closely to see that both hands move at the same time, that they move at the same rate of speed, and that they arrive at the center box at the same time. If the child is having difficulty with this type of movement, it is probable that his first approach to the problem will be to move one hand first and, after this movement is completed, move the second hand. If we allow him to continue according to this method of procedure, we will not teach him the patterns which this technique is designed to aid. Therefore, in our instructions and in the practice sessions, we will want to call his attention to such errors and ask him to correct them. He must start the movement of the hands simultaneously and continue them at the same rate of speed so that they reach the goal at the same time.

The pattern of movement presented by this subsection is perhaps the simplest of all possible patterns. In the first place, it seems probable from studies of developmental movements that movements from outside in are easier than movements from inside out. This subsection presents all patterns in the order outside in. In addition to this fact, the child in this pattern is required only to sight on a single goal, the zero box. During the initial instructions, he may change his visual fixation from 7 to 3 as frequently as he wishes and may take as much time as he needs to locate his hands on 7 and 3. He may attend to his right hand until it is on 3 and then, leaving it there, he may attend to his left hand until it is on 7. He is not required to coordinate the two sides until the performance actually begins. At the command "Bring your hands to zero," he has only to fixate on the zero box. If his only method of orientation is by sighting or aiming, he has a single point at which to aim. The aiming process can be completed in one activity, and he has only to orient his movement systems to this single control.

The simplest movement is the horizontal one starting at 7 and 3 and proceeding to zero. The next movement is the vertical movement starting at 1 and 5 and proceeding to zero. More complicated, as we have seen before, are the diagonal movements starting at 6 and 2 or 8 and 4 and proceeding to zero. A tabulation of the possible movements in this subpattern in approximate order of their difficulty is presented in Table 1 under 1(a).

b. *Movement Away from Center.* In this pattern, the child begins with both hands at the center box and upon command moves out to numbers designated by the teacher. Thus, with both hands located at *O*, he is asked to move his left hand to 7 while he moves his right hand to 3.

This pattern is somewhat more difficult than the previous pattern. Here the child is required to determine the directionality of the two hands independently. He must either look at 7 and retain this directional clue in memory while he looks at 3, or he must be able to look at the center of the circle and with the periphery of his vision be aware of the location of 7 and 3 at the same time. In pattern 1(a), we only required him to coordinate the two sides of his body toward a single directional clue. In the present pattern, we require him to orient to two directional clues at the same time and to orient the two sides of his body to these clues respectively.

TABLE 1

CLOCK GAME

Movement Combinations in Approximate Order of Difficulty

	LEFT HAND		RIGHT HAND	
	Start	Stop	Start	Stop
1 (a) Opposed movement toward center				
	7	0	3	0
	1	0	5	0
	5	0	1	0
	8	0	4	0
	6	0	2	0
(b) Opposed movement away from center				
	0	7	0	3
	0	1	0	5
	0	5	0	1
	0	8	0	4
	0	6	0	2
2 Parallel movement				
	7	0	0	3
	0	7	3	0
	1	0	0	5
	0	1	5	0
	5	0	0	1
	0	5	1	0
	8	0	0	4
	0	8	4	0
	6	0	0	2
	0	6	2	0
3 (a) Movement with cross meridians				
Movement toward center				
	7	0	1	0
	7	0	5	0
	1	0	3	0
	5	0	3	0
	8	0	1	0
	8	0	3	0
	8	0	5	0
	6	0	1	0
	6	0	3	0
	6	0	5	0
	8	0	2	0
	6	0	4	0
	7	0	2	0
	7	0	4	0
	1	0	2	0
	1	0	4	0
	5	0	2	0
	5	0	4	0

TABLE 1 (*Continued*)

LEFT HAND		RIGHT HAND	
Start	Stop	Start	Stop

(b) Movement away from center

Start	Stop	Start	Stop
0	7	0	1
0	7	0	5
0	1	0	3
0	5	0	3
0	8	0	1
0	8	0	3
0	8	0	5
0	6	0	1
0	6	0	3
0	6	0	5
0	8	0	2
0	6	0	4
0	7	0	2
0	7	0	4
0	1	0	2
0	1	0	4
0	5	0	2
0	5	0	4

4 (a) Cross movement—cross meridian
Movement left to right

Start	Stop	Start	Stop
7	0	0	1
7	0	0	5
7	0	0	2
7	0	0	4
8	0	0	3
8	0	0	5
8	0	0	1
8	0	0	2
6	0	0	3
6	0	0	1
6	0	0	4
6	0	0	5

(b) Movement right to left

Start	Stop	Start	Stop
0	7	1	0
0	7	5	0
0	7	2	0
0	7	4	0
0	8	3	0
0	8	5	0
0	8	1	0
0	8	2	0
0	6	3	0
0	6	1	0
0	6	4	0
0	6	5	0

In the early stages of training, we permit him to look back and forth from 7 to 3 as frequently as he wishes in order to determine the directions demanded. It is desirable, however, that he be able to maintain visual fixation at O and at the same time be aware of 7 and 3 with peripheral vision. Many children, in tasks involving difficulty or stress, reduce the area of their peripheral vision (Kephart and Chandler, 1956). Their visual field "tunnels down" so that the only material of which they are aware is that which lies straight ahead of them. Obviously this restriction of visual field reduces the awareness on the part of the child of many clues which would be helpful in the solution of his problem. We are interested in counteracting this tendency on the part of the child, and the present technique can be used for this purpose if we encourage him to fixate on the center of the circle and be aware of the periphery at the same time.

In this pattern, as in the previous one, the teacher must be sure that the child starts with both hands at the same time, that he proceeds at the same rate with both hands, and that he arrives at the two goals simultaneously. In activity of this type, some children will be found who give all their attention to the dominant hand and permit the non-dominant hand to take care of itself. Such children should be encouraged to pay attention to both hands at the same time and to be aware of the movement of both hands simultaneously.

As in the previous pattern, the lateral direction is the simplest, the vertical direction is next, and the diagonal directions are most difficult. A tabulation of the various combinations in their approximate order of difficulty is given in Table 1 under 1(b).

2. PARALLEL MOVEMENT

Here we require the hands to move parallel to each other. Thus, the child is asked to begin with his left hand on 7 and his right hand on O. He is then asked to move his left hand to O and his right hand to 3. Both hands are moving in a left to right direction and are moving over the same distance.

Again, the teacher should observe whether the child moves both hands simultaneously, whether he moves them at equal rates, and whether he arrives at the two goals at the same time. As in the previous patterns, it is desirable that the child pay attention to both hands and he should be encouraged to be aware of the movement of both hands at the same time. As in pattern 1(b), the present pattern can be used to aid the child in maintaining peripheral awareness during a difficult task. This is done by encouraging the child to maintain visual fixation on the center box while the movement is taking place.

We want the child to learn parallel movements in both directions (that is, right to left and left to right) and in all meridians. A table of the various combinations of movements is presented in Table 1 under 2.

3. MOVEMENT WITH CROSSED MERIDIANS

In this activity, one hand is required to move in one direction while the other hand moves in another direction. Thus, the child may be asked to place his left hand on 7 and his right hand on 1. At command, he is asked to bring both hands together at O. In order to do this, one hand must travel in a lateral direction while the other hand is traveling in a vertical direction.

In order to accomplish this activity, the child must do two things. (1) He must be able to move one side of his body in a given direction while the other side is moving in another direction. There must be enough independence of the two sides that they do not need to move in bilaterally symmetrical relationships. (2) He must be able to evaluate spatial relationships on the lateral axis according to the same scheme with which he evaluates them on the vertical axis. Thus, the distance from 7 to O must appear to him the same as the distance from 1 to O. If one of these axes appears longer than the other, the two hands will not meet in the center simultaneously. We therefore present, with this pattern, a considerably more difficult task for the child to accomplish.

As before, the teacher should observe the beginning of the movement, its speed, and whether the final goal is reached simultaneously with both hands. Again, the child should pay attention to both hands equally so that both sides of his body are under control at the same time. Attention to both sides is more necessary for the solution of the task in the present pattern than in either of the previous two. Here again, the child should be encouraged to maintain visual fixation on the O center box.

The two over-all directions of movement described above are possible in the present pattern also. Thus, the movements can be set up in such a way that both hands are moving toward the center or they can be set up so that both hands are moving away from the center. As in pattern 1, the movement toward the center is easier than the movement away from the center. Also, as we have seen before, movements in a lateral direction are easiest, vertical movements are more difficult, and diagonals are most difficult. A tabulation of the various possibilities in approximate order of their difficulty is given in Table 1. In this tabulation, movements toward the center have been presented first [section 3(a)] and movements away from the center second [section 3(b)].

4. CROSS MOVEMENT—CROSS MERIDIANS

a. *Left to Right.* In this pattern, the hands are moving in opposite directions and at the same time are moving in opposite meridians. Thus, the child is asked to begin with the left hand at 7 and the right hand at O. He is then asked to move his left hand to O and his right hand to 1. These patterns are an extension and a more difficult combination of the patterns in paragraph 3 above. The same observations and cautions are pertinent here that were described there. In the first group of patterns, the general direction of the movement is left to right.

b. *Right to Left.* These patterns are similar to those of paragraph 4(a) above except that the general direction of movement is right to left. We will want to give the child practice in both of these directions of movement since we want him to have a complete and integrated concept of direction and of movement in a given direction when these are signaled by a visual stimulus. The various movements in this pattern as well as those of pattern 4(a) are tabulated in Table 1 under 4(a) and 4(b).

When the child has become reasonably proficient with the activities described above, a circle of larger diameter can be substituted for the eighteen-inch circle. This larger circle should be approximately thirty inches in diameter. On the one hand, a larger circle requires greater skill of the child since the movements are longer and must be maintained over a longer period of time. On the other hand, it requires awareness of clues at a greater distance into the periphery of vision when the teacher requires the child to maintain fixation on the O center box while the task is being performed. In general, the further a stimulus lies from the center of vision the more difficult it becomes to recognize it or to use it as a control for general behavior (Feinberg, 1949). The larger circle is particularly desirable for increasing the aid which we provide the child in keeping his peripheral visual field operative during a stress-producing task. The same general procedure is used with the large circle that was used with the smaller circle.

For children who cannot read or who have difficulty recognizing the number symbols, substitute pictures, colors, or other materials with which the child is familiar for the numerals around the circumference of the circle. It is desirable that the child perform the task with chalk rather than with his finger or by moving his finger in the air in front of the chalkboard. The line resulting from his movement helps us and the child to determine how well he has performed.

Some children will not maintain a high level of motivation in the drawing tasks described here. For such children, other devices may be substituted to solve the motivational problem. One teacher, for example, gives the child small toy cars which he drives into the garage (the O center box) or which he delivers, two at a time, to customers' homes (numerals on the circumference of the circle).

CHALKBOARD (ORIENTATION)

Ask the child to stand before the chalkboard with a piece of chalk in each hand. Ask him to describe circular motions with both hands simultaneously. Note the direction of the movement in each hand. Then ask him to bring the chalk in contact with the board so that he is drawing circles with each hand simultaneously. He should be asked to continue drawing pairs of circles, each pair on top of the previous pair. He should continue the motion, not stopping after each circle is drawn, until he produces a series of retraced circles, one set with the right hand and one set with the left hand.

Normally we expect the child to draw his circles clockwise with the left hand and counterclockwise with the right. If he begins with these directions, we ask him to change and draw counter-clockwise with the left hand and clockwise with the right. When this movement has been established, we ask him to make his hands move parallel to each other, going clockwise with each hand. When he has established this movement, we ask him to shift and go counterclockwise with both hands. In this manner, we let him experience all combinations of direction of movement with the two hands, both those in which the movements are opposed and those in which they are parallel.

We want the child to observe the difference between movements in different directions and between different combinations of move-ment on the two sides of the body. Therefore, we will want to call his attention to the movements and the difference in the way they "feel." We can direct his attention to the movements by asking him to shift abruptly during a movement pattern. Instead of asking him to move left clockwise, right counterclockwise, and then stop, completing this task, and then asking him to move left counterclockwise, right clockwise, we will ask him to shift in the middle of the pattern. Thus, while he is moving in the left clock-wise, right counterclockwise pattern, we will call, "Change direc-tion." At this signal, he is to shift direction as rapidly as possible and without interrupting the movement. In like manner, ask him to shift from opposed to parallel patterns in the midst of the activity and to change the direction of the parallel patterns without inter-rupting the activity.

At the same time that we are showing him the difference between the movement patterns, we want him to observe that the results are circles irrespective of the directions with which they were pro-duced. Therefore, we will want to direct his attention to the prod-uct of his movement during the entire activity. His attention can be called to the trace on the board by asking him to produce good, round, smooth circles.

In most cases, a change in movement will result in a disruption of the pattern which will in turn result in a distortion of one or both of the circles. Ask the child to correct the distortion (by watching the circles he is drawing) and to smooth out the movement as rapidly as possible. When a reasonably accurate, smooth circle has been achieved, give the signal for a change of movement pattern.

Remember that the learning in this activity results from the change of direction and the reorientation of the process. As soon as the child has established correct patterns in the new direction, little further learning takes place. Therefore, little is gained by having the child continue a direction after he has mastered it. We gain more by asking him to change and readjust his perceptual-motor process. Long periods of training are not indicated; short periods with frequent changes are more effective.

Remember, however, that unless the child establishes an adequate perceptual-motor response after each change (achieves a reasonably round, smooth circle), he has not learned the relationships that we are trying to teach him. Therefore, he must be helped to achieve an acceptable (although not necessarily perfect) production at each step. If certain patterns are too difficult for him and he cannot achieve an adequate production, drop back to simpler patterns or help him by guiding the hand, tracing over heavy circles drawn previously on the board, and so forth.

THE LAZY EIGHT

An appreciation of direction of movement and of form independent of direction of movement can also be aided by use of the "lazy eight." With one continuous line, draw on the board a figure 8 lying on its side. The figure should be approximately twenty-four inches wide and approximately ten inches high. Ask the child to trace over and over this figure with one continuous line and without taking his chalk from the board. When he has achieved a smooth, free movement which is reasonably accurate, ask him to reverse directions without removing his chalk from the board or interrupting the activity.

This figure is particularly helpful since the direction of movement in the left-hand loop is the opposite of that in the right-hand loop. In spite of this difference in direction, the visual counterparts of these movements are the same when drawn or traced on the chalkboard. Such a form permits the child to observe relationships between different motor acts and perceptual products within the same figure.

The child should be asked to trace this figure in both directions with the right hand and also in both directions with the left hand. By experiencing both hands in this task, he can observe the differences and similarities between movements on one side of the body and on the other. He should be asked to stand so that the entire figure is to the right of the center of his body in some trials and so that the entire figure is to the left of his body in other trials. At other times, he should be asked to stand so that the center of his body is directly in front of the crossing point between the two loops. By varying the position of his body in all of the above combinations, we can present to him the facts of laterality related to direction of movement and perceptual products. Present all combinations of hand, direction, and body position so that the child's experience may be as diversified as possible.

As in the earlier exercises, the learning in the lazy eight exercise occurs during the adaptation to a new direction, hand, or position of the body. To continue practice after this adjustment has been made results in a decreasing rate of learning. Therefore, short periods of training with numerous changes in method are most rewarding.

DRAWING AND COPYING

In the scribbling activity which we described earlier, we presented the child with a problem in which motor activity was predominant. The child was encouraged to experiment with motor patterns and to observe the visual counterparts of these patterns as they developed in the form of marks on the chalkboard. In scribbling, the motor element was predominant and the perceptual element was secondary. The child's attention was directed from the motor to the visual.

In directional activities, as in the dotting game or the clock game, we have imposed a single visual control upon the motor activity. In these games, the child was required to make a visual orientation toward a goal. He was then required to initiate a motor pattern which would bring his hand in contact with this goal. This sort of activity requires a visual control over the initiation of the action. It involves aiming or sighting behavior and guiding a motor movement toward the sighted goal. This is, as it were, a single visual control over a motor activity. After the sighting has been accomplished and the orientation to the goal has been established, visual control may be no longer necessary. The child, in effect, establishes his perceptual control first and performs the motor movement second. Such activity is analogous to an open system of control (Brown and Campbell, 1948, p. 2), wherein the visual controls are established before the action is initiated and their control function is completed before the action takes place.

When we ask the child to draw or copy a form, we set a new task for him. We require him to exert a constant visual control over the motor movement pattern. In copying, we require him to set up a visual control which is operative throughout the motor activity. Visual control now becomes dominant and motor activity is subservient to perceptual activity. With copying, it is not possible to set up the control ahead of time. The child must constantly keep in mind the visual information and use this information to guide the motor activity at each instant of the performance. When he is copying from an actual model, the visual data are physically present. When he is drawing, he is presumably copying a mental image in which the visual data are present in memory. In either event, the perceptual data must exert a constant control over the motor activities.

It will be seen, of course, that what we have been discussing in the past few pages is the skill which has frequently been called eye-hand coordination. In the scribbling stages, we were concerned with the hand primarily and the eye only secondarily and as a means of observation. In the dotting and clock game activities, we inserted a single control over the hand by the eye. In our present drawing and copying activities, we will now attempt to bring the hand under constant control of the eye. We are attempting to set up a visual-motor feed-back (see page 60 ; also Strauss and Kephart, 1955, pp. 2–5) such that visual data can be used as a constant, closed-system control of the total activity.

THE CIRCLE

Gesell and others (Gesell, 1940; Bender, 1938; Goodenough, 1926) have shown that the first form to be reproduced by the young child is that of the circle. Our current intelligence tests place the drawing of the circle at a lower age level than the drawing of any other form (Terman and Merrill, 1937; Wechsler, 1949). The circle is the simplest form operationally since it involves a constant direction and a constant rhythm. In order to complete a circle, it is only necessary that the child set up a movement in a constant curved direction and maintain this movement until closure is made. In like manner, the rhythm of the movement is not interrupted in the process of completing the circle. We will therefore want to start our training in drawing and copying with this simplest of all forms.

MOVEMENT

Our first problem is to teach the child the circular movement itself. For this purpose, the teacher may stand in front of the child and describe a circular movement with her hand and arm. The child is asked to imitate this movement. If he experiences difficulty, we may guide his movement by asking him to touch his finger to the teacher's. As the teacher moves around in the circular motion, the contact of the finger guides the child's arm in a similar movement. By this method, some of the difficulties of the child's movement pattern can be eliminated.

Many children will have greater difficulty than can be removed by this simple method. These children will need additional tactual and kinesthetic clues to help them form a circular motion. These clues can be supplied by the use of *templates*. A template is a pattern cut out of cardboard or similar material.

The form to be studied is cut out of a sheet of cardboard. The template is then the cardboard sheet with the cut-out portion in its center. The child inserts his finger in the cut-out and runs it around the boundaries of the form. Thus, in the case of the circle, we would have a sheet of cardboard with a circular hole in its center. The child inserts his finger in this circular hole and runs it around the circumference of the circle. Through this activity, he gets tactual clues regarding the movement pattern from the contact of his finger with the edges of the template. In like manner, the template forces his hand into a prescribed motion. Whenever this forcing takes place, the muscular tensions and tonuses are changed from those which obtain when he is making the incorrect motion. Kinesthetic end organs produce sensations indicating these changes in muscle tension. These kinesthetic clues, added to the tactual clues, form a strong picture against which to compare his movement.

If the child has particular difficulty, the teacher may ask him to press hard against the template. This pressure increases both the tactual and the kinesthetic clues. When he begins to have less difficulty, the teacher may suggest that he press lightly against the sides of the template. In this manner, she can reduce the tactual and kinesthetic clues as the child becomes able to perform on his own with less and less assistance from these additional sets of clues.

TEMPLATES

When the child begins to develop an idea of the circular motion, we will want to bring this activity under visual control. Our first approach to this problem involves the use of templates held against the chalkboard. The first activity at the chalkboard is a continuation of the development of the circular movement pattern discussed above. The template is held firmly against the board by the teacher. The child is asked to place his finger inside the cut-out circle and to run it around the edge of the form. Here he is obtaining tactual and kinesthetic clues to the required movement, as previously described. In addition, he is getting further tactual information from the contact of his finger with the surface of the chalkboard as well as with the edge of the template. The teacher should encourage the child to watch his finger as it runs around the circumference of the circle.

The child is then given a piece of chalk which he is asked to place inside the template. He is then asked to run the chalk around the edge of the template in the same way in which he ran his finger around its edge. This activity results in the drawing of a circle. Here again, the task is made easier by the kinesthetic information provided by the template and the tactual information provided by the contact of the chalk with the board and with the edges of the template. When a circle is completed in this manner, the template is removed from the board so that the child can see what he has drawn.

At this point, we are introducing visual clues which we will later want to make the dominant factors in the child's control of his performance. Therefore, it is very important that at this early stage we begin to call his attention to the visual factors involved. After each attempt, the teacher will therefore remove the template from the board so that the child can see what he has drawn. He will also want to call the child's attention to the drawing and to make sure that he observes this visual trace left by the activity.

TRACING

We are now ready to introduce the problem of visual data as a guide and control for motor activity. This we do by asking the child to trace over a representation of the form which we are trying to teach. We will want to introduce this problem in stages since it represents a major learning task for the child, and we cannot ask him to jump immediately from a tactual and kinesthetic control to a visual control. We must interpose intermediate steps to help him.

a. *Visual-Tactual-Kinesthetic.* At the first stage, we will simply add visual information to the tactual and kinesthetic information which the child has already learned to use. For this purpose, we will draw a circle on the board which can be enclosed with the template. The child is then asked to place his chalk inside the template and to draw over our visual circle. To aid him in this activity, he has the tactual information from the chalk on the board and the edges of the template and the kinesthetic information from the template. At the same time, we call his attention to the visual data and encourage him to use these visual data as a guide in the process, depending as little as possible upon the tactual and kinesthetic clues.

At this early stage, we will want to make the visual information as strong as possible. Therefore, the circle which we ask him to trace will be made with very broad, heavy lines. The circumference should be drawn an inch to an inch and a half wide and the chalk should be heavy and obvious. It is desirable, if possible, to use colored chalk to increase the strength of the visual clues. Red is most suitable since it is more striking than any other color.

By using a heavy line we do two things: (1) we increase the strength of the visual stimulus by increasing its quantity, and (2) we decrease the demand for precision in the child's movements. By using bold strokes with the chalk, we increase the strength of the visual clue by increasing the brightness contrast between the circumference of the circle and the surrounding chalkboard area. If we use colored chalk, we further increase the strength of the visual clue by adding a color contrast to the brightness contrast. By these means, we make the visual data as striking, as strong, and as predominant as we possibly can. By using a wide line, we decrease the precision demands of the task. If the circumference of the circle is one inch to an inch and a half wide, the child can make a reasonably large error and still be successful in performance. Since we are introducing visual control, we are more interested at this stage in type or quality of performance than we are in precision of performance.

b. *Visual-Tactual.* In (a) above, we presented the child with three clues to the copying task: visual, tactual, and kinesthetic. Since we want him to be able eventually to perform this task on the basis of visual clues alone, we will want to remove the additional tactual and kinesthetic clues as rapidly as possible. Here again, however, we cannot remove these abruptly; we must remove them in a series of intermediate steps.

The first clue which can be removed is the kinesthetic. We do this by removing the template in the activity in (a) above. We now ask the child to trace with his finger over the circle which we draw on the board. This circle is drawn with a wide line and the visual clues are made as strong as possible. By using his finger for this tracing activity, the child obtains a maximum amount of tactual information. As it rubs over the surface of the chalkboard, his finger gives him constant and strong tactual data at the same time that he is obtaining visual data from our drawn circle. If necessary, we can increase the tactual information by asking him to press hard against the board with his finger. As he is able to perform more readily, we will want to decrease the tactual information by asking him to press more lightly. During all this activity, we want to call his attention constantly to the visual data by asking him to watch what he is doing and to stay on the circle. Since the circle has been drawn with a very broad line, the precision required to stay on its outline is reduced.

c. *Visual-Minimum Tactual.* When the child is able to perform adequately by tracing with his finger on the chalkboard, we will want to reduce this tactual clue and further reinforce the visual clue. This we can do by asking him to trace around our circle with chalk. The tactual information resulting from the chalk as it rubs against the surface of the board is less intense than that resulting from the finger when it rubs along the same surface. At the same time, a new set of visual information is introduced. The line produced by the child as he draws with his chalk is added to the visual data represented by our circle on the board. He is encouraged to observe this line while he is producing it and to compare it with ours. Here again, we are still using the circle made with broad and heavy lines so that the visual information is at a maximum and the precision required is at a minimum.

Be sure that the child maintains a smooth, free movement during the tracing. Do not permit him to slow down and tighten up his movement. Some children will move very slowly and in short spurts, checking each spurt after it has occurred. Such children are not using the visual information to guide a movement pattern. They are splitting off the motor aspects of the task from its perceptual aspects. The motor movements (spurts) are not under visual control but are produced by purely motor activity. After each spurt, the child compares his product with the model by a vision-to-vision match. Such procedures avoid the problem of perceptual-motor control and the monitoring of movement patterns by perceptual data. They are not aiding the development of a closed system of control. We will therefore want to discourage such approaches to the tracing activity since they do not result in the type of learning which we are trying to achieve.

d. *Visual.* When the child can perform with a minimum of kinesthetic and tactual clues, we can remove the tactual clue entirely and ask him to perform the task under visual guidance alone. This we do by asking him to trace the circle in the air. The child is asked to hold his finger up to the copy of the circle but not quite touching the chalkboard. He is then asked to trace the circle in the air over the copy but in front of the chalkboard. The teacher should watch carefully to see that he stays on the line even though his finger is not touching the board. Visual clues are still at a maximum since the copy we give him is still made with broad, heavy lines.

e. *Reduced Visual Clues.* Since we want the child to be able to perform the tracing task with a normal set of visual clues, we will want to remove the artificially strong visual data which we have been using up to this point. Here again, we cannot move abruptly to tracing a circle in which the circumference is drawn with a normal stroke but must move toward this goal with intermediate steps. This can be done by gradually reducing the strength of the visual clues which we offer.

The first step is to remove the color clue, drawing the broad, heavy circumference with ordinary chalk. We can then begin reducing the width of the line which we use in our copy. Thus, we may cut it down from an inch and a half to an inch, then to three-quarters of an inch, then to a half inch, etc., until we can draw a circle in which the circumference is made with a chalk line of normal width and which the child is still able to trace over with his chalk.

Do not forget that as you reduce the width of the line, you are not only reducing the strength of the visual clues; you are also increasing the precision of movement required of the child. Therefore, the process of reducing the width of the line is determined both by the child's ability to use reduced visual clues and by his ability to make more precise movements.

COPYING

When we ask the child to copy a circle, we have introduced a new variable which was not present in the task of tracing a circle. In the task of tracing, the visual data were constantly present at each instant of the performance. As he traced around the circle, at any instant, the visual data required to guide the next instant of performance were immediately before him. When he is asked to copy, however, the visual data are in one position on the board and his production is in another position. He must therefore introduce mental images of the visual data to serve as immediate guides to his performance. The copy supplies the general set of visual data, but its application must be accomplished through the use of memory information.

The difficulty interposed by this memory requirement is frequently seen in the trouble which the child has in achieving a closure. The end of his circular motion does not meet the beginning. As a result, his production is not closed but there is an overlap or a gap in his circle between the starting point and the ending point. In order to close his circle in the copying task, the child must remember his beginning point and must keep in mind the total movement pattern so that previous activities are remembered and have an effect on present activities.

In the tracing performance, as soon as the child has traversed a portion of the circumference, he can if he wishes forget all about this portion and simply continue his activity guided by the copy which lies directly in front of him. When he is required to copy, however, this immediacy of response is inadequate. Past activities must continue to influence present activities so that the child keeps the starting point always in mind and, upon completion of the activity, comes back to it. Only in this way can a closure be achieved. In copying, no instant of activity can remain independent but must be integrated with remembered previous activity and anticipated future activity.

We can help the child to achieve closure by calling special attention to the beginning and ending point of his activity. Thus, we may make a large bold X on the board. We ask the child to begin his circle at the X and to end it at the X. As he progresses with his activity, this strong stimulus helps him to keep in mind the point at which he began and the point at which he must end. We can also aid him by verbally calling to his attention the starting X and the ending X. Thus, we add auditory and verbal clues to the visual clues. As he becomes more proficient, we will want to reduce these artificial clues until he can operate without them. Obviously we can reduce the clues by reducing the number of verbal hints which we give him and by gradually reducing the size of the X which we give him as a clue.

REPRODUCTION

When the child can copy a form, we want him to be able to reproduce it from memory. Thus, we want to be able to say to him, "Draw me a circle," and we want him to be able to reproduce an adequate circle from this verbal clue alone. In this activity, we have inserted a further demand upon his performance. In tracing, we gave him continuous visual clues as a guide to his activity; in copying, we required the substitution of remembered clues for part of the visual clues. Since he could look back and forth to the copy, we offered him help whenever his memory clues weakened or failed him. When we ask him to reproduce a circle on verbal instructions alone, however, we ask him to guide his total performance on the basis of a mental image or a set of remembered data. In this performance, all of the guiding of the motor movement must result from memory images. Thus, reproduction of the circle represents the highest type of performance where all of the control of the activity has become cortical and intellectual.

VARIATION

All of the activities discussed above have been very specific and could be applied to a specific circle. We want the child to develop a generalized concept of a circle rather than a specific concept of a given circle. Therefore, if we go through the stages of chalkboard activity with a particular circle, we are in danger of teaching the child how to reproduce a *particular circle* but failing to teach him the generalized concept of the circle. Therefore, we will want to vary the activities described above in terms of the variables in the circular form itself. There are a number of these variables, and in our activities we will want to use circles varying in all of the aspects with which we want the child to become acquainted.

a. *Size.* The child must learn that the characteristic aspect of a circle is its shape. Therefore, we will want to vary the sizes of the circles which we offer him as examples. In all of the activities above, we should present circles of varying sizes. Do not use the same size circle in all sessions or in all activities of one session. Present sometimes small circles, sometimes large circles, and sometimes intermediate sizes. These variations should, however, be kept within a reasonable range. Obviously we do not wish to give the child a circle so large that he cannot comprehend all of its parts at one time. On the other hand, if we make the circles too small, we may drive him back into the "splinter" type of activity discussed in our description of scribbling techniques.

b. *Speed.* The child must learn that the circle is drawn with a constant rhythm (as opposed to squares and other forms in which the rhythm must be interrupted). Again, we want him to realize that the constancy of rhythm (Piaget and Inhelder, 1956, p. 65) is the important factor and not the rhythm itself. Therefore, we should vary speed in our activities just as we varied size. Sometimes we will ask him to draw circles rapidly, sometimes we will ask him to draw them slowly, etc.

c. *Solid vs. Outline Figures.* The child must learn how to see a form as a figure on a background. This is more difficult in the case of outline forms than in the case of solid or colored-in forms. In the case of the outline form, the area enclosed by the contour is objectively similar to the area lying outside the contour. If form perception is adequate, the child disregards this similarity and the area within the contour comes to stand out and appear different from the area outside the contour (Kephart, 1958). In this way, he develops the concepts of figure-ground. With many children, however, this figure-ground relationship does not arise spontaneously. We will want to help these children develop the figure-ground relationship. If we do not pay attention to this problem, we are in danger of teaching them how to reproduce the contour of the figure without seeing or responding to the figure as a form.

Therefore, we will want in the course of chalkboard training in drawing to incorporate training in figure-ground relationships. This can best be done by coloring in the area bounded by the figure. When the form is colored in, the inside area stands out against the outside area since it is different in either brightness, color, or both. Such additional clues aid the child in developing the figure-ground relationship.

For this reason we will want, in teaching the child the drawing of a circle, to vary the figure-ground relationship. Part of the time we will ask him to color in the circle, and part of the time we will ask him to draw it in outline. The coloring-in problem presents some of the same difficulties that we have discussed in terms of outline drawing. Thus, we will want to provide the child with templates so that tactual and kinesthetic clues can be added to his performance, and we will want to offer him increased visual clues by the use of broad lines and strong visual data just as we did for his outline-drawing performance. In all of the types of activity discussed above, we will sometimes ask him to draw in outline and sometimes ask him to color in. Here again, always call attention to what he has done. Ask him to step away and look at the product which he has made when he has finished it.

d. *Direction.* We want the child to know that a circle is the same thing if you draw it in a clockwise direction as it is if you draw it in a counterclockwise direction. Therefore, in our training, we will want to vary the direction in which the child draws. Sometimes we will ask him to draw clockwise, sometimes we will ask him to draw counterclockwise. Again, call his attention to the fact that the circle is the same regardless of the direction in which it is produced.

e. *Hand.* We also want the child to know that a circular motion produced by the right hand is the same thing as a circular motion produced by the left hand. Therefore, we will want to vary the hand which we ask him to use. Sometimes we will ask him to draw or trace with the right hand, and sometimes with the left hand. Again, we call his attention to the fact that the product is the same regardless of the hand which is used.

We will also want to present all of the combinations of direction and hand. As we have seen earlier, a clockwise movement with the right hand is different from a clockwise movement with the left hand. The motor patterns presented by these two movements differ. We want the child to know the different ways in which he can produce a circular motion and to recognize that regardless of how it is produced it still is a circle. Therefore, in our activities, we will ask him sometimes to draw clockwise with the right hand, counterclockwise with the right hand, clockwise with the left hand, and counterclockwise with the left hand. In this manner, we present all of the combinations of movement patterns of the hands which result in a circular product.

f. *Other Body Parts.* We also want the child to know that the circular movement remains circular independent of the body part with which it is produced. Thus, in addition to asking him to produce circles with his hands, we will ask him to draw circles with his toe in sand or other soft material. We may ask him to hold a pencil or crayon in his teeth and draw a circle with his head. Many children do not appreciate the circular pattern as applied to parts of the body other than the hand. It is important that the child realize that a circle is a generalized pattern and can be produced by any body part which is capable of a circular motion.

VERBAL COMPONENT

Throughout all our activity in drawing and copying, we will want to be sure that the child attaches the verbal symbol to the productions which he is making. Language and communication demand the use of a verbal symbol which must stand for a motor pattern, an image of a motor pattern, or the data from motor patterns particularly as these are combined with sensory elements to form perceptions (Piaget and Inhelder, 1956, p. 453). Therefore, we will want from the beginning to increase the symbolic value of the verbal symbol by attaching it to all experiences in which it is applicable. Therefore, in drawing a circle we will want to attach the word *circle* to all of the activities that we can. Thus, in our instructions, we will use the word *circle;* in calling attention to the productions of the child, we will use the word *circle.* In like manner, we will ask him what he is going to draw, what he has drawn, and what the production which he has made is called. In this way, we keep the verbal symbol constantly in relationship to the child's activities.

OTHER FORMS

We have seen that the simplest form for the child to reproduce and the one which appears earliest in the developmental process is the circle. Other simple geometrical forms appear characteristically later in the developmental process. Table 2 is adapted from Gesell (Gesell, 1940) and indicates the order of appearance of these forms as he has observed from his research. From this table, it will be seen that the order of appearance of ability to copy the various forms is as follows: circle, cross, triangle, diamond. Gesell does not list the ability to copy a square in this table, since he found extreme variability depending on the method of duplication which the child used. From his further observations and those of other workers (Bender, 1938; Terman and Merrill, 1939), however, it would seem that the square appears at approximately the four-year level.

TABLE 2

Age of Appearance in Developmental Sequence of Ability to Copy Simple Geometric Forms (Adapted from Gesell, 1940).

Age	Ability
36 months	Copies circle
48 months	Copies cross
60 months	Copies triangle
66 months	Prints a few letters
72 months	Copies diamond

In helping the child to develop drawing and copying ability, we will want to follow the order of forms represented by this developmental sequence. We will therefore wish to present forms in the order in which they appear in Table 2. We have already discussed the circle as the simplest form. The next form would be the cross.

THE CROSS

The cross involves three principles which were not present in the circle: (1) the construction of a vertical line, (2) the construction of a horizontal line, and (3) the problem of bisecting a line. We will want to help the child with each of these problems separately.

THE VERTICAL LINE

In his spontaneous scribbling, the child normally produces vertical lines before he produces horizontal lines. Gesell (1928) places imitation of a vertical stroke at the twenty-four to thirty month level, imitation of a horizontal stroke at the thirty-six to forty month level. Most frequently the direction of these vertical lines is from top to bottom. Ask the child, therefore, to copy the vertical leg of the cross first. If he has difficulty, begin with the problem of drawing a vertical line.

In helping the child construct a vertical line, we can use many of the devices which we have used previously in helping him draw a circle. Thus, the initial step would become that of establishing the concept of a straight, vertical line. Again, as in the case of the circle, ask him to move his hand up and down in a vertical direction so as to establish the vertical movement. If he has difficulty, we can guide his hand or ask him to keep the tip of his finger in contact with our finger as we describe a vertical motion.

His first vertical performances on the chalkboard can be aided by the use of templates. In this case, the template consists of a straight line. A straight narrow groove is cut out of the template material so that when the chalk is placed inside the groove and moved in a vertical direction a straight line results. This pattern is frequently overlooked in the construction of templates. However, the teacher will find the use of a straight-line template very rewarding.

When the child can produce a straight line with a template, in which erroneous movements to either the right or the left are prevented, he is given a ruler or straight edge in which only erroneous movements in one direction are prevented. Thus, we can increase the difficulty of the task by easy stages.

When he is able to produce a straight line with the ruler, we can then remove these supports and ask him to produce a straight vertical line without external aids in a free situation where he must develop all of the control himself. As a further aid at this latter stage, we may give him a broad, heavy colored line to trace over. In this manner, we can increase the tactual, kinesthetic, and visual relationships.

THE HORIZONTAL LINE

The horizontal line is taught in the same manner as the vertical line. Ask the child to copy the horizontal leg of the cross. If he has difficulty, help him in the same manner as before. Present first a complete template, then the ruler or straight edge, then the strong visual clues, and finally free copying.

Most children will show a preference for horizontal lines drawn in the left-to-right direction. The child should be encouraged to experiment with horizontal lines drawn in both directions. He must learn that a horizontal line is the same independently of the direction in which it is drawn. However, since many of our cultural activities proceed from left to right, we will want, when we are sure that he has the complete concept, to encourage the child's preference for the left-to-right direction.

AVOIDING DIAGONALS

The cross used in this exercise is one in which the arms are vertical and horizontal. Do not rotate this cross so that the arms are diagonal. As we will see later, this diagonal orientation is much more difficult. The cross with which we are concerned here is a plus sign, not an "X." The point of intersection of the two lines is such that each is bisected. Thus, all four of the arms of the cross are of the same length. Again, the cross is like a plus sign, not like a "T."

DEVELOPING CONCEPTS OF LENGTH

Many children who can adequately produce the vertical and horizontal lines alone will be found to have difficulty orienting these two lines to each other in the proper relationship. Thus, the horizontal line may be placed too high or too low on the vertical axis or the horizontal line may be too long either on the left or, more frequently, on the right. These deviations indicate that the child is having difficulty with the problem of the relationships between the parts of this figure and particularly with the problem of bisecting a line. In certain cases, where one arm is drawn markedly longer than its counterpart, he may also be having difficulty stopping. The problem of stopping will be dealt with in more detail in our discussion of the square.

The problem of bisecting involves the concepts of "longer," "shorter," and "equal" as these apply to linear lengths. These concepts are a more difficult type of generalization than we usually consider them. The child requires a great deal of information on the basis of which to develop such concepts.

"Long" v. "Short." We begin with the concept of "long" versus "short." We want the child to appreciate the difference between two unequal lines in three areas: kinesthetic, tactual, and visual. Draw two horizontal lines on the chalkboard, one longer than the other. We give the child kinesthetic information by asking him to "bound" the lines with his hands. In this procedure, the child is asked to place his left hand at the left end of the long line and his right hand at the right end of the line. He is then asked to transfer to the short line and perform the same operation. His attention is called to the difference between the position of his hands when he bounds the short line and when he bounds the long line. We point out to him that when his hands are closer together the line is shorter and when they are farther apart the line is longer.

We may wish to increase his kinesthetic information concerning lengths by asking him to compare in a similar "bounding" manner various objects about the room. We will also want him to experiment with lines of different lengths rather than with a single pair of lines so that he will generalize his information rather than learning specifically the difference between two members of a specific pair.

We can increase his tactual awareness of length by asking him to trace over the lines which we have drawn. Tactual information in such an activity is related to time. With the longer of the two lines he gains tactual information over a longer period of time, whereas with the shorter of the two lines he gains the same tactual information for a shorter period of time. Ask the child to trace at an even rate over the longer line and then at the same rate over the shorter line. Then ask him to compare these two experiences, pointing out the difference between the two. His appreciation of this difference can be increased by adding auditory stimulation to the tactual and kinesthetic stimulation. Thus, we may count or chant as he traces the length of a line. Here again, we are increasing the awareness of the time over which the tactual stimulation is operative. Counting or chanting serves to structure the time interval and provide an additional basis for comparing the tactual stimuli.

During all of the above activities, we encourage the child to look at the lines while he is experimenting with them. We want him eventually to be able to make the comparison of length on the basis of the visual stimuli alone. When we have helped him to compare by adding kinesthetic and tactual stimuli to the visual, we can ask him to make his judgments on the basis of the visual stimuli alone. In this case, we will ask him to look at the two lines and tell us which is the shorter. He can then check his judgments by the tactual and kinesthetic methods which he has previously learned. Here again, we will want to present a wide variety of different pairs of lines, beginning with those in which the difference in length is marked and progressing to pairs in which the difference in length is less marked. Only in this way can we assure generalization of the concepts which we are attempting to develop.

The Concept of Equality. When the child has become aware of "longer" and "shorter," he can move on to the concept of "equal," which is neither longer nor shorter. His concept of equality in length can be aided by the same procedures which we used to increase his concept of "long" versus "short." Bounding of two lines with his hands and observing that he need not change the position of his hands when he goes from one to another will help him to appreciate equal lengths in lines. In like manner, tracing with his finger and observing that the same amount of time is consumed in tracing one line as in tracing the second line will help him to establish the concept of equality.

He can then be asked to make a line which is the same length as one which the teacher has placed on the board and check his product by the tactual and kinesthetic methods. He can also be asked to divide a line in two parts such that the left part will be equal to the right part. Here again, he can be asked to check his visual judgment with kinesthetic and tactual judgments. We can then ask him to copy the cross in such a way that the vertical line will divide the horizontal line in half and the horizontal line will divide the vertical line in half.

EQUALIZING THE TWO LINES

Many children will be found who are able to produce a cross in which all paired arms are of equal length but in which the vertical arms are longer than the horizontal arms or vice versa. Although the relationships within the figure have been properly reproduced, the vertical and horizontal relationships are not equal. Such a production frequently indicates that the child has not matched vertical length to horizontal length. A visual stimulus in a vertical orientation does not appear to be the same length as that same stimulus when it occurs in a horizontal orientation. For this child, visual clues to length are unequal when they are in different meridia.

To aid such a child, we must teach him how to compare vertical length with horizontal length. In this problem, we can use the same techniques which we used in teaching him "long" versus "short." Thus, we may ask him to bound a vertical line with his hands and then perform the same operation with a horizontal line, comparing the two kinesthetic patterns. In like manner, we can ask him to trace over a vertical line and subsequently to trace over a horizontal line and compare the tactual stimulation. It may require a considerable number of such experiences before the child is able to make a judgment of equality between a horizontal and a vertical line. He should experiment with lines of different lengths in the different orientations and also with lines of the same length in the different orientations. As soon as he is able to make judgments, we encourage him to make predominant use of the visual data. We can increase the significance of the visual data by asking him to make his judgments on the visual information first and subsequently to check it by kinesthetic or tactual information.

THE SQUARE

The square adds a new element with which the child has not previously had experience, namely, corners. Executing a corner involves two additional types of activity. The first of these is stopping a movement at a prescribed point, and the second is changing the direction of a movement. The child must learn first to stop at a corner and then to turn a corner.

THE PROBLEM OF STOPPING

As we have seen earlier in this discussion, the problem of stopping a movement is as difficult as the problem of starting a movement. The activities involved in stopping are essentially the same as those involved in starting and demand a re-patterning of the neurological impulses guiding muscular activity. The child must not only reverse this neural patterning, but reverse it at a given time and at a given place. The stimulation for such stopping behavior is not strong and is only in part a direct perceptual stimulation. The child must learn to stop where he wants the corner to be. This point is determined in part by perceptual data from the paper itself and in part from anticipated data concerned with the length of the line which he desires to produce. Thus, the stopping point or stimulus for stopping is very weak and is a combination of perceptual data and imagery. In most children, we find the difficulty arising primarily from this latter problem. The child is able to stop but he is not able to anticipate the point of stopping. He does not get a sufficiently strong stimulus for the stopping activity.

We can help the child with the problem of stopping by increasing the number of clues which are available to him. Thus, we can increase the visual clues by providing a wide, heavy, and preferably colored line as a stopping point. On the right side of the chalkboard draw a heavy line approximately an inch and a half to two inches wide. Have the child place his chalk about eighteen inches to the left of this line. Ask him to draw to the line and stop before he crosses it. If he still has difficulty in stopping, place a ruler or straight edge along the right-hand side of the broad line as a "stopper." The child then draws his line until the ruler prevents him from going further. He is encouraged to stop before he hits the ruler and to stop on the broad, heavy line. Motivation may be increased by asking the child to imagine that his chalk is an automobile. He is asked to drive his car onto the street but not across the street. He must not hit the "curb" (ruler) on the other side of the street. As the child becomes more adept, the ruler is removed and the width of the line is decreased.

THE PROBLEM OF TURNING

When the child is able to stop within a reasonable distance, we can shift our attention to the problem of turning the corner. In this task, the child must change the direction of a movement without completely terminating the task. He must alter direction in a movement which is a part of a total motor activity and, in the process of changing direction, must not lose sight of the total activity.

In this problem also, we can help him by increasing the clues to the new direction. Again draw a broad, heavy colored line on the right-hand side of the chalkboard. Ask the child to place his chalk about eighteen inches to the left of this line. Then ask him to draw over to the line and go down in the new direction without getting off the line. If he has difficulty, again use a ruler as a "stop." The child then draws over to the ruler and proceeds down its length. If he still has difficulty, provide two rulers, one on each side of the broad, heavy line. The child then draws over to the line and proceeds down between the two rulers.

When the child begins to develop some skill in turning this corner, we can first remove the ruler and then decrease the width of the line. Eventually we can ask him to execute this corner without these additional clues. By this activity, he can be taught to draw a corner (which is one of the elements of a square) by himself. During the learning process, when the wide line is in use, motivation can be provided by asking the child to imagine that his chalk is a car, as we did before. The child then drives his car over to the road, turns and drives down the road without getting off.

STRENGTHENING FORM PERCEPTION

The execution of the square also presents a greater demand for form perception than was required by either the circle or the cross. As we have seen earlier, form perception develops by differentiating out of a globular mass, elements of a form which are subsequently recombined into an integrated or constructive figure. The elements of the square, as Hebb (Hebb, 1949, p. 83) would suggest, are the lines and the angles. We have previously helped the child to execute each of these elements. We must now call his attention to the presence of the elements in the square form, helping him to differentiate them out of the globular mass and helping him to re-integrate these elements into a constructive figure.

To help the child differentiate the elements out of the globular figure, we will call his attention to the corners. This can be done with a template or a square cut from wood or cardboard. To the visual information regarding the corners we add tactual and kinesthetic information by asking the child to feel these characteristics of the form. We want him to feel these in order around the contour of the figure so that he is aware that there are four such elements in a certain relationship to each other. We may also add auditory information by asking the child to count the corners or to give an auditory signal when he arrives at a corner.

We can help the child preserve the relationships between the elements by asking him to complete the total square figure. This he does by establishing a temporal order of events which corresponds to the spatial simultaneous order of events represented by the copy figure. Thus, we ask him to draw a square. We encourage him to complete this figure with one continuous line and we call attention to the order in which the elements appear. We call attention to each corner as he approaches it and point out its relationship to the previous element and to the next element.

SUPPLYING ADDITIONAL CLUES

As in the case of the circle, we will need to aid the child in this drawing behavior by supplying additional sensory clues. Kinesthetic clues may be supplied by the use of the template, tactual clues by the activity of tracing, and increased visual clues by the use of broad, heavy colored lines. We will use these clues in combination and remove them in order as the child's ability increases. Thus, we will want to use with the square the same general series of activities outlined above for the circle.

GENERALIZING THE CONCEPT

As in the case of the circle, we want the child to generalize the concept of square and therefore we will alter the size, the rhythm or speed, the direction, and the starting point. In order to increase the figure-ground relationship, we will sometimes ask him to color in the square form and sometimes ask him to draw the circumference of the form. Thus, we will carry him through the several stages: tracing with a template, tracing with the finger, tracing with chalk, copying, and reproducing.

AVOIDING DIAGONALS

Care should be taken to keep the square form always in the vertical and horizontal orientation, never in the diagonal orientation. If the square is rotated through 45 degrees, its sides become diagonal lines instead of vertical and horizontal lines. As we shall see, the reproduction of diagonal lines is much more difficult and occurs much later in the developmental process than the reproduction of horizontal and vertical lines. We will want, therefore, to avoid the diagonal directions during training with the square form. Diagonal directions will be important in the drawing of triangles and diamonds and should be postponed until these figures are introduced.

THE RECTANGLE

The rectangle introduces another new problem for the child, that of disproportion of size among the various sides. The child must learn that opposite sides of the rectangle are parallel and that two of these parallel lines are longer than the other two. Furthermore, he must learn that the differences between the length of the sides are proportional.

DEVELOPING THE CONCEPT OF "PARALLEL"

The problem of parallelism between opposite sides of the figure becomes more important in the case of the rectangle than it was in the case of the square. Although opposite sides of the square were also parallel, this parallelism could be achieved in large part by merely paying proper attention to the length of the sides. If the sides are of equal length and the corners are right angles, parallelism is assured in the case of the square. In the case of the rectangle, this parallelism is not so easily accomplished. Since the sides differ in length, the concept of parallel lines is much more useful in the reproduction of the rectangle than in the reproduction of the square.

It is therefore desirable that we help the child with the concept of "parallel" when he reaches the rectangle. Here again, we can help him if we can increase the clues to parallelism. The visual clues can be enhanced by the addition of tactual and kinesthetic clues. In this procedure, we will ask the child to trace with his finger the two opposite sides of the rectangle simultaneously. Thus, he will trace one side with his right hand and one side with his left hand. Call his attention to the fact that his hands remain the same distance apart during the entire tracing activity. Draw an angle on the board and ask him to trace the two sides of the angle simultaneously. Call his attention to the fact that in the case of the angle (non-parallel lines) his hands come together or grow wider apart, whereas in the case of the parallel lines they remain the same distance apart. Ask him to try this tracing activity on the two long sides of the rectangle and also on the two short sides. Call his attention to the fact that the same parallel relationship is present between the two long sides that is present between the two short sides.

THE PROBLEM OF PROPORTIONALITY

We have already described techniques by which we can help the child observe differences in the length of lines (see the cross above). These same procedures can be used again to help him to observe the difference between the long side of the rectangle and the short side.

In the case of the rectangle, however, another problem is presented. Not only are the sides different in length but the difference in length is proportional. It is not sufficient to observe that one side is long and the other short. The length of the two sides must be proportional. A failure to recognize this proportionality leads the child to draw highly elongated rectangles in which the long side is disproportionately longer than the short side. Such attempts have been observed by any teacher in the elementary grades. The child must recognize that the nature of the rectangle is due to the proportionate differences in length rather than to differences in length per se. This problem of proportionality has been discussed at length by Piaget (Piaget and Inhelder, 1956).

We can help the child to observe the problem of proportionality if we can teach him to use the additional clues, which we have previously given him to judge differences in length, as measuring devices. Thus, we may ask him to bound with his hands the short side of the rectangle and, without moving the position of his two hands, lay this distance along the long side of the rectangle. If the rectangle is, for example, twice as long as it is high, he can observe that he lays his hands out twice along the long side. We can then call his attention to the fact that the long side is "twice as long" as the short side. The same procedure can be used with the tactual stimulation of tracing with the finger. He can observe that it takes him twice as long to trace the long side as it does to trace the short side. Here we have helped him to establish subjective measuring units by kinesthetic and tactual information.

GENERALIZING THE CONCEPT

We will want to use similar rectangles of various sizes. Thus, we might present a figure six inches by twelve inches. At a later point, we would present the same figure nine inches by eighteen inches. Both of these figures are similar rectangles since they are twice as long as they are high. However, they differ in absolute size and the objective measurements are different. We want to call the child's attention to the fact that these figures are similar even though their over-all lengths are different. We want him to observe that the basic concept of the rectangle is the proportion between the two sides and not the absolute length of the two sides. We will need, therefore, to present a large number of figures, some of which are similar and some of which are dissimilar, and ask him to observe the similarities and dissimilarities, pointing out that these are a function of the proportionate differences between the sides.

In this connection, we will also want to present the rectangle in the two primary orientations, one in which the long side is horizontal and one in which the short side is horizontal. Here again, we want the child to come to appreciate the general concept of a rectangle. We must therefore present it in both orientations so that he learns that a rectangle is the same figure regardless of which side becomes the base.

STRENGTHENING FORM PERCEPTION

As with the square, the child must learn to differentiate the elements of the rectangular figure and to re-integrate these elements into a constructive form. Here again, we will want to call his attention to the elements of the figure (lines and angles) and to the relationships between these. We will want to use the same series of procedures which we used in the case of the square and the circle. Ask him to trace with his finger around a template, to trace with chalk around a template, to trace a broad heavy line with his finger and with chalk, to copy the form, and to reproduce the form. In all of these activities, call particular attention to the sides and angles. This can be done auditorily by chanting, as well as tactually and kinesthetically. If the child produces a sound or a word in connection with each side and if the word or sound associated with the long side occupies a longer period of time than in the case of the short side, this auditory information can be added to the visual, tactual, and kinesthetic information to help him keep the elements of this figure separate and to keep their relationships in mind.

Since we are attempting to teach the general concept of "rectangle," we will want to vary the size and the proportions of the figures which we present him. We will also want to help him establish the figure-ground relationship by asking him sometimes to color in the figure and sometimes to draw its contour.

FIGURES WITH DIAGONAL LINES

As we have seen so often previously, the production of diagonal lines is more difficult than the production of either vertical or horizontal lines. It would appear that diagonal movements occur later in the developmental process than other types of movement (Gesell, 1940). Bender found that vertical lines were copied approximately correctly at five or six, whereas oblique lines were not copied correctly until nine or ten years (Bender, 1938). The age levels quoted by Bender are somewhat higher than those quoted by Gesell owing to differences in the complexity of the tasks which they presented to the child. However, there is general agreement between these two workers regarding the order in which directional lines are achieved. Piaget and Inhelder, on the other hand, were unable to observe a difference between the age of acquiring verticals and the age of acquiring horizontals (Piaget and Inhelder, 1956, p. 400). However, they found diagonals developing later than either verticals or horizontals (*ibid.*, p. 74). We will therefore not present the child with figures involving diagonal lines until he has learned to reproduce figures involving horizontal and vertical lines. Among the common geometrical forms involving diagonal lines are the triangle and the diamond.

Since the new problem in these figures is the diagonal direction, we will want to give the child special help with this movement. As in previous activities, we can use templates and tracing techniques to increase his awareness of the diagonal. It will be found desirable to present the child first with a diagonal line alone. Ask him to draw across the chalkboard in a diagonal direction. If he is unable to accomplish this drawing adequately, we may increase the visual clues by providing him with a wide heavy line which we ask him to trace. If he still has difficulty, we can add a ruler or a template as a guide, thereby adding tactual and kinesthetic clues to the visual clues. We can then help him to learn the diagonal movement by the same techniques which we used to help him learn the circular movement.

THE TRIANGLE

When the child has mastered the diagonal movement itself, we can present him with the triangle. It will be found easiest if we first present him the triangle with its base down and its apex up. This would appear to be the most natural orientation for this figure and the one which the child appreciates most readily. Helping him with the triangular figure will follow the same steps outlined above in our discussion of the square. First, we can provide him with templates and a broad, heavy line, giving him maximum clues. As he is able to perform in this situation, we can remove the template, reducing the clues to visual and tactual. Later, we can reduce the intensity of the visual clues until he is tracing in a normal fashion. From this stage, he can proceed to copying and reproduction.

As in other forms discussed above, we want to be sure that the child gains the concept of "triangle" rather than learning the reproduction of a specific figure. For this reason, we will want to vary the size of the triangle and, to aid him in his figure-ground relationship, we will want sometimes to ask him to color in the figure and sometimes to trace around its periphery. When the child has begun to learn the triangle in its upright orientation, we will want to present it in the opposite orientation with the apex down. He should recognize that the triangular form is the same regardless of its directional orientation.

THE DIAMOND

The most difficult of the common geometrical forms for the young child is the diamond. Reference to Table 2 will indicate that the normal child does not copy this form until seventy-two months of age. It can be seen that the diamond form magnifies the difficulties of diagonal movement which we first encountered in the triangle. In the case of the diamond, the child must at each point in the form transfer from one diagonal direction to another. All of the elements of this figure represent diagonals. Frequently we see the child displaying his difficulty when he changes direction from one diagonal to another. Thus, as he approaches a corner of the diamond he may make a number of false starts and, only after he has started the movement, recognize that it is proceeding in a wrong direction. Through this experimental motor activity, he produces "ears" on his form, a problem which will be recognized by any elementary school teacher.

The steps in teaching the diamond are the same as those in teaching the square and the triangle. Begin first with maximum clues, using templates, a broad, heavy line, and maximum tactual stimulation. As the child progresses, gradually reduce these clues, removing first the template and then reducing the strength of the visual stimulus. Finally, ask the child to copy the form and then to reproduce it from memory.

As always, we will want to present the diamond in various sizes. We will also present it in both orientations: first with its long dimension vertically and then with its long dimension horizontally. It will be found that ability to produce this form in one orientation does not guarantee ability to produce it in the other orientation. It will be found frequently that when the diamond is rotated through 90 degrees, the child will appear to be presented with an entirely new task and the steps in teaching the form in its original orientation will need to be repeated in whole or in part in this new orientation.

In the diamond figure, as in other forms, we will want to help the child with his figure-ground construction by asking him to color in the form part of the time. He should also learn that the diamond is the result of two triangles with their bases together. We can aid in the development of these relationships by drawing a line bisecting the diamond figure and asking him to reproduce the two halves separately, pointing out that they are triangular figures. In like manner, we can give him cut-outs of triangles which, when placed base to base, form the diamond figure.

It will be noted that both the order of presentation of simple geometric forms and the stages in teaching these forms follow very closely those recommended by Jolles (Jolles, 1958).

COMPLEX FORMS—LETTERS AND WORDS

When the simple geometrical forms discussed above have been learned by the child, he has all of the basic patterns required for the reproduction of more complex forms. Now such figures as the Maltese cross, the divided rectangle, and similar forms, either symmetrical or asymmetrical, can be understood by the child. He will still need help in organizing the elements of these more complex forms into adequate wholes, but the basic patterns for their recognition and reproduction are now present.

LETTERS

Among such complex forms are the twenty-six specific figures which we know as the letters of our alphabet. It therefore follows that at this stage the child can begin to learn the reproduction and recognition of letters. If, in some of the more complicated letter forms, he continues to have difficulty, we can help him by techniques similar to those used to present the more simple geometrical forms. Thus, templates and tracing can be used to help the child learn to reproduce single letters. It should be borne in mind that we are here teaching the child the problem of form in the individual letters. We are not concerned at this point with teaching the alphabet or with individual letters as a prelude to reading. Our concern is wholly with the ability of the child to recognize the form of the letter. It is felt that such forms cannot be fully appreciated until they can be reproduced and until the visual data represented by the letter on paper come to have meaning in terms of the movement patterns of the child's organism.

WORDS

Like letters, words represent complex forms. Therefore, at this stage the child can learn to reproduce and recognize simple words and phrases. Here again, we are interested in the child's development of a full appreciation of the form represented by the word.

It is felt that this can best be accomplished by using as many clues to the development of this form as possible. Therefore, just as with simple geometric forms, the child should trace the word either with or without templates, depending upon his ability, should then copy the word, and finally reproduce it. After he has learned to reproduce a word, he should be able to recognize it on paper or on the chalkboard. If he has difficulty in recognizing the word as produced by someone else (reading the word), we can aid his recognition by using the process of reproduction as a clue to recognition. Thus, for the word which is not recognized, we would ask the child to trace over it or to reproduce it on the chalkboard. Such procedures are recommended by Fernald and have been found very useful in early stages of teaching reading (Fernald, 1943).

Throughout all of the activities described above, one of the factors toward which we have been working is the use of these concepts of form and pattern in the later activities of reading. Reading involves the association of a verbal and auditory pattern with the visual pattern. For this reason, we will want to encourage the child to verbalize during all of the drawing and copying processes. We will want to encourage him continually to associate a verbal pattern with the motor activity in drawing and copying. For this reason, it is desirable to call the child's attention to the verbal association in all of the training activities in this area. Thus, we may use the word *square* in association with his production of a square; we can ask him what he is drawing, and when he has finished, we can ask him what he has drawn. It will be found helpful at all stages in learning to draw a square to associate continually the word *square* with the process of producing the figure and also with the figure when it has been produced. This verbal component becomes particularly important when we reach the stage of letters and words. Here we are coming much closer to the reading process itself and we will want to establish the habit of associating verbal components with such activities. We will therefore ask the child to say the letter or word as he is writing it. When he has completed his writing, we will ask him to read what he has written (Fernald, 1943).

FROM CHALKBOARD TO PAPER

All of the activities which we have been describing have been carried out on the chalkboard. The chalkboard differs from paper and pencil in two fundamental ways: (1) it is oriented vertically, and (2) the sizes are consistently larger. However, our final goal is the reproduction of these forms and figures on paper at a table or desk.

The table or desk represents a different orientation from that of the chalkboard. On the chalkboard, the orientation was vertical and the top of the chalkboard was "up." In like manner, the top of all of the forms which the child reproduced on the chalkboard was a vertical "up." When we pass from the chalkboard to the horizontal orientation of the desk, however, the top of the paper changes from a true vertical "up" to a conventional "up" which is a direction away from the child. The child needs to learn that the orientation on the desk is a conventional one and he must learn to make the transition from the true "up" of the vertical orientation to the horizontal "up" of the horizontal orientation. Most elementary school teachers have observed the child who, when asked to put a mark on the bottom of the paper, turns the paper over and puts his mark on the backside. He has translated the concept "top" and "bottom" in terms of the vertical orientation and has not learned to appreciate the conventional orientation of paper on a desk (see Strauss and Kephart, 1955, p. 179).

In order to help the child make this transition, it will be found useful to bridge the gap by degrees. Thus, if the chalkboard is one which can be tilted, we can move it toward the horizontal orientation a bit at a time and let the child work his way through from the vertical "up" to the "up" of desk and paper. Thus, we would ask him to perform with the chalkboard vertical, then we would tilt it ten degrees toward the horizontal and ask him to perform again, then tilt it twenty degrees, etc., until it became horizontal.

In like manner, the size of the reproductions which we ask the child to make on paper are considerably smaller than those which we ask him to make on the chalkboard. He must learn to translate the movement patterns that he has established into the more precise and less extensive patterns required to produce smaller figures. At the same time, he must not lose these patterns as a part of the total motor system.

We can help him in making this size transition by approaching it through easy stages. At first, the teacher may want to use large sheets of newsprint on a table, permitting the child to reproduce his figures in approximately the same sizes that he used on the chalkboard. We can move from the large newsprint and crayons to paper of letter head size and pencils. We can also carry him gradually from large figures covering the entire sheet to smaller figures of the size we desire, reproduced in order on the page.

When he has made this transition and is ready for letters and words, we can provide him with primary tablet paper. This paper has lines which are approximately twice the size of the normal ruled tablet paper. We can then ask the child to fit his letters into these wide lines. When he has been able to reproduce at this primary size, we can provide him with ordinary tablet paper and ask him to reduce the size of his figures again until they will fit within the lines of such paper. We must be careful at each of these stages to see to it that the new size of drawings develops out of the total motor pattern which we began to establish on the chalkboard and continued to encourage on the large sheets of paper. Smaller drawing and copying tasks should not be entered into as a new type of activity which is accomplished by a new and unrelated series of motor performances. These finer and more precise patterns must develop out of and remain related to the more gross movement patterns.

chapter 8

Sensory-Motor Training

THE WALKING BOARD

We have previously discussed the walking board as a method of observing the behavior of the child. This device may also be used as a training device. By adapting many of the activities described in our earlier discussion of the walking board, we can provide experiences which will aid the child in the development of dynamic balance and contribute to the learning of laterality and directionality. The walking board has been used for many years in kindergarten and elementary school activities (see Jones, Morgan and Stevens, 1957, pp. 60, 64). We must remember, however, that the contribution of the walking board results from its implications for teaching balance and laterality rather than in the development of skill on the walking board itself. As with so many other activities, the child must be helped to generalize rather than merely to acquire a specific skill. Thus, from our point of view, the child who walks across the board and does not lose his balance is not learning from the activity. Only when he loses his balance and is required to correct it, does he learn.

The walking board is a section of two-by-four measuring eight to twelve feet in length. Each end of the board is fitted into a bracket which serves as a brace and prevents the board from tipping over. When fitted into place, the board is raised approximately two inches off the floor. Each bracket has a combination fitting so that the board can either be set in flat with the wide surface up or be set in on its edge with the narrow surface up.

The walking board technique is a modification of walking a fence or walking railroad ties, activities which were common in our childhood. The child is asked to start at one end of the board and walk slowly to the other. For beginners or those having difficulty, the four-inch surface is used. As the child becomes more adept, the board is turned on edge and the two-inch surface is used. For the child who has extreme difficulty, a two-by-six or even larger board can be substituted. When the task is difficult, the adult should help the child by holding onto his hand. The child should be encouraged to dispense with this help as soon as he is able. However, he should not be forced, since he may develop a fear reaction which will interfere with further training.

WALKING FORWARD

The child first learns to walk the board forward. Care must be taken to see that he walks slowly and maintains balance at all times. By running across the board, he may be able to perform the task without the necessity for balance. Since balance is the function being trained by the technique, we must see that he does not avoid the problem by running or otherwise changing the procedure. He should place each foot squarely on the board so that both toe and heel make contact at each step.

WALKING BACKWARD

After the child has learned to walk the board forward, he learns to walk it backward. At this point, he will probably need help again from the adult. As before, he is encouraged to dispense with this help as soon as possible. He is allowed to look back to see where the next step should be but is encouraged to learn where the board is behind him without having to look. He will soon find that the task becomes more difficult when he has to look and is easier if he can keep his eyes ahead while walking backward. He may have to explore with his toe before each step to locate the board behind him. He is allowed to do this but is encouraged to learn the direction "straight back" so that such preliminary explorations will no longer be necessary.

WALKING SIDEWISE

The child can now learn to walk the board sidewise. To do this, he stands with feet together facing across the board and on the left end. He then moves his right foot out, shifts his weight, and moves his left foot until his feet are together again. This sequence is repeated until he has crossed the board. After each step, the feet are brought together again. When he returns from right to left across the board, the sequence of actions is reversed. Again, care must be taken to see that he moves slowly and maintains balance at all times.

TURNING AND BOUNCING

When he has learned these three basic procedures, the child can be taught to turn on the board. He is asked to walk across the board and, without stepping off, to turn and walk back sidewise. When he has mastered this half turn, he can be asked to walk forward across, turn, and return walking forward. The most difficult task is to walk backward across the board, turn, and return walking backward. This latter task requires maintaining the difficult backward directionality while turning. Variations and combinations of these routines can be introduced to maintain interest and also to reduce anticipation. Thus, he learns to maintain balance under conditions which cannot be completely foreseen.

The ability to maintain balance under conditions which are not predictable can be further cultivated by asking the child to walk to the center of the board, turn, and walk back.   All combinations of direction and turn can be repeated in the center of the board. Under these conditions, the spring of the board becomes an additional factor which must be considered in maintaining balance.   The child should be encouraged to experience this spring and the resulting sensations.   Allow him to "bounce" on the board and discover how it feels to be on a springy surface.   Help him, if necessary, but encourage him to learn to maintain balance under conditions that, for him, are unusual.

For children in whom number concepts are beginning to develop, elementary concepts in this area can be combined with balance training.   Maximum spring is experienced at the center of the board. When the child is asked to walk out *halfway* on the board, this springing sensation can reinforce the visual and other clues to "halfway."   He can be asked to count the steps required to walk across the board, then the steps required to walk halfway across, halfway across and back, etc.   The child can be aided to a fuller understanding of quantitative concepts by the use of the total body in their demonstration.

LATERALITY AND DIRECTIONALITY

The primary purpose of the walking board is to aid in teaching the child balance and postural responses.   Maintaining balance on the board requires an accurate knowledge of the difference between the right side of the body and the left.   The technique thus aids in the development of laterality.   As we have seen, laterality is necessary in such activities as reading (where a left-to-right progression across the line of print must be sustained) and writing.   It is probable that many reversals of words or letters are due to inadequate laterality.

The board also aids in the development of directionality.   Added to the experiences of right and left in maintaining balance are the experiences of forward and backward in progress across the board. Lateral direction is separated from fore and aft direction.   The former is used in balance, while the latter figures in the goal of the activity. When the spring of the board is added to the activity, the directions up and down are also added.

SPECIAL ADAPTATIONS

For the child who is having exceptional difficulty, the task of walking the two-by-four may prove too difficult. For such a child, we may have to decrease the difficulty of the task . As mentioned above, we can use a two-by-six or two-by-eight instead of the narrower two-by-four. In some cases, however, even these boards may be too difficult. We may need to start with a paper alley, constructed by laying a strip of wrapping paper along the floor, or a "street," marked out by two parallel paper strips placed along the floor with the width between them adjusted to the needs of the child. The child is then required only to walk within the alley or "street" without getting off. In this manner, we teach the child to control the gross direction of his movement before we introduce more complicated concepts of balance.

When the child has learned control under these rather simple demands, we can begin to increase the demands by reducing the width of the "street." As he is able to perform, he can then be asked to perform on the boards, beginning with the two-by-eight and proceeding to the two-by-six and finally the two-by-four.

Children displaying such gross lack of control will be found to be apprehensive of any task requiring more refined control. Thus, they will require the presence and support of the teacher. They may wish, for example, to hold his hand. (See Bender, 1956.) The teacher should offer such support and be very careful of requiring greater control than the child possesses. At the same time, he should encourage the child to dispense with such support as soon as his control develops to the point where he no longer needs it.

For the same reason, such children may fear the height of the two-by-four, even though it is only two or three inches off the floor. For such children, it is desirable to start with activities where there is no height from the floor. Thus, a four-inch strip of paper may be substituted for the board. In like manner, the child can be started with the board flat on the floor and only later be introduced to the board off the floor on the braces.

THE BALANCE BOARD

Another device which will be found useful in helping the child to learn balance and accompanying skills is the balance board. With this device, we can help him to pinpoint the center of gravity of his body and, through requiring him to maintain both fore-and-aft and left-to-right balance, we can offer him a more dynamic problem than in the case of the walking board. It will usually be found desirable to develop relatively adequate ability with the walking board before attempting the balance board, since performing on the latter is a somewhat more difficult task.

The balance board is a square platform sixteen by sixteen inches. Underneath and in the middle of the board is a balance post three inches in height. Three sizes of balance posts are provided: three by three inches, four by four inches, and five by five inches. These posts can be interchanged by means of a simple wing nut so that the task can be made easier for the child who is having greater difficulty. Some children may have to begin with the board flat on the floor with no post at all until they become accustomed to the task and to the idea of being off the floor.

Start the child with the largest post and, when he can balance without difficulty, change to the middle post. When he can use the middle post with ease, change to the smallest post. If the child has difficulty, pin up a picture or other visual target at his eye level and several feet in front of him. Ask him to keep looking at the picture while balancing on the board. The task is easier if the eyes are held still. Encourage the child to rock the board both in the right-left direction and in the fore-aft direction. Let him experience a shift of weight and of the center of gravity and observe how such shifts are accomplished and controlled. It will be found that children enjoy such experimentation in situations like this where there is no danger.

SPECIAL TASKS

When the child has achieved skill in the simple balancing performance, ask him to perform other neuro-muscular tasks while balancing on the board. Let him bounce a rubber ball on the floor

A balance board helps develop a flexible postural adjustment (Courtesy Highland School, Lafayette, Indiana. Photographer: Howard R. Knaus).

in front of him and catch it. Begin with a large beach ball and decrease the size until he can use a tennis ball. Let him bounce and catch the ball with both hands, then with the right hand, then with the left.

While the child is balancing on the board, ask him to throw objects at a target (bean bag, ring toss, etc.). Suspend a ball by a string from the ceiling so that it swings in front of him like a pendulum about arm's reach away. Ask him to strike out and touch it with his finger as it swings past.

Ask the child to perform simple calesthenics while balancing on the board. Some children are even able to jump rope on the board.

Use the board to help increase awareness of the body and its parts. While he is balanced on the board, ask the child to touch his shoulders, hips, knees, ankles, toes. Gross identification can be aided by commands such as "Touch your left knee with your right hand." Combining maintenance of balance with movements of identification helps to create body image.

TRAMPOLINE

One of the most helpful training devices in the area of coordination and muscular control is the trampoline. This device is a sturdily constructed metal frame within which a heavy canvas is attached by means of springs. The canvas serves as a performing surface. When the child jumps on the trampoline, the spring of the canvas surface throws him into the air and permits him to be free of the earth for a few seconds by counteracting the forces of gravity. This freedom and this new orientation to his own body and its activities can be experienced without danger and provides a most exhilarating sensation for the child.

LEARNING DYNAMIC BALANCE

One of the most important contributions of the trampoline is the development of total bodily coordination throughout the gross muscle systems. When standing on a firm surface, the child can avoid the problems of dynamic balance by distributing the weight masses of the body around the center of gravity and making only minimum necessary adjustments. As he rises into the air from the surface of the trampoline, such minimum balancing adjustments are not adequate. His body is free of the ground and he must locate the center of gravity under unfamiliar and much less stable circumstances. He must then maintain a dynamic coordination of all of the major muscle groups around this center of gravity in order to maintain balance. If he is unable to maintain such a dynamic balance, either he falls harmlessly on the canvas or the spring of the canvas is snubbed and the activity is reduced.

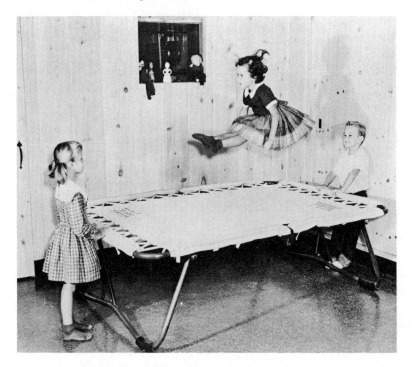

The trampoline helps develop motor patterns which can be used as the basis for future learning (Courtesy Nissen Trampoline Company, Cedar Rapids, Iowa).

LEARNING COORDINATION

Not only must the child learn a dynamic relationship to the center of gravity and maintain a dynamic balance, but he must maintain these coordinations under changing relationships. In addition, the changes in these relationships are not the result of his own efforts directly but are dependent in large part on the trampoline and its functions. Thus, the timing and rhythm of his activity are dictated by the spring of the trampoline rather than directly determined by his own movements. Here is another important teaching aspect of this device. In activities on the ground, the child can adjust his movements to the rhythm patterns of his muscles. Thus, if the neurological innervation to one or more muscle groups loses its rhythm, he merely adjusts his movement to this change. On the trampoline, such adjustment is not possible since the rhythm is dictated by the device. Therefore, he must learn to maintain adequate and constant rhythms in his neuro-muscular coordination which are demanded in few other activities.

DISCOVERING INADEQUACIES

Very frequently such experiences serve to teach the child that his neuro-muscular rhythm is inadequate and to point out to him the situations and activities in which his rhythm becomes distorted. Thus, when a child seven years of age demonstrated a neuro-muscular problem in the right leg, the trampoline helped him to appreciate the problem. As he was bouncing, this leg would go out of phase and its rhythm would display a faster rate than that of the rest of his body. This alteration in rhythm on one side would stop the trampoline and interfere with his performance. In walking and similar situations, he would merely adjust to this change in rhythm by limping and would not be completely aware of when the alteration occurred or the nature of the alteration. The trampoline, through its insistence on the maintenance of a prescribed rhythm, pointed out to him these difficulties which he had not been able to appreciate fully in more normal activities.

DEVELOPING BODY IMAGE

When the child is thrown clear of the canvas, he must learn to balance not only in a right-and-left direction but also in a fore-and-aft direction. The former of these balancing problems is closely related to the problem of laterality which we have discussed previously. The latter is closely related to directionality and to appreciation of a third dimensional axis through the body. Thus, the mere activity of bouncing on the trampoline contributes to body image and spatial relationships within the body. These relationships are further emphasized in more complicated trampoline stunts such as the seat drop, the knee drop, or the back drop. These more advanced activities help to teach the child the location of various portions of his body and their relationship to each other both in the upright position and in less customary positions. Certain relationships can be observed which are very difficult to observe under more normal conditions. Thus, in the seat drop the relationship of height between his seat and his feet can be observed through the difference in timing between bouncing on his seat and bouncing on his feet. In like manner, the height from the ground to the shoulders or the back can be observed in trampoline activities.

Simple activities on the trampoline are suitable for young children. If an adult is present to watch the child and if certain simple rules are followed, there is no danger in this equipment. The teacher will find that, for the most part, children will not attempt activities which are beyond their ability.

BOUNCING

The simplest activity on the trampoline is straight bouncing. The child stands in the center of the canvas and jumps up and down, permitting the canvas to add to the force of his jump and therefore lift him higher off the surface (LaDue and Norman, 1956). The child should stand on the canvas with his feet about shoulder width apart. As he rises from the bed, the legs should be kept straight and, if better form is desired, the feet should be brought together. As the child descends toward the canvas, the knees should be slightly bent to cushion the shock and the feet should return to the shoulder width position. The child should anticipate contact with the canvas and begin preparations for his next jump as he descends.

Stress should be placed upon controlled bouncing in one spot. Do not permit the child to inch forward or backward but encourage him to jump in the same spot. For this purpose, most trampolines are equipped with an X mark in the center of the canvas to indicate the target of the jump.

In early stages of training, it will be found desirable to hold the child's hands as he jumps. This support gives him additional confidence and, perhaps more important, gives him a clue to his center of gravity and the relationship of his body to it. Do not try for height or form in the early phases of bouncing. It is important that the child get the feel of being unsupported and recognize the dynamic factors of balance involved.

When the child can bounce easily for a series of jumps without support, ask him to bounce on one foot only. This alteration in procedure alters the requirements for balance in much the same way that standing on one foot on the floor altered the requirement in some of our earlier activities. He should learn to bounce on the right foot alone and also on the left foot alone.

When the child has learned to bounce on each foot alone, ask him to alternate feet (to jump once on the left foot, once on the right foot, once on the left foot, etc.). When he has learned this simple alternation, ask him to try more complicated patterns, such as jumping twice on the left foot, twice on the right foot, twice on the left foot, etc. When he has accomplished these symmetrical patterns, we can introduce asymmetrical patterns such as those described in the jumping activities of the examination sequence.

When the child has learned straight bouncing, activities can be introduced in which he is asked to turn in the air while he is bouncing. Thus, we can ask him to jump up, turn 90 degrees, and land. It can be seen that such activities make rather severe demands on the child's control and orientation. He must change his balance relationships while in the air, and at the same time he must maintain his orientation to the ground and to the trampoline. When he has learned to turn through 90 degrees, we can ask him to turn through 180 degrees and, when he has learned this, we can introduce intermediate angles between these coordinates.

During all the bouncing activities, the child's attention should be called to the rhythm which is demanded. We can do this by asking him to count his jumps. Be sure that his counting is related to the activity of jumping and is not a purely independent counting task. He must count as he hits the canvas of the trampoline. At a somewhat later stage, we can ask him to count a certain number of jumps and then stop. Such activities can help him to estimate time and to anticipate events in time.

TRAMPOLINE STUNTS

Seat Drop. One of the easiest stunts on the trampoline is the seat drop. The child lands on the bed in a sitting position with the legs fully extended forward so that the entire backs of the legs contact the canvas simultaneously. The trunk is slightly inclined backward from the vertical. Hands are flat on the bed six to eight inches in back of the hips. The fingers are pointed toward the feet and the arms are slightly bent. The child bounces once or twice and then performs the seat drop, springing back into the standing position.

Knee Drop. The child lands on the bed in a kneeling position with the contact point being the knees, shins, and instep. He is instructed to keep the body directly above the knees when landing in the knee-drop position. He then springs back to a standing position.

Back Drop. The child lands on the bed in a supine position with legs straight and vertically inclined. He places his hands either on the sides and fronts of the legs just above the knees or free of the legs, semi-extended forward and upward. He is instructed to keep the chin on the chest throughout this trick. Attempt the stunt first from a standing position. Raise one leg and fall backward to the back-drop position. After he lands on his back, the child springs back to a standing position.

Front Drop. Land on the bed in a prone position. Extend the arms forward with the elbows extended sideward and palms of the hands downward. The following contact points should land simultaneously: palms, forearms, abdomen, and thighs.

Other Stunts. A kit of materials describing the trampoline and activities with which it may be used may be obtained from the Nissen Trampoline Company, Cedar Rapids, Iowa. The simple stunts described above, and particularly straight bouncing, will be found most useful with elementary school children. Most of the learnings in which we are particularly interested can be fostered by these very simple activities. As we have mentioned above, the motivational value of the trampoline is very high and some of the children will be interested in learning more complicated tricks. These stunts and methods of teaching them are described in the kit.

BED SPRINGS AND MATTRESS

In the absence of a trampoline, many of the learning situations described above can be provided by the use of bed springs. Obtain a set of bed springs and a mattress which are highly resilient. Tie the mattress to the springs so that it will not slip off. Many of the stunts described above can be performed on this bed-spring apparatus. Since the resiliency of the bed springs is not as great as that of the trampoline, the same degree of activity cannot be obtained. However, many of the desired experiences can be presented to the child with this equipment. It is highly desirable that the child be permitted to experience the sensation of bouncing and being free of gravity. For this reason, some type of equipment which permits such experience will be found very useful in training.

ANGELS-IN-THE-SNOW

This technique is a modification of the childhood game of the same name. The child lies down in the snow and moves his arms and legs. He then gets up and looks at the patterns created in the snow as a result of his movements. This old game has many elements which can be used to aid the child's development. The original game has been modified for use indoors but the activities required of the child remain basically unchanged. We have previously described the use of this activity as a testing technique. It will also be found highly useful as a training method.

BILATERAL MOVEMENTS

The child lies flat on his back on the floor with his arms at his sides and his feet together. He is then asked to move his feet apart as far as he can, keeping his knees stiff. He is then asked to move his arms along the floor until his hands come together above his head, keeping his elbows stiff. Encourage the child to press against the floor with his heels as he moves his legs and with his hands and wrists as he moves his arms. He should be aware of his hands and feet and their positions at all times during the exercise. The tactual sensation from contact with the floor will increase this awareness.

Children may be found who are unable to make these simple movements or who can move one side at a time but not both together. Other children may be able to make the movements but cannot change time—"move fast" and then "move slow." In these cases, the adult may have to help the child by moving the arm or leg with his hands. The child should be encouraged, however, to learn to perform the movement without help as soon as possible.

When the child brings his feet together, encourage him to "click his heels." When he brings his arms down to his sides, encourage him to slap his sides. By this means, awareness of body parts can be increased through the addition of tactual stimulation. Also, awareness of the difference between a body-body contact and a body-outside object contact can be heightened.

When he has learned to make bilateral leg and arm movements easily and smoothly and equally on each side, ask him to combine the leg and arm movements. In this phase, he is asked to move his legs apart and at the same time move his arms over his head. He then moves his legs together and at the same time brings his arms down to his sides. He is asked to coordinate these two movement patterns so that his legs are apart *at the same time* that his hands come together above his head. As his heels touch, *at the same time* his hands touch his sides. He is thus asked to time each pattern so that it is synchronized with the others. Both leg and arm movements must be smooth and the arm movement must take as long as, and no longer than, the leg movements. Be sure he keeps his movements smooth. He may try to avoid the problem of the exercise by moving one limb or pair of limbs independently and then "catching-up" with the others.

UNILATERAL AND CROSS-LATERAL MOVEMENTS

When the child has learned how to make these bilateral movements and has become aware of his body in the various positions, introduce unilateral and cross-lateral movements. Ask the child to move his right leg only to the extended position. Then ask him to return it. Always stop at the end of any movement to allow him to appreciate the new posture. Then ask him to do the same with his left leg only, then his right arm only, then his left arm only.

Some children will have difficulty moving one leg or one arm without moving the other. In this case, hold one foot down while the other leg is being moved. It is desirable to hold the foot in a firm grip so that the child maintains tactual awareness of this limb while he moves the other. Encourage the child to complete the single movement without help as soon as possible. Pressing the non-moving foot against the floor will increase tactual stimulation and help him make the transition.

Some children will be found who cannot identify the leg or arm to be moved if we merely point to it. They cannot make the translation from a visual awareness to a tactual-kinesthetic awareness of the limb so that movement can be initiated. These children will need the additional help that results from the teacher's touching the limb to be moved. Press firmly against the selected limb so that a strong tactual stimulus is provided upon which to base a choice. As a result of this tactual stimulus, the translation from visual to tactual-kinesthetic is made unnecessary. However, encourage the child to make the translation and to initiate the movement on the basis of the visual stimulus alone as soon as possible. Such encouragement can be provided by being sure that the child has awareness of the visual stimulus before the tactual is added. For this reason, point to the limb and stop, waiting for him to become fully aware of the visual stimulus and to attempt to initiate the movement. Add the tactual stimulus only if he has trouble or makes an error. The intensity of the tactual stimulus can be gradually decreased by using a lighter and lighter touch as he progresses.

When the child has mastered these simple unilateral movements, introduce more complicated unilateral movements. Ask the child to move his right leg and right arm together. Next ask him to move his left leg and left arm.

When he has mastered these movements, introduce cross-lateral movements. Ask him to move his left leg and right arm together. Then ask him to move his right leg and left arm. In all of these exercises, timing and the synchronization of timing are important and must be given constant attention.

ALTERING TIME AND POSITION

When these basic movements have been completed, alter the time factor itself. Ask the child to move fast, then slow, then in rhythm to a beat or count. All the types of movement discussed above should be repeated with this timing factor added.

Ask the child to turn over face-down on the floor and repeat all the exercises in this new position. Then place a hassock or pillow under his abdomen so that by raising his shoulders and legs he can be free of the floor except for the pivot provided by the support. The entire series of exercises should be repeated in this position. Now he has an added anti-gravity factor which requires a greater muscle tonus throughout all the muscle systems involved in posturing. The child is required to perform all the former tasks while maintaining this increased tonus of the postural muscles. Do not forget that this position is *very tiring*. Therefore, the periods of practice in this posture should be short. Do not ask the child to maintain this posture continuously for more than one or two minutes at the outside.

PURPOSE OF EXERCISE

This exercise is designed to help the child learn laterality and to increase his awareness of his body image. It can assist him in discovering his extremities and becoming aware of their position in space relative to his body. Movements directed toward the two sides of the body develop an awareness of laterality and teach him to use this awareness in directing activities. Asking him to make movements in time sequence or rhythms helps him to gain good bilateral control in which each side maintains its independence but is integrated with the other. Timed movements also help him to translate spatial changes into temporal sequences of action. He can see his response both as a sequence in time and as a change in space and he learns the relationships between these two methods of seeing the same act. Body image is increased since individual identification and control of limbs alone and in combination is required.

STUNTS AND GAMES

Certain stunts and games used in elementary physical education classes will be found useful in aiding the child to develop body image and motor control. Many of these stunts require the child to reverse normal patterns of movement so that the resulting over-all movement takes place in unusual directions or in unusual positions. Thus, the duck walk or rabbit hop require the child to move forward through space but with motor patterns somewhat different from those normally used in walking or running. By the use of such stunts, the child can be taught variations in movement patterns and elaborations of his customary patterns. Laterality and directionality are required to carry out the task and must be maintained while the usual postural and balance relationships are altered.

Parts of the body are required to assume different relative positions and different functions during these stunts. This alteration of the customary body schema can be used to point out more strongly to the child the location and functions of the various limbs. By this means, his body image may be strengthened.

Since these stunts and games are discussed in textbooks on elementary physical education (Neilson and VanHagen, 1939), only a few examples will be described here. The reader is referred to these texts for further materials.

Duck Walk. Ask the child to place his hands on his knees and perform a deep knee bend. In this position, ask him to walk forward. He may also place his hands behind his back with his palms together and his fingers pointing backward in imitation of a duck's tail.

Rabbit Hop. Ask the child to place his hands on the floor and perform a deep knee bend. Have him move his hands forward and, keeping his hands on the floor, bring his feet forward between his hands with a jump. He then moves his hands forward again and repeats the process as he progresses across the room.

Crab Walk. Ask the child to squat down reaching backward and putting both hands flat on the floor behind him without sitting down. Ask him to walk or run in this position. He should keep his head, neck, and body in a straight line.

Measuring Worm. Ask the child to place his hands on the floor in front of him and about shoulder width apart. His legs should be stretched out straight behind him with the weight of the body supported on the arms and toes. The arms should be kept straight and the body should be straight from head to heels. Keeping his hands stationary and knees straight, ask him to bring his feet up by little steps until they are as close to his hands as possible. Next, keeping his feet stationary, ask him to move his hands forward with little steps until he has reached the starting position again. This series of movements is repeated as the child progresses forward across the room.

Elephant Walk. Two children are required for this game. The first child grasps the second at the hips. The second child then jumps upward and locks his legs high around the hips of the first. He then drops backward and works his head, shoulders, and arms between the legs of the first child. The first child then drops forward onto his hands keeping his arms and legs stiff. Both children hold these positions while the first child walks forward.

RHYTHM

Many of the problems of form perception and of figure-ground relationships which have been investigated over a number of years in the field of visual perception exist also in other areas. The investigation of form perception in the past has been largely concerned with spatial relationships and with foreground-background relationships in space. It seems probable that similar types of relationships exist in time. When figure-ground for form is encountered in the dimension of time, we know it as rhythm. Rhythm is important in kinesthetic and tactual problems since much of the information which we obtain from the senses is probably aided and militated by ability to establish and maintain rhythm relationships. In the auditory field, information is kept classified and organized through the imposition of rhythm upon auditory stimuli.

It is felt that many of the problems of auditory span, temporal order in series information and the like, may be related to weaknesses in ability to establish and/or maintain rhythm patterns. As in all other perceptual activities, rhythm in various sensory-motor areas must be integrated so that the child has a concept of rhythm in the total organism. Kinesthetic rhythms must be integrated with tactual rhythms and with auditory rhythms. In any complex task, all of the rhythmic relationships in all of the areas must coincide and the same rhythm pattern must be dominant throughout.

RHYTHMS ON ONE SIDE OF THE BODY ONLY

Many children find it difficult to maintain a rhythm pattern when the rhythmical activities alternate from one side of the body to the other. They are able to establish a rhythm when they are required to beat it out with one hand, for example, but encounter difficulty when two hands must be used and movement of the rhythm must pass from one hand to the other and back again. Therefore, in beginning training in the area of rhythm, it is desirable to start with rhythms on one side of the body only.

Obtain a set of bongo drums or similar materials such that when struck with the hand a strong characteristic sound is produced. (For the present activities, only one such instrument is necessary, but for later techniques it will be desirable to have pairs such that the tone produced by each is distinctively different.) Two sets of these materials are desirable, one for the child and one for the teacher.

Give the child one of the drums while you take the other. Beat out a constant rhythm pattern in which all of the beats are of equal length and equally spaced (*da-da-da-da*). Ask the child to repeat on his drum what you have produced.

In the early stages of training, permit the child to watch you and to beat his drum along with you. In this way, you afford him visual information concerning rhythm as well as auditory, kinesthetic, and tactual information. Alter the rhythm pattern by increasing or decreasing the over-all rate; that is to say, beat a fast constant rhythm, then beat a slow constant rhythm, etc. When the child is able to identify the rhythm and to reproduce it while watching you, ask him to close his eyes and listen to your beat and then reproduce it. In this activity, we are asking him to recognize and establish a rhythm pattern on the basis of auditory information alone.

When he is able to recognize and establish simple constant rhythm patterns of the type described above, we can move on to more complex rhythms. Present next a simple two-beat rhythm (*da-dit, da-dit, da-dit*). Again vary the speed of the over-all rhythm and begin by permitting him to watch as well as listen until he is able to pick up the rhythm from the auditory clues alone.

We can next go to three-stage rhythms (*da-dit-dit-da-dit-dit*). These three-beat rhythms can be altered in various combinations of two items taken three at a time (thus, *dit-da-dit, dit-da-dit, dit-da-dit*). As the child is able to master these three-beat rhythms, we can move on to four-beat, five-beat, six-beat, etc.

In all these rhythm exercises, be sure that the child establishes a smooth rhythmic flow. In three, four, and greater numbers of beats, we have a rhythm imposed upon a rhythm. Thus, *da-dit-dit, da-dit-dit, da-dit-dit* is a series of triads. The child must learn to establish not only the rhythm within the triad (*da-dit-dit*) but the over-all rhythm among the triads (*da-dit-dit, da-dit-dit, da-dit-dit*).

In order to learn to generalize these rhythm patterns, the child should produce them in various ways. Thus, in addition to beating the drum with his dominant hand, he should learn to produce the same rhythm by beating with the non-dominant hand. Then he should learn to establish the same rhythm with both hands together. He should also beat the rhythm with his feet, produce it with his vocal cords by a series of vocal sounds, etc. We want him to generalize the concept of these rhythms so that any activities of his organism which can be grouped in time may be used to produce the same rhythm.

BILATERAL RHYTHMS

When the child has learned to establish rhythm patterns on one side of the body and with one part of the body alone, he must learn to establish the same type of rhythm pattern when both sides of the body are used or when the part used to produce the rhythm alternates from one side to the other. Thus, we will want him to learn to beat out rhythm patterns with both hands, with both feet, etc.

For this bilateral activity, pairs of bongo drums are used. Give the child one pair of drums while you take the other pair. Beat out a simple alternating rhythm in which the beats are of equal length and are equally spaced: thus, *R-L-R-L*. The rhythm should alternate regularly from right to left. Ask the child to reproduce this rhythm pattern.

In the early stages of training, let him watch you as well as listen to you. In this way, he can make use of maximum clues (visual, auditory, kinesthetic, tactual) in establishing his rhythm. When he has been able to establish the rhythm on the basis of all of these clues, ask him to close his eyes and develop the rhythm on the basis of the auditory information alone. Vary the over-all speed of the rhythm: sometimes beat a fast rhythm, sometimes a slow rhythm, etc. Be sure that the child flows smoothly from the right to the left so that the rhythm is smooth and constant, not jerky or accented. Be sure that the flow between the sides of the body is back and forth, not split up into a flow in one direction only (thus, we want *R-L-R-L*, not *RL-RL-RL*).

When the simple *R-L-R* alternation has been mastered, present rhythms in which two beats with each hand are alternated: thus, *R-R-L-L-R-R*. Again, be sure that the flow of the rhythm is smooth and that the rhythmic pattern is not interrupted when it crosses from one side of the body to the other. When the double alternation has been mastered, present alternating series of three (*R-R-R-L-L-L*), four (*R-R-R-R-L-L-L-L*), and five. Whenever the child has difficulty, permit him to watch you as well as listen. However, as soon as he is able to do so, ask him to develop the rhythm pattern on the basis of the auditory stimuli alone. Do not present single series (*R-R-L-L*) but present continuous series of sufficient length to be sure that the child has established the cross-body flow (*R-R-L-L-R-R-L-L*, etc.).

When these regular rhythms have been mastered, we can present irregular rhythms (*R-R-L-R-R-L*). These irregular patterns can be altered in all combinations of two items taken three at a time. When simple irregular rhythms have been established, we can move on to irregularities involving four beats, five beats, six beats, etc. It is desirable that the child learn to establish these rhythm patterns up to as many as ten or twelve beats, both in the previous activity where all of the rhythm was on one side and in the present activity where the rhythm alters from one side to the other.

Here again, we want the child to generalize the rhythm to all types of bodily activity. Thus, we will ask him to beat it out with his feet, either using the drums or tapping out the rhythm on the floor. We will ask him to beat with the right hand and the right foot and also with the left hand and the left foot. In like manner, we will ask him to beat with the right hand and the left foot and with the left hand and the right foot.

chapter 9

Training Ocular Control

Training techniques in the area of control of the eyes are very similar to testing techniques in this area. The general procedure is to move a target in front of the child and ask him to follow it with his eyes. Care is taken to watch the child's eyes carefully to see that he is following the target and that his eyes are moving smoothly and with coordination. In the event of any continued jerkiness or lack of control, the training is discontinued and some other means of helping the child is undertaken.

As noted earlier, the control of the eyes must be matched to the general motor and kinesthetic patterns of the organism. The stimulus variables resulting from visual stimuli do not give adequate information for location and orientation in space. These spatial judgments result from matching kinesthetic information from the eye with the general pattern of orientation developed in the organism. It is therefore apparent that a certain amount of motor and kinesthetic orientation is necessary in the organism as a whole before ocular control can be adequately achieved. The child must have a reasonably solid motor pattern to which to match ocular motor patterns before ocular control can be used to further spatial

and orientational information. For this reason, ocular-pursuit training should not be started until such time as the child has developed
sufficient laterality and directionality to form the basis for a reasonably adequate matching.

STAGES IN OCULAR-PURSUIT TRAINING

Stage 1. In the initial approach to pursuit training, the testing
techniques described in Part II are used as a training device.
The teacher moves the same pencil target used in the testing procedure before the child's eyes in the principal meridia (lateral, vertical, diagonal, and rotary). However, instead of a single trial with
a judgment of adequacy of performance, the target is moved repeatedly and the child is urged to increase the adequacy of his
performance. As noted previously, lateral and vertical movements
are easier than diagonal or rotary movements. Therefore, begin
training with these easier movements and proceed, as the child is
able, to the more difficult directions.

It is very important in ocular-pursuit training that the child make
progress readily in the training activity used. If he continues to
follow the target with uncontrolled movements, he is in danger of
merely practicing his errors and the training procedure defeats its
own purpose. For this reason, the adult should be particularly alert
for progress in control during the early stages of the training period.

If the child does not show observable improvement within a few
trials (four to eight), it is doubtful that the training procedure used
will be effective if continued. Therefore, in this early stage of
training, be alert for improvement and if, within the first few trials,
such improvement is not apparent, this training activity should be
discontinued and the training should drop down to stage two.

Stage 2. Stage two is identical with stage one except that the
target used is a penlight. Obtain a small pen-shaped flashlight such
as those sold in drug and hardware stores. A penlight in which
the bulb or a plastic shield for the bulb (which permits light to
pass through) projects beyond the barrel of the light is desirable.
With this type of light, the source of light is visible when the penlight is held in a vertical position at the child's eye level. The penlight target is moved in the principal meridia in the same manner

as the pencil target in stage one. The same observations should be made and the same procedure recommended in stage one should be followed.

The purpose of stage two is to increase the intensity of the visual stimulus. Whereas the pencil target was visible through reflected light and presented a relatively weak visual stimulus, the penlight presents its stimuli through direct light rays and is a much stronger visual stimulus.

As in stage one, observe carefully to note progress in the child's ability to control. If such progress is not noted within a few trials, then stage two should be discontinued and training should proceed to stage three.

Stage 3. In stage three, the child is asked to point to the target and to follow it with his finger as he follows it with his eyes. The penlight target is used as in stage two and the target is still moved in the principal meridia.

Following the moving target with the finger as it is followed with the eyes adds a kinesthetic clue to the visual clues used in stages one and two. As we said earlier, it is necessary to match the kinesthetic information from the extra-ocular muscles with the general kinesthetic pattern of the body in order to develop the desired ocular control. Such matching is made easier and more direct if a correlated kinesthetic stimulus is added to the visual stimulus. It is this correlation of kinesthetic and visual information which is achieved by the technique of this stage.

As in the earlier procedures, observe the performance of the child carefully. If he does not show demonstrable improvement within a few trials, this process is discontinued and the training moves on to stage four.

Stage 4. Stage four is identical with stage three except that the child is asked to place his finger on the light and move his finger in contact with the penlight as the light moves. He is urged to offer a certain resistance to the movement of the light by saying to him, "Press down hard. Try to keep the light from moving." The light is then moved in the principal meridia as in the earlier procedures.

The purpose of stage four is to increase the kinesthetic stimulation. In stage two, the intensity of the visual stimulus was increased while in stage three a coordinated kinesthetic and visual clue was presented. In stage four, the kinesthetic variable is emphasized while maintaining the kinesthetic-visual parallel. It is for this reason that the child is asked to press hard on the light and to offer a certain resistance to its movement. This increased pressure and the development of resistance increases the tactual and kinesthetic information resulting from the activity.

As before, the performance of the child is observed carefully. If no observable improvement is noticed within a few trials, the training moves on to stage five.

Stage 5. In this stage, the target is a ball. Begin with a large ball such as a beach ball or a playground ball. As training progresses and as the child improves, decrease the size of the ball. The adult places both of his hands, palms flat, on one side of the ball. The child places both of his hands flat against the other side of the ball and directly opposed to the hands of the adult. Thus, the ball is held between the two pairs of hands. The adult then begins to move the ball in the principal meridia carrying the child's hands along with him. The child is encouraged to watch the ball and to keep it in sight as it moves.

In this stage of training, the kinesthetic and tactual information is again increased. Both hands are used and, since the hands of the child are opposed to the hands of the adult, the adult can produce as much resistance and as much tactual information as he likes by simply pressing harder against the ball. At the same time, the visual stimulus is increased in strength by providing a larger target. Thus, in stage five the child is given maximum information with which to develop his skill.

As before, the adult watches very carefully to see how well the child is able to control his eye movements. Here again, if improvement is not observed within a few trials, the training is discontinued.

If the child does not show improvement at stage five, he should be referred to a professional eye man for specialized help. If at this stage of training the child has not yet begun to show improvement, it is probable that a more severe problem than inadequacy in learning is present and that there is some neurological, physiological, or anatomical problem which must be solved before the learning problem can be attacked. These more severe problems require extensive treatment and their solution should be referred to a professional man in the area of visual care.

In beginning ocular-pursuit training, work down through the stages described above until a level is found at which the child can start to learn. Once this level has been identified use the activity of that stage as a training device, helping the child to achieve the desired degree of control through this type of activity. As soon as he has achieved control with one type of activity, move upward through the stages to the next type of activity until, at the end of the training, he is able to follow adequately the pencil target prescribed in stage one.

As was pointed out earlier, some of the movements will be more difficult than others. The stage at which a child can perform will therefore vary from one meridian to another. A child may be found who can perform adequately in the lateral direction at stage one but who, in diagonal direction, must have the additional help provided by stage four or five. In the training of such a child, use whatever activity is appropriate for the particular movement which is being trained. However, move up through the stages as rapidly as possible until the child is able to perform at stage one in all meridia.

EXTENT OF MOVEMENT

It will be found that many children can follow the moving target adequately within a rather restricted range of movements. For example, the child may be able to follow the target with ease if it is moved two or three inches to the right or left. If, however, the movement of the target extends beyond this restricted range, the child may experience difficulty and his skill may break down. Ocular control is more difficult the further it extends toward the periphery in either direction. On the one hand, the child has had more incidental practice with restricted movements near the center of the line of sight than he has with wider movements near the periphery of the area of sight. On the other hand, all muscular control is more difficult as it extends toward the extremes of movement in any direction. For these two reasons, it should be expected that ocular control will become more difficult the further it is extended from the midline in any direction.

As stated earlier, we do not want the child to practice his own errors. Therefore, training procedures should begin by training movements in those areas in which the child can perform adequately. This may be a very restricted area near the center of the line of vision. As he becomes more proficient in this limited area, training will gradually move out in all directions, increasing the extent of the movement required. In this manner, the area within which he has control can be gradually expanded. It will be found, therefore, that with many children the broad movements prescribed under testing will not be possible, but restricted movements within a narrow area will be performed reasonably well. In such cases, the movement of the target will need to be restricted to the area in which the child can operate. Long excursions such as those used in testing (and which will eventually be used in training) are given up and short excursions within the range in which the child can operate are substituted. This range and the extent of the movements are gradually increased as the child becomes able to perform further from the center of his visual field.

At this point another problem frequently presents itself. As we have mentioned earlier, the kinesthetic-visual matching must be reversed every time the child crosses the midline of his body. This reversal in matching frequently causes the child difficulty in ocular control as well as in the eye-hand control which we saw in chalkboard training. Therefore, many children will be found who have difficulty in the center of the visual field because they are required to cross the midline. Such children cannot be trained on one side of the midline alone since this would increase the difficulty which they are already experiencing.

Therefore, with such children it is necessary to give special practice in crossing the midline at the same time that we are attempting to extend the area over which they show control of eye movements. In the process of increasing the extent of control, the extent of movement in either direction is gradually increased. In so doing, however, the midline must be crossed in order to keep the movement balanced. When the midline is crossed, the child has difficulty.

In such cases, proceed as described above to increase the range of control but at the same time give special help whenever he crosses the midline. It may be necessary to use a lower stage of training at or near the midline so that he is able to smooth down his midline control before the extent of movement can be increased. Since two problems are being attacked at once, the child frequently requires activities of a lower level of skill demand (lower stages of training) than will be necessary when either one or both of these problems begin to be solved.

KNOWLEDGE OF RESULTS

One difficulty encountered in ocular-pursuit training techniques in young children is the problem of helping the child to know when he is performing adequately. Since he has little information regarding the operation of his eyes, he has no way of knowing when they are out of control. Since he has not established an adequate pattern of kinesthetic information from the extra-ocular muscles, he has no data with which to judge the smoothness of his pursuit movements. He will need to be given some information by which he can determine when he is "on target" and when he is not.

The purpose of a pursuit movement is to keep the target centered on the fovea or central portion of the retina. This fovea is the area of clearest vision and, when the image is adequately centered thereon, the child has a clear, sharp image of the target. If the image is centered on some portion of the retina other than the fovea, the image is less clear, less sharp, and less detailed. If the ocular-pursuit mechanism is so far out of control that the image does not fall on the retina at all, the child has no image of the target; he "loses" the target. These facts concerning the image of the target can be used to help the child determine when his pursuit movements are adequate.

Watch the eyes carefully to determine when they are pointed toward the target. If the child has lost the target, immediately stop the movement of the target and ask the child to re-fixate it. Such remarks as "Where is it?" "Where did it go?" "Look at it," will usually catch the child's attention and cause him to fixate the target again. When he has had a few such experiences and has learned that he should be able to see the target clearly and sharply at all times, ask him to use this information to determine the status of his control. Thus, he can be instructed to keep the target in view all the time or not to lose the target.

During all training activities be sure that the child is constantly "on target." Do not continue the training at any time if he is "off target." Whenever it appears that the child's eyes are not adequately centered on the target, training should stop and he should be requested to re-fixate the target. When he has re-centered on the target, training can begin again. It is essential that the child learn that it is possible to keep the target in view at all times and never to "lose" it. It is imperative that the child learn how to maintain this type of control. If he is permitted to perform without the target adequately centered, we are permitting him to practice his errors and our training is doing no good and may be doing harm.

In some cases, when binocular training is being undertaken, one eye will lose its fixation while the other continues to fixate the target. In such cases, cover the eye which is fixating properly. The child is then left without a clear image of the target since the eye with which he is now looking is not adequately centered upon it. Then the statement "Where is it?" will cause him to re-fixate with the eye which has been "off target." The other eye can then be uncovered and training can proceed. At no time in binocular training should the child be allowed to follow with one eye while the other eye is not properly pursuing the target. Covering one eye will show him the problem and permit him to correct the error.

BINOCULAR AND MONOCULAR TRAINING

In the normal course of development of ocular control in young children, the child develops control of a single eye first and, when control of each eye separately has been established, he integrates the two eyes together and establishes binocular control. For this reason we would expect, normally, that monocular control would come before binocular control. It is essential that the child develop the skills necessary to control each eye separately and that he integrate these skills for binocular control. Therefore, in helping him to gain ocular control we will want to follow the normal course of development. For this reason, we will wish to train him with the right eye alone, with the left eye alone, and with both eyes together.

In certain cases, children will be found in whom binocular control is superior to monocular control. These children will show apparently good control when tested with both eyes together. However, when tested with either eye alone, their control breaks down and they show considerable difficulty. If our statements concerning the development of ocular control are correct, cases such as these should not be expected. It is felt that such children have made an adaptation to the pressures of the environment surrounding them (which requires binocular responses) when they have not developed the necessary skills for these responses. As a result, they have developed an apparent binocularity which is achieved by simply tying the two eyes together rather than integrating the two control patterns. This apparent binocularity is not efficient and these children are frequently found to have difficulty with demanding visual tasks such as reading. (For a further discussion of this phenomenon see Getman and Kephart, 1958.)

FATIGUE

It will be found that children who have difficulty with ocular control will easily become fatigued in these pursuit-training activities. It should be remembered that the control of the eyes is a very complex neuro-muscular problem. It must also be remembered that the precision which we require in such training activities is extremely high. For these reasons, pursuit-training activities are easily fatiguing and should not be carried on for long periods of time.

In addition to the problem of fatigue, the greatest amount of learning in pursuit activities occurs while the child is adjusting the neuro-muscular apparatus to the task. Therefore, the period of most rapid learning is early in the training session and the amount of learning per unit of time decreases as the session proceeds. It is recommended that pursuit-training sessions be limited to approximately ten minutes. This time should allow roughly three minutes for training of the right eye, three minutes for training of the left eye, and three minutes for training of both eyes.

Training Ocular Control in the School Classroom (Courtesy Highland School, Lafayette, Indiana. Photographer: Howard R. Knaus).

OCCLUSION

When monocular training is undertaken, it is necessary that the eye which is not being trained be covered. For this purpose, some kind of occluder or cover will be needed. A suitable device can be made from a paper towel or a strip of felt. A hole is cut in the paper or felt so that when the strip is held up to the face the eye will be directly behind this hole and the hole will be of such a size that the child has unimpaired vision through it. A rubber band is broken in two and is tied through small holes at the narrow edges of the band so that it can pass behind the child's head. The child then places the occluder over his face leaving one eye free to see through the hole with the rubber band behind his head to hold the device in place. When training is changed to the other eye, the child removes the occluder, turns it through 180 degrees and replaces it with the opposite eye now in position behind the hole. Such devices can be made very easily and have been found satisfactory. Decorated to represent the Lone Ranger or other interesting characters, they also provide good motivational devices for the training.

CLASSROOM TECHNIQUES

The teacher, confronted with the problem of a large number of children in a classroom who must be kept occupied during the school day, will find it desirable to integrate these special training techniques with the regular activities of the classroom. Although some children will be found who need individual attention and whose problems are so severe that they can only be dealt with in an individual setting, other children will be found whose problems are less severe and who can be helped in small group situations. Also, as the children develop in the learning of pursuit skills, their training can shift from individual situations to small group situations. As with many other neuro-muscular skills, a period of important initial learning is experienced. During this initial learning, great care must be taken to see that the child absorbs the fundamentals of the skill on which he is working. Also during this period, progress is rapid and performance improves markedly.

Following this initial spurt, however, there is a long period in which practice and repeated, less intensive training are required. This latter period serves to establish and fix the learning initiated in the former period. The period of "overlearning" of the skill is extremely important since the child must internalize the specific skills which he has learned and come to use them continuously in all the activities in which he engages. During this latter period, left to his own devices, he is apt to slip back into the poor habits which he had established formerly. Therefore, it is necessary that training be continued for a considerable period of time after the initial skills have been learned. During this long period of "overlearning," however, group activities and activities involving less of the teacher's time are possible.

Activities in Small Groups. When pursuit training has reached the level of stages one and two, training is possible in small groups. Usually, in the lower elementary grades the teacher establishes reading groups of six to eight children. Those children requiring additional training in ocular pursuits can be grouped together as one of the reading groups. The teacher can then arrange the children in a semi-circle around her chair, can move the target before the children in much the same way as she would do in the case of a single child for training, and ask the children to follow the target. She can then carry on much the same type of training activities, recommended earlier for individual children, in this small group situation. It is, of course, essential that she watch carefully the performance of the children and, should any child experience difficulty, remove him from the group and give him individual attention until his difficulty is overcome.

A complete series of pursuit-training activities, including right eye, left eye, and binocular, can be carried through in such groups. Small training groups substituted for all or part of the reading circle activity for these children have been used successfully in first grade classrooms in the public schools at Lafayette, Indiana (Simpson, 1960).

During the later stages of pursuit training and particularly during the period when skills are being internalized, it is possible to arrange conditions so that the children can assist in training each other. It has been found most practical to arrange the children in pairs. One child moves the target for the other child, observes his eyes as he follows the target, and in general performs most of the functions previously undertaken by the teacher in the more difficult stages of training. When the first child has been trained, the children reverse places and the first child now trains the second.

It will be found that children become very adept at helping each other. They watch each other's eyes very carefully and spot difficulties readily. This paired training has the additional advantage that the child who is performing the training is also receiving training himself since he must move the target smoothly and therefore must exert similar neuro-muscular control to perform his function that is required of the child being trained. Under these circumstances, the child gets an even clearer concept of ocular control and what it can do than he obtains when the teacher is moving the target for him.

CHALKBOARD AIDS

Another activity which is very useful in training ocular pursuits and which can be adapted to use in the classroom involves the chalkboard. The teacher draws on the chalkboard a "road," using the flat side of a piece of chalk and drawing a strip about an inch to an inch and a half wide on the chalkboard. The child is given a plastic model of a vehicle which he is asked to "drive" by pushing it along with his hand on the road. Two-wheeled vehicles such as motorcycles have been found more satisfactory than four-wheeled vehicles such as automobiles since the former requires more attention to keep it on the road. The two-wheeled models can be turned more easily and as a result must be attended to more constantly to correct minor errors in direction. Begin with straight roads and proceed to curved and wavy roads which require considerable skill to negotiate. (Compare with Kirk and Johnson, 1951, p. 173.)

This type of pursuit activity can be used in the classroom situation either individually or in small groups. A series of roads can be constructed and, among a small group of children, each child can work on his particular road. Here again, pairs of children with one monitoring the other can be used. This technique can be extremely useful since it combines activity of the hand with activity of the eye.

PLAY ACTIVITIES

Many types of play activities are very useful in developing ocular-pursuit skills. Any game or sports activity which involves following a moving object and requires the child to keep the moving object constantly in view can be used to aid in ocular control. Volley ball, basketball, kick ball, and similar sports are useful in this connection. It will be found that the child having difficulty with ocular control will gravitate to a position in these games where such control is not required. Thus, in football he will be found playing in the line; in baseball he will be found either as pitcher or catcher; he tends to avoid basketball but if he does engage in this game, he will play guard. Care must therefore be taken to see that the child enters into those phases of the activity which require following the moving object.

A number of commercial toys are available which involve marbles or other objects that roll along a surface or down inclines. Most

of these toys are too small to provide the latitude of movement
necessary for the training activities in which we are interested. Such
toys, however, will be found very useful if they can be obtained in
a suitable size.[1] It will be found that the children are fascinated
by these devices and that they use them in a very specific manner
for aid in their ocular-pursuit problems.

THE MARSDEN BALL

A soft rubber ball about the size of a tennis ball is suspended by
a string from the ceiling or, if the technique is used outdoors, from
an overhanging tree limb or similar support. The string can be
attached to the ball by driving a small cup hook into the rubber
and tying the string to this. When the opposite end of the string is
attached to the ceiling, the ball swings like a pendulum. It can be
swung laterally before the child, it can be swung in a back and
forth direction, or it can be swung with a circular motion around
him. By altering the length of the string, the timing of the swing
can be slowed or made more rapid. Larger balls may be used initially for younger children or children having particular difficulty.
As they become more adept, the size of the ball can be decreased
(Marsden, 1953).

The child stands at one side about arm's length from the ball and
with the pivot line of the string directly in front of him. Pull the
ball to one side and release it, letting it swing across in front of the
child by its own weight. Do not throw or push the ball. Allow it
to swing as a free pendulum. As the ball passes in front of him,
the child is instructed to reach out and touch it with his finger. He
must reach out and contact the ball directly in one movement. He
is not allowed to thrust his finger into the path of the ball and wait
for it to hit his finger.

He is given a starting point for his finger each time so that he
thrusts out with a definite, prescribed movement. The first starting
position will be the shoulder. The child is instructed to hold his
hand beside his shoulder with his finger pointed ahead. When the

---

[1] An effective rolling marble game may be obtained from Baugh and Reser
Hardware, Inc., 432 Columbia, Lafayette, Indiana.

ball passes, he is to thrust out and touch the ball. Other starting positions will be the eyes and the hip. Always he is to thrust out in one steady movement, not to wander or search for the ball. He is to keep his head still, following the ball with his eyes, and to keep his head pointed forward.

This technique requires that the child follow a moving target and respond in terms of the position of the target. It requires accurate timing and a synthesis between the visual system and the motor system. It aids the child in developing the vital translation between kinesthetic-tactual data and visual data. He must follow the ball with his eyes as though he were following it with his finger and must learn to obtain the same information through this ocular following that he earlier received through manual following.

Preliminary Techniques. Many children will be found who have difficulty in performing this task. For them, it may be necessary to start with simplified versions of the task and gradually, as they gain skill, increase its difficulty. Thus, the child may need first to learn to reach out and touch the ball while it is standing still. For such a child, use a preliminary technique in which the ball is not swung but is allowed to hang motionless. Allow the child to position his finger within an inch or two of the ball before he thrusts at it. Then gradually, being sure he masters each stage before proceeding to the next, move the starting position back until he can thrust from his shoulder.

The ball may need to be swung through a very small arc at first to permit the child to achieve. Increase the length of the arc gradually until accurate following and anticipation are achieved. He may need to follow the ball with his finger at first so that he can learn to match visual following with manual following. Later he can be asked to begin translating from one to the other by waiting until the ball starts swinging before he begins following it with his finger. He can thus be moved along until he can use visual data alone.

Varying the Procedure. When the child has become adept at the task of hitting the ball, be sure that he is following it continuously and not just depending on a split-second awareness of the ball in a certain position to guide his aim. Certain children will learn how to avoid the demands of the swinging ball task by paying attention only to a small area directly in front of them. When they see the ball in this area, they thrust out. They have not followed the ball but have depended upon speed in a single perception for their performance. It is like looking for a single frame in a movie film instead of following the action. If a child has good perceptual speed, he may be able to perform well in the task by this method. He can be forced out of this restricted method by varying the procedure.

Instruct the child to thrust when you call out "Now." He does not know when you are going to give the signal, and he must thrust immediately when he hears you. Under these conditions, he is required to maintain readiness to respond at all times. Only by following the ball can he be ready at any time you may signal. It is well to insert this variation into the training procedure as soon as possible to insure that the proper method is being used. Be sure that he follows with his eyes and not with his head. He should be instructed not to move his head.

When the child has mastered the ball as it swings laterally to his body, we can move on to a fore and aft direction. In this procedure, pull the ball on a line directly in front of the child and let it swing. The ball then moves toward and away from the child. The child reaches out with his hand underneath the ball and with his finger pointed upward. He then moves his hand up so that his finger touches the ball from underneath. He should start in the prescribed starting position and execute the response in one continuous movement. He should hit the ball squarely from underneath, not position his finger and wait for the ball to swing into it. By paying attention to his thrusts, he can observe the direction and extent of his miss on each trial.

When the child begins to learn the task with his finger, he may be given a short bat with which to bunt the ball. It is desirable that these ball techniques be learned with the finger first. The tactual stimulation of the finger actually touching the ball, added to the visual stimulation, makes early learning more rapid and more thorough. When the bat is used, the child is encouraged to reach out and meet the ball, not to hold his bat out and let the ball hit it.

To train judgments over longer distances, this bat or a long, thin pointer can also be used with the ball swinging laterally. In this case, the child stands farther from the swinging ball and thrusts out with the pointer, touching the ball with its tip in the same manner that he formerly did with his finger. The pointer thus becomes an extension of the arm and the task requires spatial judgments beyond arm's reach. Here again, in the preliminary exercises the child should first experience tactual stimulation through the finger because of the value of this stimulation in the learning process.

The process of bunting the ball with the bat involves a spatial judgment and a process of following a target in the fore and aft direction in addition to the problems presented by the laterally swinging ball. Also, timing and rhythm are involved and the technique can be useful in the training of these factors.

Training Ocular Pursuit. Ocular-pursuit movements without accompanying gross muscle movement can be trained with the Marsden Ball by asking the child simply to watch the ball as it swings back and forth. He should be cautioned to hold his head still and follow the ball with his eyes alone. He should be encouraged not to lose sight of the ball at any time. For older children, we may paste cut-out letters of the alphabet on the surface of the ball. As it swings, the child is asked to find as quickly as he can an *a*, then a *b*, etc. The ball should be seen clearly at all times.

The ball is swung laterally and in a fore and aft direction as before. It can then be swung diagonally (as from far left to near right). These diagonal movements are the most difficult to master. Therefore, they should not be introduced until skill in the lateral movements has been achieved. Later, the child is asked to lie on his back on the floor and the ball is swung in a circular movement above him as he follows it. During all of these procedures, watch the child's eyes to ensure that the following movements are smooth and accurate. When movements are not smooth, encourage the child to "keep his eye on the ball." In these latter exercises, the swinging ball becomes the moving target of the earlier pursuit-training techniques and serves the same purposes. It has the advantage that the child can work alone and thus requires less constant supervision. Obviously the gross problems of control must be solved before such relatively unsupervised practice can be effective.

chapter 10

Training Form Perception

PUZZLES

Help for the child with deficiencies in the development of constructive form perception can be provided by the use of puzzles of the jigsaw or cut-out type. Care must be taken in the use of these materials to ensure that the child completes the puzzle on the basis of evaluation of the total form rather than on the basis of a simple matching of some few specific elements in the form. For example, in the common form board task the child may pick up a triangular shaped piece. He may then match the apex angle of the piece to a similar angle of the cutout by placing these two elements together. He then completes the task by simply letting go of the piece and permitting the rest of the form to drop into place by itself. Such a child has, in all probability, dealt with only one element of the form, the apex angle. He has not seen nor attended to the remaining elements of the figure. He has been able by this method to solve the form board problem without constructing the form of the pieces or of the cut-out sections. His performance has been on the basis of a matching of single elements, not on a matching of total forms. If we permit the child to persist in such behavior, he will not learn form perception but will continue to use single elements as a basis for the solution of the task.

For this reason, it will be found that commercial puzzles in which the form or picture is more striking than the shape of the individual pieces will be most useful. Puzzles should be selected in which the picture presents a single form or a limited number of separated forms. Thus, puzzles involving a picture of a child, such as the mannequin puzzle, are most useful. Other puzzles which present more than one figure but have each figure separate from the others and have each figure stand out sharply against a relatively undetailed background are useful. Avoid puzzles in which the figures are complicated, in which they overlap each other, and in which they are not sharply delimited from the background. The cutouts should follow the outline of the pictured form rather than representing randomly shaped pieces having little or no relation to the picture itself. The use of these simple artistic devices emphasizes the figure-ground quality for the child and helps him to keep the picture figure dominant in the process of solving the puzzle.

Watch the child carefully as he works on his puzzle. If he tries to fit a piece from one pictured figure into a different figure and is obviously paying more attention to the pieces than to the picture, he should be stopped. If he attempts to match edges of the pieces rather than considering the piece in terms of the pictured form, or if he is obviously paying attention to the irregularities of the piece rather than to the picture which he is completing, he should be stopped and his attention should be directed to the form qualities of the picture rather than to the detail qualities. He should be encouraged to attack the problem in terms of the picture as a whole rather than peculiarities of the individual pieces.

PROVIDING ADDITIONAL HELP

Additional help can be given if the child is permitted to break down the form for himself before he attempts to build it up. Thus, a simple but very effective puzzle can be constructed by asking the child to choose a picture from a magazine. Help him direct his choice toward the kind of a picture which will have simple, clear forms which stand out sharply from the background. When he has selected his picture, draw lines with a heavy crayon outlining pieces to be cut out. Then give the child scissors and ask him to cut out the pieces along the lines which you have drawn. Particularly in the early stages of such training, be sure that you outline the pieces in such a manner that the form remains dominant. The lines outlining the piece should be simple, straight lines and simple curves, not complicated with many zigzags and curlycues which he can use for matching purposes. Outline the cut-out areas so that they contain complete figures or parts of figures which obviously are related to the remainder of the figure, such as a head or an arm or a foot from a figure of a person. By these means, we keep the figure more dominant than the details of the cut-out piece. When the child has completed the cutting out process, he is then asked to assemble the pieces into the total picture again. The experience of having observed the entire picture and of having it called to his attention before it was cut apart helps him to retain the total form as the dominant portion of the task.

Inevitably in such puzzles, details of the picture will be severed by the cut of the paper. Thus, a line of an arm may run across the cut which the child has made. These details occurring on each adjacent piece can also be matched by the child. Thus, instead of matching the total form of the arm to the total form of the body, he may match the line of the arm on one piece to its extension on the other piece. Here again, he is paying more attention to the elements of the figure than he is to the total form. For this reason, we will want to use a large number of different pictures rather than using the same picture or puzzle a number of times. Through a variation in the forms used, the details are changed frequently. It therefore becomes more difficult for the child to solve the problem on the basis of matching details than on the basis of construction of a total form. By this means, he is encouraged to abandon details as a clue and to develop total forms as clues.

CONSTRUCTING SIMPLE PUZZLES

The teacher can also construct for the child simple puzzles which are useful in this type of training. The most satisfactory puzzle consists of a simple picture from a magazine following the principles of strong figure-ground relationships outlined above. Paste this picture on cardboard or heavy paper backing. Cut a straight horizontal line through the middle of the card so that the upper half is exactly equal to the lower half. Ask the child to assemble the two halves of the picture. Since the two halves are identical, if he tries to match edges, he finds that he can match the two cut edges together but also that he can match the top edge and the bottom edge. One of these solutions is correct and one is in error. Therefore, in assembling the puzzle, he is forced to pay attention to the picture as opposed to the shape of the pieces. The task can be made more complicated by cutting the card into four or more equal pieces, by making straight cuts properly spaced horizontally, vertically, or both.

This simple type of puzzle will be found very useful. It can be used with picture materials as described above. As the child becomes more proficient, it can be used with outline drawings of simple geometric forms and, when the child has progressed sufficiently, with letters and figures as outlined by Strauss and Lehtinen (Strauss and Lehtinen, 1947, pp. 176–77).

STICK FIGURES

Match sticks (with heads removed) are used to construct simple geometric figures. The teacher will find it desirable to prepare a series of forms in which the elements (sticks) are glued down to a piece of wood or cardboard. Prepare the forms illustrated in Figure 9. Give the child thirty match sticks with which to construct his figures.

In figures of this type, elements of the form (lines) are broken down and presented to the child separately as sticks. He is required to supply the integration of these elements, all of which are alike, which will result in a product representing accurately the figure presented to him. He must develop and execute for himself the constructive aspects of the forms. The task does not require the coordination demanded in drawing or copying and, at the same time, emphasizes the constructive aspects of form perception while demanding less attention to the elements themselves. A series of tasks, increasing in difficulty, will be found helpful in the use of such materials to aid form perception. For a discussion of the developmental variables in the match stick task, see Piaget and Inhelder (1956).

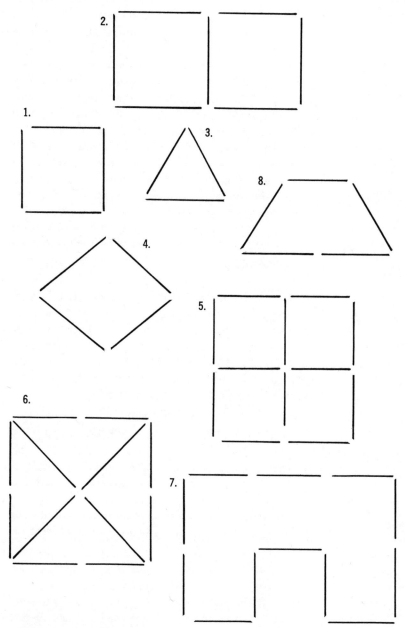

FIGURE 9. Match-stick forms.

A. Task 1 (square).

    1. Lay the square pattern before the child on a desk or table. Be sure that it is centered directly in front of him and far enough away so that he can work between the pattern and the front of the table. Say, "Make one just like this." Pattern is in full view of the child and laid flat on the table in the same orientation as his production. Observe the order in which he places his sticks. If he does not do so at once, ask, "Can you go right around, this way?" Outline with your finger a continuous counterclockwise progression around the contour. If he is still unable, ask him to run his finger around the contour of the model. Call special attention to the corners and the change of direction at each. To ensure that he does not learn this order as a specific task element but learns the concept of continuity of direction, require him to go sometimes clockwise, sometimes counterclockwise in a random order.

    2. Hold the pattern vertically before the child. Say, "Now make one like it." If failure occurs, lay the pattern horizontally and let him feel around the contour. Then have him make one. Now raise the pattern at a 10 degree angle to the horizontal. Have him make one. If he is successful, raise the pattern to 20 degrees and repeat. Continue until he can reproduce from the vertically oriented pattern.

    3. Remove the pattern from the child's view. Say, "Now make one like it." If there is an error, show him the pattern again and let him correct his error.

    4. With the pattern out of sight, ask him to make one twice as large. If there is an error, reintroduce the pattern and ask, "Is yours just like this?" If he recognizes the error, help him correct it. If he does not recognize the error, ask about the specific point or points of error. Then help him correct his form.

B. Task 2 (rectangle).

    1. Repeat steps A(1), A(2), A(3), and A(4), using the rectangular form. If the child has difficulty with the rectangular shape (for example, produces a square instead of a rectangle), ask him to run his finger over the long edge of the pattern

and then over the corresponding edge of his figure and compare these two movements. Then ask him to correct his figure. In order to relate this comparison to total form rather than only one element (side), ask him to run his finger around the square pattern, then around the rectangular pattern, and compare the differences in the total contours. Introducing an auditory rhythm (as 1, 2, turn; 1, turn; 1, 2, turn; 1, turn) may aid him in observing the differences in length and long-short relationships of the four sides.

2. Present the pattern rotated 90 degrees so that one of the short sides is nearest the child. Repeat steps A(1), A(2), A(3), and A(4) in this rotated position.

3. Show the child the pattern with a long side on the base. Say, "This is the way the figure looks when it is right side up." Rotate it 90 degrees. Say, "Now I have turned it on its side. You make me one that is right side up."

4. Repeat A(4) with figure rotated 90 degrees.

C. Task 3 (triangle).

1. Present the triangle with its base toward the child. Repeat steps A(1), A(2), A(3), A(4).

2. Repeat B(2) and B(3) only rotate the triangle 180 degrees so that its apex is toward the child.

D. Task 4 (diamond).

1. Repeat steps A(1), A(2), A(3), A(4).

2. Repeat steps B(3) and B(4) with the diamond rotated 90 degrees.

E. Task 5 (divided square).

1. Repeat steps A(1), A(2), and A(3).

2. Show the square form of task one. Ask, "Can you find this figure in the one you have made?" If he answers "No," ask him to run his finger around the contour of item one. Then run his finger around one of the small squares of item five. If he still cannot see the small square in the large square, pull it out by removing these four sticks from the total figure. When he can recognize task one in this context, put it back into item five. Let him run his finger around it again. Repeat until he can recognize task one in one of the squares of item five. Continue until he sees that there are four small squares combined in task five.

F. Task 6 (diagonals).
   1. Repeat steps A(1), A(2), and A(3) using the square form with two diagonals.
G. Task 7 (irregular rectangle).
   1. Repeat steps A(1), A(2), and A(3) using the irregular rectangle
   2. Repeat step B(2) with pattern rotated 90, 180, and 270 degrees.
   3. Repeat step B(3) with pattern rotated 90, 180, and 270 degrees.
   4. Repeat step E(2). Ask, "Can you add one more stick and make one like this (small square) in the one you have (irregular rectangle)?" Help him find all three possibilities.
   5. Repeat step G(4) using the rectangular form of task two. Help him find both possibilities.
H. Task 8 (trapezoid).
   1. Repeat steps A(1), A(2), A(3), and A(4) using the trapezoid.
   2. Repeat step G(2).
   3. Repeat step G(3).

THE PEGBOARD

The pegboard is a modification of the Strauss Marble Board (Strauss and Lehtinen, 1947; Strauss and Kephart, 1955). It serves the same functions and provides the same activities as the earlier equipment, but it will be found easier to use since the pegs remain more firmly in the board than do the marbles. The pegboard consists of a square board in which rows of holes have been drilled. It will be found desirable to use a relatively large board (at least twelve by twelve inches). It will also be found desirable to ensure that the holes are not too small (one-eighth of an inch in diameter has been found adequate) and that the holes are not too close together (a half inch between centers). A square piece of acoustic ceiling tile will make a very adequate pegboard. Select a square in which the holes are arranged in straight vertical and horizontal rows. Tile of this kind has twenty-two holes in each direction and provides adequate space and an adequate number of holes for rather elaborate forms to be laid out.

Important figure-ground relationships can be learned with pegboards. (Courtesy A. Devaney, Inc.).

The device will be found to work better if the pegs are relatively large. Pegs of extremely small diameter and extremely short pegs require too much manipulative ability from the child and distract him from the problem of form. It will be found that golf tees make excellent pegs for use with the ceiling tile. Clip off a half inch from the sharp end of the tee so that there will be less danger of the child's hurting himself and so that the length will be more adequate. Golf tees have an additional advantage in that they have a relatively large head. When these tees are set in a row in the pegboard, the heads of adjacent tees come close together. By bringing the units of the form (pegs) closer together, the form problem

is made simpler since the units are not as distinct. Such a simplification can only be accomplished with heads on the pegs since
bringing the shafts of the pegs closer together to decrease the intervening space increases the number of units in the form and also
increases the manipulative problem.

DIFFICULTY OF THE TASK

It will be seen that the pegboard presents a somewhat more difficult form perception problem than either of the two techniques
previously described. In the case of puzzles and form boards, it
was only necessary to match one form to another. The child
could solve the problem by matching the block to the cut-out de-
pression in the board. With the match stick problems, the elements
of the form were maintained intact. The elements in this problem
are lines and each line is represented by one stick so that the number of pieces in the completed product is no greater than the number of lines in the form. In the case of the pegboard, however, the
elements themselves (lines and angles) are broken down into units
(pegs). Thus, in completing the pegboard task, the child is required
to build up elements of the form from homogeneous units.

The pegboard, therefore, offers a difficult form perception problem for two reasons. In the first place, the form is broken up into
a large number of units. The number of units is larger and the
form is more completely broken up than is normally the case.
The child must hold the form against an exaggerated distraction of
units. In the second place, the task is elongated in time. It requires
more time to place pegs in a pegboard than it does to place match
sticks or to draw lines with a pencil or crayon. For this reason,
the spatial-temporal translation problem is increased with pegboard
materials. The child must hold the form over a longer period of
time and in the face of greater temporal distractions than is the
case with other materials.

For these reasons, it will be found that pegboards are very useful in helping the child develop form perception. They represent a difficult task and permit us to offer more difficult types of
training. When form perception has begun, it can be solidified
and can be "over-learned" through such training. This "over-learn-
ing" can operate as a margin of safety for the child in his daily

activities. If form is extremely solid, we can be sure that it will consistently emerge and will be available in normal activities. It is obvious, however, that the pegboards will be found too difficult for the child who has little form perception or only the beginnings of form perception. The more simple activities (copying and match sticks) should be used first to ensure that the child has enough form perception to be able to handle the pegboard tasks. For a discussion of the relationships between pegboard activities and mental ability, see Werner and Strauss, 1939; Werner, 1944; Crain and Werner, 1950.

STAGES OF TRAINING

Two boards and two sets of pegs are provided, one for the child and one for the adult. The pegs should be of a color contrasting with the background. In this way, the form can be made to stand out more sharply against the background and the difficulty of the task is kept reasonable. On his board, the adult outlines a simple figure (square, oblong, triangle, etc.). This figure is then shown to the child and he is asked to make one like it on his board.

There are two stages in the training activity. In the first stage, the board with the model figure on it is left in full view of the child. He may consult it whenever he has difficulty and he may constantly compare his production with the model. In the second stage of training, the model figure is shown to the child only briefly. When the child begins to work, the model is removed and the child is asked to complete the activity with no further reference to the model.

With any individual form (such as a square), it will be desirable to move from the first stage to the second stage as rapidly as possible. The child who has little form perception will tend to attack the problem of the pegboard on the basis of the units themselves. Thus, he will, by counting holes, determine the placement of the first peg. He will then orient the second peg to the first peg or, in some cases, he may resort to counting holes again to locate the second peg. In this peg-by-peg fashion, he will proceed around the form. It will be seen that this type of activity can be carried out with little reference to the total form itself. The child can deal with each peg independently and can produce a reasonable replica of the model without having seen or attended to the total form. He can achieve a production without integrating the units or constructing the form. Obviously it is undesirable for him to proceed in this fashion since the training which is desired is not being achieved. Such a unit-by-unit solution becomes much more difficult when the model is removed from view. Therefore, by moving from the first to the second stage as soon as possible, the child is forced out of the disconnected unit approach and is encouraged to construct the form and use it as a basis of his procedure.

The order of difficulty of simple forms on the pegboard follows roughly the order of difficulty discussed earlier in connection with chalkboard drawing. We saw in the earlier discussion that the circle was the simplest form to draw or copy. On the pegboard, a circle represents specific difficulties because of the placement of the holes. Therefore, it should not be used in pegboard activities or, if it is used, should be introduced very late in the process. In pegboard activities, the straight line replaces the circle as the simplest type of form.

Maintaining Form against Background. Some children will have difficulty holding the form represented by a straight line against the distraction represented by the large number of additional holes in the pegboard. Thus, they may start to construct a straight line of pegs and be drawn off into slanting or angle lines. It should be remembered that the structure represented by the holes in the pegboard is much more obtrusive than the structure represented by normal background materials. Therefore, the child may need help in overcoming the distraction represented by this structure which he would not need in drawing or other activities where the background is less highly structured. He can be given aid in maintaining form against this background by the use of a template for a straight line as described under chalkboard training. A cardboard or plastic template is prepared in which a long, narrow opening representing a straight line has been cut out. This template is laid along the pegboard in the prescribed direction, and the child places his pegs within the cut-out area of the template. As a result of this activity, he is able to construct a straight line which he can then observe and evaluate. When he has learned to construct a straight line with the maximum assistance represented by the template, remove the template and lay a straight edge such as a ruler across the pegboard. Under these conditions, the child is required to maintain the straight line form against distraction in one direction but is given help in overcoming the distraction in the opposite direction. This intermediate step may help him to make the transition between the straight line produced with the template and a straight line produced by free activity on the pegboard.

Constructing Lines. The child should learn to produce a straight, horizontal line completely across the pegboard. He should also learn to produce a straight, vertical line extending over the length of the pegboard. He should learn to produce these lines in various positions on the pegboard. Straight lines near an edge are easier since the edge represents a guide. Straight lines near the center of the board are more difficult because the guiding effect of the edge of the board is further removed. Do not use diagonal lines at this stage of training since they are considerably more difficult and it will be found that the simple square and rectangle form can be presented and learned as soon as a straight line can be achieved. The use of these simple straight line forms will make the problem of the diagonal less difficult at a later stage in training.

When the child has learned to construct a straight line, he must learn the problem of achieving a line of a given length. This problem involves the same difficulty of stopping which we discussed earlier in connection with chalkboard activities. In the pegboard, the row of holes extending ahead of the point at which he is working tends to draw the child on, so that the problem of stopping becomes more severe in pegboard activities. The child has a tendency, when he has learned to follow a row of holes, to follow it on to the edge of the board.

He can be given aid in learning to stop by being presented with a line shorter than the length of the board. When he has begun his production in the proper position, lay a ruler or other device in the opposite direction at the point where he should stop. He then follows the row of holes until he comes to this obstacle and stops there. The ruler then presents a strong stimulus for the act of stopping. When he has learned to stop with a ruler, place the last peg in the row for him. He then follows along the row of holes until he comes to the pre-placed peg. This peg then represents a stimulus for stopping. It will be found useful to outline the line which he is to construct by placing beforehand the first peg and the last peg. The child is then asked only to fill in the intermediate pegs. He should be encouraged as soon as possible to learn to stop when his line is of the prescribed length without these additional clues.

Constructing Squares and Rectangles. When the straight line has been mastered, a square can be presented for reproduction. With this new form, the child may again become distracted by the structured background. It may therefore be necessary again to provide him with a template so that the distraction of the background will be partially overcome. He should be encouraged to dispense with the template as soon as possible. It will also be found useful in helping him overcome the background problem if a solid square constructed by filling in the entire square area with pegs is presented. This form with its mass in contrast with the background is a stronger figure-background combination than an outline form in which only lines contrast with the background. It may be found that the child can perform more easily with these solid squares than with the outline square. They will therefore represent a valuable intermediate step in the training process. The square models should be varied in size as in chalkboard training to ensure that the child develops the concept of "square" rather than learning to reproduce a specific figure.

When the square has been mastered, the rectangle can be presented. The same problems discussed in chalkboard construction of a rectangle should be considered in the pegboard construction of a rectangle. The rectangle should be presented in both orientations, one with the long side as the base and one with the short side as the base. The problem of proportionality within the rectangle will need to be considered also.

The Problem of Orientation. The pegboard presents two background problems. The board itself is a background and, as we have seen, is a structured background. In addition, since the board is relatively small in relation to the total visual field, it constitutes a secondary form on a background represented by the table top and the rest of the visual surroundings. Therefore, the child should learn to deal with the pegboard as an intermediate background situation. For this reason, he should pay attention to the orientation of his production in relationship to the board itself. Therefore, ask him to construct a figure where the model has been placed in the upper left-hand corner, in the lower center portion of the board, etc. Ask the child to make his figure just like yours, not only in terms of the form itself, but in terms of the position of the figure on the board. The first problem of the form board is the construction of the figure itself. Therefore, pay attention to this problem first and be sure that the child is able to construct the figure. Then move on to the problem of orientation of the figure on the board and ask him to orient his figure to the peg-board in the same way that yours is oriented.

Constructing Diagonals. At this stage in the training process, the diagonal line may be introduced. It will be found that all of the problems encountered in the learning of the horizontal or vertical line will be encountered again when the diagonal line is presented. As we have seen frequently before, diagonals are more difficult than verticals and horizontals. It will therefore be expected that the child will have difficulty in constructing diagonal lines. In addition to these problems, the construction of the pegboard is such that the diagonal line is increased in difficulty with this device. The centers of the holes on the diagonal are farther apart on the pegboard and the space relationships of holes on the diagonal are different from the space relationships on the horizontal or vertical. In many cases, it will be found necessary to return to the straight-line template or to the ruler as aids in helping the child to construct diagonal lines. The problem of stopping may occur again and can be aided by the same methods used with horizontal and vertical lines. When the diagonal line has been mastered, the triangle and diamond figures can be presented.

After these basic, simple forms are learned, more complex forms involving extensions and combinations of the simple forms can be presented. If it is felt desirable, a series of complex forms can be devised and even letters and numbers can be designed for use on the pegboard (see Jolles, 1958).

Multiple Forms. When single forms have been mastered, the form perception problem can be increased in difficulty by presenting two forms on the board at once. Begin by constructing two figures which lie adjacent to each other. That is to say, one or more pegs of the second form are adjacent to one or more pegs of the first form (see Figure 10). This arrangement of forms presents a further difficulty for the child. When he is engaged

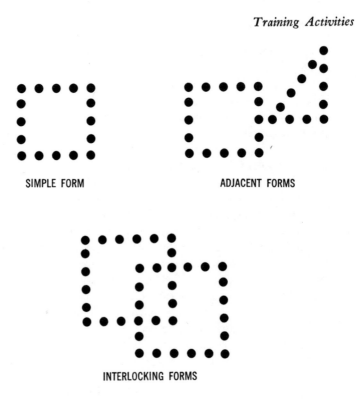

SIMPLE FORM   ADJACENT FORMS

INTERLOCKING FORMS

FIGURE 10.   Illustrations of Pegboard figures.

in completing one of the forms, the second form represents a distraction and he may be carried off in a wrong direction by the stimulus of the second form. Observe whether, in his work with adjacent forms, the child completes one form first and then moves on to the second form. Such a procedure indicates that he has seen this design as two independent forms adjacent to each other. If he constructs one line of the first form and then a line of the second form or splits his approach in some similar manner, it may be suspected that he has not seen or dealt with these two forms as separate wholes. Encourage him to recognize each form and to deal with each separately. It may be found that kinesthetic information will aid in separating the two forms. Ask the child to run his finger around the square form (Figure 10). If necessary, guide his hand so that he will not be led off by the distraction of the triangular form. Then ask him to reproduce this square. Next ask him to run his finger around the triangle and reproduce that figure. When he can perform with this kinesthetic help, ask him merely to look at the square, name it, and reproduce it. Then have him look at the triangle, name it, and reproduce it. Finally, ask him to look at the total figure, name the two forms, and reproduce each in proper orientation for himself.

Interlocking Forms. A further complication can be introduced by the use of interlocking forms. In this design, one form includes a portion of the second form (see Figure 10). With interlocking forms, it is desirable that the child again complete each form separately. Many children work their way around the outside edges of the two forms and fill in the central common area later. This procedure would indicate that they have dealt with one form involving complications rather than two forms interrelated with each other. The child should be encouraged to complete one form and then the other. In this way, we can be sure that he understands that two forms are present and we can be sure that he is able to manipulate the relationships between these two forms. The same intermediate steps recommended for adjacent forms will be found useful with interlocking forms.

In all training activities involving two forms either adjacent or interlocking, it is desirable that the second stage of training, where the model is shown the child but is removed while he is constructing his forms, be used as soon as possible. Because of the difficulty of this task, children have a tendency to look back and forth from their construction to the model, checking each line or each peg. This type of behavior indicates a concern with elements or detail rather than with the total form. The child should be encouraged to dispense with this method as soon as possible and care should be taken to see that he is required to deal with the forms as wholes. Such encouragement can be provided by removing the model and by noting carefully the method of construction which he uses. Examples of methods of construction based on reproduction of elements rather than total forms can be found in Strauss and Lehtinen, 1947, pp. 33–34.

CHAPTER ILLUSTRATIONS

References

Abbott, W. *The Theory and Practice of Perspective.* London: Blackie and Son, 1950.

Baltzer, F. "Beiträge zur Sinnesphysiologie und Psychologie der Webespinnen." Bern: Mitt. Naturf. Ges., 1923.

Bartley, S. H. *Principles of Perception.* New York: Harper & Bros., 1958.

Bender, L. *Psychopathology of Children with Organic Brain Disorders.* Springfield: Charles C Thomas, 1956.

———. *Visual Motor Gestalt Test and Its Clinical Use.* New York: American Orthopsychiatric Association, 1938.

Bexton, W. H., W. Heron, and T. H. Scott. "Effects of Decreased Variation in the Sensory Environment," *Canad. J. Psychol.,* VIII (1954), 70–76.

Brown, G. S. and D. P. Campbell. *Principles of Servomechanisms.* New York: John Wiley & Sons, Inc., 1948.

Bühler, K. *The Mental Development of the Child.* London: Routledge and Kegan Paul, 1930.

Cinat-Tomson, H. "Die geschlechtliche Zuchtwahl beim Wellensittich (Melopsittacus undalatus Shaw)," *Biol. Zbl.,* XLVI (1926), 543–52.

Coghill, G. E. *Anatomy and the Problem of Behavior.* Cambridge: Cambridge University Press, 1929.

Cowell, C. C. and H. W. Hazelton. *Curriculum Designs in Physical Education.* Englewood Cliffs, N. J.: Prentice-Hall, Inc., 1955.

Craik, K. J. W. *The Nature of Explanation.* Cambridge: Cambridge University Press, 1952.

Crain, L. and H. Werner. "The Development of Visuo-Motor Performance on the Marble Board in Normal Children," *J. Genet. Psychol.,* LXXVII (1950), 217–29.

Dennis, W. (ed.). *Current Trends in Psychological Theory.* Pittsburgh: University of Pittsburgh Press, 1951.

Dusser de Barenne, J. G. "The Labyrinthine and Postural Mechanisms," in *Handbook of General Experimental Psychology,* ed. C. Murchison. Worcester: Clark University Press, 1934, pp. 204–46.

Ellis, W. D. (ed.). *A Source Book of Gestalt Psychology.* New York: Harcourt, Brace & Co., 1938.

Feinberg, R. "A Study of Some Aspects of Peripheral Visual Acuity," *Amer. J. Optom.,* LXII (1949), 62.

Fernald, G. M. *Remedial Techniques in Basic School Subjects.* New York: McGraw-Hill Book Co., 1943.

Freeman, F. N. *Psychology of the Common Branches.* Boston: Houghton Mifflin Co., 1916.

Fulton, J. F. *Physiology of the Nervous System* (3rd ed.). New York: Oxford University Press, 1949.

Gelb, A. and K. Goldstein. "Analysis of a Case of Figural Blindness," in *A Source Book of Gestalt Psychology,* ed. W. D. Ellis. New York: Harcourt, Brace & Co., 1938.

Gesell, A. *Infancy and Human Growth.* New York: Macmillan Co., 1928.

———. *The First Five Years of Life.* New York: Harper & Bros., 1940.

Gesell, A., F. L. Ilg, and G. E. Bullis. *Vision—Its Development in Infant and Child.* New York: Paul B. Hoeber, Inc., 1941.

Getman, G. N. and N. C. Kephart. "The Analysis of Ocular Fixation," *Optometric Extension Program Papers,* XXX (1958), 25–31.

Gibson, E. J. "Improvement in Perceptual Judgments As a Function of Controlled Practice or Training," *Psychol. Bull.,* L (1953), 401–31.

Gibson, J. J. *The Perception of the Visual World.* New York: Houghton Mifflin Co., 1950.

Gibson, J. J. and E. J. Gibson. "Perceptual Learning: Differentiation or Enrichment," *Psychol. Rev.,* LXII (1955), 32–41.

Gilhousen, H. C. "An Investigation of 'Insight' in Rats," *Science,* LXXIII (1931), 711–12.

Goodenough, F. L. *The Measurement of Intelligence by Drawings.* Yonkers-on-Hudson: World Book Co., 1926.

Gottschaldt, K. "Uber den Einfluss der Erfahrung auf die Wahrnehmung von Figuren 1: uber den Einfluss Gehaufter Einpragung auf ihre Sichtbarkeit in Unfassenden Konfigurationen," *Psychol. Forach.*, VIII (1926), 261–317.

Graham, C. H. "Visual Perception," in *Handbook of Experimental Psychology*, ed. S. S. Stevens. New York: John Wiley & Sons, Inc., 1951, pp. 868–920.

Guilford, J. P. *Fundamental Statistics in Psychology and Education* (2nd ed.). New York: McGraw-Hill Book Co., 1950.

Guilford, J. P., R. C. Wilson, P. R. Christensen, and D. J. Lewis. "A Factor Analytic Study of Creative Thinking. II. Administration of Tests and Analysis of Results," *Psychometrika*, XIX (1954), 297–311.

Halsey, E. and L. Porter. *Physical Education in the Elementary Schools: A Developmental Program.* New York: Henry Holt & Co., Inc., 1958.

Harlow, H. F. "Learning Theories," in *Current Trends in Psychological Theory*, ed. W. Dennis. Pittsburgh: University of Pittsburgh Press, 1951.

Harris, D. B. (ed.). *The Concept of Development.* Minneapolis: University of Minnesota Press, 1957.

Hebb, D. O. *The Organization of Behavior.* New York: John Wiley & Sons, Inc., 1949.

Helson, H. "Insight in the White Rat." *J. Exp. Psychol.*, X (1927), 378–97.

Hempelmann, F. *Tierpsychologie.* 1926.

Higginson, G. D. "Visual Perception in the White Rat." *J. Exp. Psychol.*, IX (1926), 337–47.

Hsiao, H. H. "An Experimental Study of the Rat's 'Insight' within a Spatial Complex," *Univ. Calif. Publ. Psychol.*, IV (1929), 57–70.

Hurlock, E. B. *Child Development.* New York: McGraw-Hill Book Co., 1942.

Itard, J. M. G. *The Wild Boy of Aveyron.* New York: Appleton-Century-Crofts, Inc., 1932.

Jeffries, L. A. (ed.). *Cerebral Mechanisms in Behavior.* New York: John Wiley & Sons, Inc., 1951.

Jersild, A. T. *Child Psychology.* Englewood Cliffs, N. J.: Prentice-Hall, Inc., 1954.

Jolles, I. "A Teaching Sequence for the Training of Visual and Motor Perception," *Amer. J. Ment. Def.*, LXIII (1958), 252–55.

Jones, E., E. Morgan, and G. Stevens. *Methods and Materials in Elementary Physical Education.* Yonkers-on-Hudson: World Book Co., 1957.

Kagerer, R. L. "The Relationship between the Kraus-Weber Test for Minimum Muscular Fitness and School Achievement." Unpublished Master's thesis, Purdue University, 1958.

Keller, F. S. and L. M. Hill. "Another 'Insight' Experiment," *J. Genet. Psychol.*, XLVIII (1936), 484–89.

Kephart, N. C. "Visual Behavior of the Retarded Child," *Amer. J. Optom.*, XXXV (1958), 125–33.

Kephart, N. C. and R. E. Chandler. "Changes in the Visual Field in a Pursuit Tracking Task," *Optom. Weekly*, XLVII (1956), 507–9.

Kirk, S. A. and G. O. Johnson. *Educating the Retarded Child.* New York: Houghton Mifflin Co., 1951.

Koffka, K. *The Growth of the Mind.* New York: Humanities Press, 1951.

Kraus, H. and R. P. Hirschland. "Minimum Muscular Fitness Tests in School Children," *Res. Quart.*, XXV (1954), 178–88.

Krech, D. and R. S. Crutchfield. *Elements of Psychology.* New York: Alfred A. Knopf, Inc., 1958.

LaDue, F. and J. Norman. *This Is Trampolining.* (2nd ed.). Cedar Rapids, Iowa: Nissen Trampoline Company, 1956.

Lorente de No, R. *A Study of Nerve Physiology.* New York: Rockefeller Institute for Medical Research, Vols. 131, 132, 1947.

Lotz, R. H. *Medicinische Psychologie oder Physiologie der Seele.* Leipzig: Weidmann'sche Buchandlung, 1852.

Lowder, R. G. *Perceptual Ability and School Achievement.* Available from Winter Haven Lion's Club, Winter Haven, Florida, 1956.

Marsden, C. D. "The Marsden Ball," in *Visual Training at Work. Optometric Extension Program Papers*, XXV, No. 8 (1953).

McCulloch, W. S. "Why the Mind Is in the Head," in *Cerebral Mechanisms in Behavior*, ed. L. A. Jeffries. New York: John Wiley & Sons, Inc., 1951.

Munn, N. L. *Psychological Development.* Boston: Houghton Mifflin Co., 1938.

Murchison, C. (ed.). *A Handbook of Child Psychology.* Worcester: Clark University Press, 1931.

———. (ed.). *Handbook of General Experimental Psychology.* Worcester: Clark University Press, 1934.

Osborn, A. F. *Applied Imagination.* New York: Charles Scribner's Sons, 1953.

Paterson, D. G. *Physique and Intellect.* New York: Century House, 1930.

Piaget, J. *The Origins of Intelligence in Children.* New York: International Universities Press, 1952.

Piaget, J. and B. Inhelder. *The Child's Conception of Space.* London: Routledge and Kegan Paul, 1956.

Potter, M. C. "Perception of Symbol Orientation and Early Reading Success," Teachers College, Columbia University Contributions to Education, No. 939, 1949.

Prudden, B. *Is Your Child Really Fit.* New York: Harper & Bros., 1956.

Riesen, A. H. "The Development of Visual Perception in Man and Chimpanzee." *Science,* CVI (1947), 107–8.

Robinson, H. M., M. C. Letton, L. Mozzi, and A. A. Rosenbloom. "An Evaluation of the Children's Visual Achievement Forms at Grade 1," *Amer. J. Optom.,* XXXV (1958), 515–25.

Russell, D. H. *Children's Thinking.* Boston: Ginn & Co., 1956.

Schilder, P. *The Image and Appearance of the Human Body.* New York: International Universities Press, 1935.

Schjelderup-Ebbe, T. "Weitere Beiträge zur Social- und Individual-Psychologie des Haushuhns," Z. *Psychol.,* CXXX (1932), 289–303.

Seguin, E. *Idiocy and Its Treatment by the Physiological Method.* New York: Columbia University Press, 1907.

Senden, M. *Raum- und Gestaltauffassung bei operierten Blindgeborenen vor und nach der Operation.* Leipzig: Barth, 1932.

Sherman, M. and I. C. Sherman. *The Process of Human Behavior.* Boston: W. W. Norton & Co., Inc., 1929.

Sherrington, C. *Man on His Nature.* Cambridge: Cambridge University Press, 1951.

Shinn, M. W. *The Biography of a Baby.* Boston: Houghton Mifflin Co., 1900.

Simpson, Dorothy. "Perceptual Problems of Elementary School Children." Ph.D. dissertation, Purdue University, 1960.

Small, V. H. "Ocular Pursuit Abilities and Readiness for Reading." Unpublished Ph.D. dissertation, Purdue University, 1958.

Stern, C. *Children Discover Arithmetic.* New York: Harper & Bros., 1949.

Stevens, S. S. (ed.). *Handbook of Experimental Psychology.* New York: John Wiley & Sons, Inc., 1951.

Strauss, A. A. and N. C. Kephart. *Psychopathology and Education of the Brain Injured Child.* Volume II: "Progress in Theory and Clinic." New York: Grune & Stratton, Inc., 1955.

Strauss, A. A. and L. E. Lehtinen. *Psychopathology and Education of the Brain Injured Child.* New York: Grune & Stratton, Inc., 1947.

Street, R. F. *A Gestalt Completion Test.* (Teachers College, Columbia University Contributions to Education, No. 481.) New York: Teachers College, Columbia University, 1931.

Terman, L. M. and M. A. Merrill. *Measuring Intelligence.* New York: Houghton Mifflin Co., 1937.

Thorpe, W. H. *Learning and Instinct in Animals.* Cambridge: Harvard University Press, 1956.

Tolman, E. C. and C. H. Honzik. "Insight in Rats," *Univ. Calif. Publ. Psychol.,* IV (1930), 215–32.

Valentine, C. W. *The Psychology of Early Childhood.* London: Methuen, 1942.

Valentine, W. L. "Visual Perception in the White Rat," *J. Comp. Psychol.,* VIII (1928), 369–75.

Vernon, M. D. *A Further Study of Visual Perception.* Cambridge: Cambridge University Press, 1952.

———. *Backwardness in Reading.* Cambridge: Cambridge University Press, 1957.

Wechsler, D. *Wechsler Intelligence Scale for Children.* New York: Psychological Corporation, 1949.

Welch, L. "The Transition from Simple to Complex Forms of Learning," *J. Genet. Psychol.,* LXXI (1947), 223–51.

Wellman, B. L. "Physical Growth and Motor Development and Their Relationship to Mental Development in Children," in *A Handbook of Child Psychology,* ed. C. Murchison. Worcester: Clark University Press, 1931.

Werner, H. *Comparative Psychology of Mental Development.* New York: International Universities Press, 1948.

———. "Development of Visuo-Motor Performance on the Marble Board Test in Mentally Retarded Children," *J. Genet. Psychol.,* LXIV (1944), 269–79.

———. "The Concept of Development from a Comparative and Organismic Point of View," in *The Concept of Development,* ed. D. B. Harris. Minneapolis: University of Minnesota Press, 1957, pp. 125–48.

Werner, H. and A. A. Strauss. "Types of Visuo-Motor Activity in Their Relationship to Low and High Performance Ages," *Proc. Am. Assoc. Ment. Def.,* XLIV (1939), 163–8.

Wiener, N. *Cybernetics.* New York: John Wiley & Sons, Inc., 1948.

Woodworth, R. S. and H. Schlosberg. *Experimental Psychology.* New York: Henry Holt & Co., Inc., 1954.

Zubek, J. P. and P. A. Solberg. *Human Development.* New York: McGraw-Hill Book Co., 1954.

Zuk, G. H. "Perceptual Processes in Normal Development, Brain Injury and Mental Retardation," *Amer. J. Ment. Def.,* LXIII (1958), 256–59.

Index of Names

Subject Index